THE **DEATH** OF **CAPITAL**

HOW CREATIVE POLICY
CAN RESTORE STABILITY

MICHAEL E. **LEWITT**

WILEY

John Wiley & Sons, Inc.

Published by John Wiley & Sons, Inc., Hoboken, New Jersey.
Published simultaneously in Canada.

For general information on our other products and services or for technical support, please contact our Customer Care Department within the United States at (800) 762-2974, outside the United States at (317) 572-3993 or fax (317) 572-4002.

Wiley also publishes its books in a variety of electronic formats. Some content that appears in print may not be available in electronic books. For more information about Wiley products, visit our web site at www.wiley.com.

Library of Congress Cataloging-in-Publication Data

Lewitt, Michael E.
    The death of capital: how creative policy can restore stability/Michael E. Lewitt.
        p.cm.
    Includes bibliographical references and index.
    ISBN 978-0-470-46650-6 (cloth)
    1. Capital. 2. Capitalism–United States. 3. Finance–United States. 4. Global Financial Crisis, 2008-2009. I. Title.
    HB501.L4125 2010
    332′.041–dc22   2009049432
Printed in the United States of America.

10 9 8 7 6 5 4 3 2 1

To my family,
who continually challenge me to
try to make the world a better place

CONTENTS

ACKNOWLEDGMENTS

When I started writing *The HCM Market Letter* over 10 years ago, I had no idea whether anybody would be interested in what I had to say. But somehow the newsletter has assumed a life of its own, and I am very grateful for all of those who have taken the time to read it and send me encouragement to continue writing. I especially appreciate the criticism, for writing a monthly publication does not always leave sufficient time for other people to review my material prior to publication. The newsletter has become a collaboration between myself and my readers, and for that I am deeply appreciative.

I have been strongly influenced by a number of financial writers and intellectuals in my writing. In particular, James Grant, editor of the indispensable *Grant's Interest Rate Observer*, has extended me numerous kindnesses over the years and remains a true gentleman of the old school in a world that could use more of them. John Mauldin is another extremely generous man who has exposed my work to a wider audience than I could have gained myself and continues to provide investors with more valuable information than virtually anybody else in the world today. Kate Welling has also been extremely generous by interviewing me and including my writings in her indispensable publication, *welling@weeden*.

I have also been strongly influenced by the example of Stephen Roach, whose weekly research is sorely missed as he continues on his Asian journey; Christopher Wood, who first made me believe in the power of contrary thinking and financial journalism with his great book *Boom and Bust* (New York: Atheneum, 1989); Mark C. Taylor, the chairman of the Religious Studies Department at Columbia University, author of the incredibly insightful *Confidence Games: Money and Markets in a World without Redemption* (Chicago: University of Chicago Press, 2004), wise man and, I hope, friend. Last but really first in my heart and mind, Arnold Weinstein, Edna and Richard Salomon Distinguished Professor of Comparative Literature at my alma mater, Brown University, and his wife Ann, who started teaching me more than 30 years ago about both life and literature have never stopped sharing their brilliance and humanity with me and their other students.

In the business world, I have had the privilege of working with some giants. First and foremost, I must thank my partner Joseph Harch. I spent a lot of time in school, but I hadn't really learned anything until I entered the "School of Harch" in 1988 as a newly varnished associate in Drexel Burnham Lambert, Inc.'s Corporate Finance Department in Beverly Hills, California. Joe became my mentor and has remained my mentor and one of my closest friends since then. Joe is an investment savant; ask him about something and you better bring your sleeping bag because he will speak to you with an enthusiasm and knowledge second to none for as long as you let him. It has been one of the great honors and thrills of my life to work beside him for almost 20 years, and there is no end in sight. I am also indebted to the team that Joe and I have worked with at Harch Capital Management, LLC, over the past two decades: Jeffrey Hill; James DiDonato; Gabriel "Buddy" Gengler; Adam Sternberg; Susan Crouse (who also helped tremendously with the preparation of this book); Mary Ide; James O'Neil; Vicky Zimmerman; Thomas Crawford; and Peter Ventry. G. Chris Andersen has also been an important teacher and friend to me over the years and remains one of the most original thinkers in the investment banking business.

I would also like to thank Pedro J. Ramirez, the publisher of *El Mundo*, for offering me the opportunity to write for his newspaper. Pedro is a true citizen of the world, a scholar and a gentleman, and I am honored to have been welcomed into the *El Mundo* family as well as the Ramirez family.

During the period that I was writing this book, I was also fortunate enough to have the opportunity to learn from one of the greatest investors of our generation, Leon Cooperman, as well as his partner Stephen Einhorn, at Omega Advisors, Inc. Lee combines the best qualities of intellectual rigor and focus with the old-fashioned moral virtues of honesty and outspokenness in a way that few men do. I consider him both a mentor and a friend. I also owe a debt of gratitude to the great people at John Wiley & Sons who helped me bring this project to fruition, from Debra Englander, who talked me into writing a book in the first place; to Kelly O'Connor, Stacey Fischkelta, and Adrianna Johnson, who had to put up with my perfectionism. These are true professions with whom any first-time author is privileged to work.

Finally, my family must come first in my thanks. This book has taken me away from them more than I would have liked. All of my writing is intended to contribute to a better future for them as well as everybody else's children. I love you guys and appreciate that you stuck with me through this.

This disposition to admire, and almost to worship, the rich and the powerful, and to despise, or, at least, to neglect, persons of poor and mean condition, though necessary both to establish and to maintain the distinction of ranks and the order of society, is, at the same time, the great and most universal cause of the corruption of our moral sentiments.

—Adam Smith

For historians each event is unique. Economics, however, maintains that forces in society and nature behave in repetitive ways. History is particular; economics is general.

—Charles Kindleberger

INTRODUCTION

The 2008 Crisis—Tragedy or Farce?

I n 1852, Karl Marx wrote that history tends to repeat itself—the first time as tragedy, the second as farce.[1] Nowhere has this warning about man's compulsion to repeat his mistakes been more frustrating to witness than in the world of finance. When it comes to finance, there is only one certainty: Mistakes will be repeated again and again until their perpetrators have lost their minds, their jobs, their money, or all of the above. If the working definition of insanity is repeating the same act over and over again while getting the same bad result, then Wall Street is a living exemplar of an insane asylum. Not only do the denizens of Broad and Wall Streets repeat their mistakes, they always manage to commit larger, more expensive and more reckless mistakes each time around.

While driving to work at the Beverly Hills offices of the investment bank Drexel Burnham Lambert, Inc., early one morning in February 1990, I wasn't thinking about Marx's dictum. But by the time I drove

1

home that afternoon (earlier than planned), I was living it. The last thing I expected that morning was to be called into a meeting and told that one of the most powerful firms on Wall Street was going to declare bankruptcy later that day. I was blown away. At the time, Drexel had all of $3.5 billion in assets and was the biggest underwriter of junk bonds in the world. At the time, it all seemed like a very big deal.

Less than two decades later, what happened at Drexel seems like small potatoes. In September 2008, Lehman Brothers Holdings, Inc., became the first large investment bank to fail since Drexel, except it was 200 times larger than my former employer, holding approximately $600 billion of assets. It also conducted business with virtually every significant financial entity in the world. And Lehman Brothers was only the tip of the iceberg. The Bush administration and the Federal Reserve were simultaneously facing an even bigger problem that required their immediate attention. Just a couple of days later, the government was forced to step up and infuse the insurance giant American International Group (the now infamous AIG) with $85 billion of capital to avoid what would have likely been an extinction-level-event for the global financial system had AIG been allowed to go under.

In the immediate wake of Lehman's bankruptcy and AIG's near-collapse, capital died. Economic activity came to a grinding halt around the world. Financial markets collapsed. Lenders stopped lending. The global financial system was facing its most severe crisis in a century as the flow of capital ceased. Figures of economic authority had lost their credibility. The reassuring words offered by Federal Reserve Chairman Ben Bernanke and Treasury Secretary Hank Paulson rang hollow. President Bush was nowhere to be found. And other important financial firms were facing new threats every day.

The Goldman Sachs Group, Inc., and Morgan Stanley, once considered among the strongest financial institutions in the world, were pushed to the brink by speculators in their credit default swaps and a complete loss of confidence by the markets in their business models and credit-worthiness. Merrill Lynch, once known as the "Thundering Herd," was revealed to be the "Dundering Herd" and was sold overnight to Bank of America in a hasty transaction that raised many legal and ethical questions whose niceties were ignored during the press of the crisis. The U.S. government scrambled to figure out what to do, and ended up engaging in a prolonged and unprecedented series of interventions into the economy that will ultimately cost more than $10 trillion and have numerous repercussions, many of them impossible to predict and most of them highly likely to be negative.

The world was learning another hard lesson about financial markets being built on nothing more than a thin tissue of confidence and the belief that promises and commitments will be kept. Tragedy or farce, call it what you will, this crisis was the real deal. People were angry. They shook their heads and asked, "How could things have come to this?" They should have been asking instead, "How could we have reasonably expected things to turn out otherwise?" Some of us had been warning that the world would face the death of capital sooner or later, although we took little pleasure in seeing our worst fears materialize. As this is being written toward the end of 2009, stability has returned to the surface of the financial markets. But the underlying economies on which these markets must ultimately depend remain structurally weak, and the path toward sustained economic growth is difficult to articulate. In order to forge a productive future, we need to understand the sources of instability that caused the financial system to fail us in the past.

Seeds of Instability

The Death of Capital explores three key characteristics of modern economies and markets that contribute to their instability and ultimately led to the crisis that permanently wounded world capitalism in 2008.[2] These characteristics are the following:

Finance Dominates Industry. The financial markets have overtaken the industrial and manufacturing sectors as the dominant force in the global economy. Finance, which I would define as applied economics, is a force that dominates not only the economy but culture, politics, science, and virtually all human endeavors. Finance dominates industry and manufacturing as the motive force of modern Western economies.[3] Some historians, such as Fernand Braudel, have argued that the dominance of finance is a sign of a civilization's waning power. Whether that will prove to be the case for the

United States and Europe remains to be seen, but there is abundant evidence that Western economies that are dominated by finance are increasingly ceding their hegemony to the rising manufacturing and industrial powers in the East.

Markets Are Governed By Flawed Intellectual Assumptions. Despite overwhelming evidence to the contrary, the financial system is structured on the assumptions that markets are efficient and investors are rational. Both assumptions are patently false. Furthermore, the laws that govern investor behavior require them to focus on narrow short-term economic considerations at the expense of long-term economic and social considerations that would contribute to a more equitable and, in the long run, wealthier global economy. Many current investment approaches are based on concepts such as diversification and correlation that need to be revised in light of market changes and recent historical experience. The work of the great economic thinkers—in particular Adam Smith, Karl Marx, John Maynard Keynes, and Hyman Minsky—must be reread to come to a proper understanding that capital is a highly unstable process that can be managed and regulated far more effectively than it has been in the recent past.

Speculation Trumps Productive Investment. As a result of the rise of finance and weak regulation of the financial services industry, an increasing amount of financial and intellectual capital in recent years has been devoted to speculation rather than to production. As the size and importance of the financial sector increased over the past three decades, this largely deregulated industry limited the flow of funds into activities that add to the long-term growth of the economy (such as energy, education, and infrastructure projects) and maximized investments in unproductive activities such as leveraged buyouts of twilight industries that needed to be retooled rather than weighed down with new debt. By the mid-2000s, massive amounts of capital were used to leverage up the balance sheets of dying animals such as newspapers and automobile manufacturers in what could only generously be termed a lost cause and might truly be deemed a farce (in Marx's sense of the word). Had that capital been devoted to more productive uses, far fewer jobs might have been lost and far fewer factories would sit idle today.

A Word on Speculation

Speculation is one of the most important concepts discussed in this book. Speculation describes economic activities that do not add to the capital stock of the economy or increase the productive capacity of the economy. Instead, financial speculation involves economic activity that is not intended to create lasting economic value but is merely intended to generate short-term financial profits. Whether or not such activities are *intended* to be productive is another question, but by and large economic actors do not pay attention to such questions in their quest for immediate gratification. The growth of finance has contributed to a deeply unfortunate trend in Western societies in which an incalculable amount of brain power and economic power are devoted to activities that do not contribute to the productive capacity of the global economy or to the improvement of the human condition.

Speculation is hardly new to the U.S. economy. In fact, as Lawrence E. Mitchell describes in his recent book, *The Speculation Economy*, speculation is hard-wired into the legal structure of American business. Professor Mitchell dates this phenomenon back to the end of the nineteenth century.

> [I]t was only during the last few years of the nineteenth century that business distress combined with surplus capital searching for investment opportunities, changes in state corporation laws, and the creative greed of private bankers, trust promoters and the newly evolving investment banks created the perfect storm that shifted the production goals of American industry from goods and services to manufacturing and selling stock.[4]

The type of speculation that Professor Mitchell describes is endemic to the very capital structure of the American corporation. "Waves of watered stock created by the giant modern corporation brought average Americans into the market for the first time. The instability of these new securities and the corporations that issued them provided enormous opportunity, both intended and not, for ordinary people and professionals alike to speculate, leading sometimes to mere bull runs and sometimes to widespread panic."[5] The instability inherent in corporate capital structures is a microcosm of the systemic instability described by Hyman

Minsky in his "financial-instability hypothesis," a subject discussed in Chapter 2 of this book. The important point to understand is that speculation leaves room for capital to make mischief. Rather than finding a home in productive uses, speculative capital nests in areas where it sits and festers, creating imbalances that later come home to roost.

The great economic historian Charles Kindleberger defined "pure speculation" as "buying for resale rather than use in the case of commodities, or for resale rather than income in the case of financial assets."[6] This is a polite description of what is colloquially known as the "Greater Fool Theory," which has gained an increasingly prominent role in financial markets during the series of expanding bubbles that have characterized the U.S. economy and financial markets over the past 30 years. Buying on the basis that someone else will come along and pay more for your assets became a national pastime in the U.S. housing market in the first decade of the twenty-first century, and threatened to make a quick return to the American stock and credit markets in the wake of the 2008 crisis when investors began to bid up prices of stocks and bonds to extremely rich valuations after the markets hit their bottom in March 2009.

Even in the immediate wake of the financial crisis, speculation continued apace. As U.S. GDP began to creep into positive territory in the second half of 2009 (entirely as a result of government stimulus in the U.S., Europe, and particularly in China, the latter of which accounted for a disproportionately large share of global growth beginning in the second quarter of the year), the nation's banks remained reluctant lenders to consumers and businesses but avid speculators with their own capital. Goldman Sachs, which in 2009 was earning approximately 80 percent of its revenues from risk-based activities, reported record earnings for the second and third quarters of 2009 based largely on its proprietary trading prowess (for example, the firm earned more than $100 million on 116 of the 194 trading days between January 1, 2009 and September 30, 2009). JPMorgan Chase, by all accounts the nation's strongest bank, also announced impressive second and third quarter earnings that were aided by healthy trading profits. While these firms were figuring out how to divide the spoils among their employees, they were overlooking the fact that their success was far less attributable to the intellectual and trading acumen of their about-to-be-overcompensated executives than their ability to take advantage of record low interest rates that the government was forced to provide in order to ensure that the economy did not sink into depression. The fact that these institutions were more focused on using these government-sponsored profits to overcompensate their employees than bolstering their balance sheets suggests that they would have to be dragged kicking and screaming into reforming their business practices.

As the United States struggled to emerge from the financial crisis, questions abounded about what could be done to encourage banks to increase lending to consumers and businesses. Rather than lending, the nation's largest institutions were devoting increasing amounts of capital to their trading businesses, which are inherently speculative in nature. In other words, they were using their capital, which had effectively become government insured, to speculate in securities rather than lend it to businesses that could create jobs and fund research and development and otherwise add to the productive capacity of the economy.[7] As a business proposition, choosing speculation over production makes a great deal of short-term sense—the returns offered by speculating in government-supported financial markets are far richer than the profits that could be earned making loans to shaky consumers and businesses reeling from a deep recession. But financial institutions serve a dual role in society; they do not merely exist to earn profits but also serve a public utility function whereby they are empowered to make capital available to support a healthy economy. It is with respect to this public utility function that they receive government licensure. It is also ostensibly for the purpose of fulfilling this role that the U.S. government bailed out these institutions to the tune of trillions of dollars in 2008 after their business practices proved to have been reckless and threatened the entire financial system with ruin.[8] Society has yet to draw a clear line between the business-for-profit and public utility function of its largest financial institutions, but this may be the most important issue facing post-crisis economies in the wake of the death of capital in 2008.

Financialization

In addition to the four key destabilizing characteristics of modern markets and economies described above, a series of changes within the

actual business of finance were key contributors to the systemic instability whose only logical outcome was crisis. All of these changes come
under the common heading of financialization, which in its broadest
sense speaks to the increasingly dominant role that finance has assumed
in Western economies. These features include the following:

- The transition of financial institutions, in particular banks, from
  deposit-taking and lending institutions into risk-taking institutions.
- The increasing utilization of debt instead of equity as a source of
  capital at all levels of the private and public sector.
- The growth of an unregulated "shadow banking system" that consisted of a nexus of private equity funds, hedge funds, money market
  funds, nonbanks such as GE Capital, and special purpose entities
  such as collateralized debt obligations (CDOs) and structured investment vehicles (SIVs) that moved control of the money supply
  beyond the reach of central banks.
- Dramatic changes in the short-term money markets that included
  the utilization of riskier assets in products that were marketed as
  low risk.
- The explosion of credit derivatives, structured credit products and
  other derivative financial instruments that supplanted cash securities.
- Enormous growth in the private equity business.
- Increased reliance on mathematical models to govern investment
  decisions.[9]

These changes were all manifestations of three trends: an overall shift
in economic activity away from production and in favor of speculation;
toward opacity and away from transparency; and toward debt and away
from equity. The result was an emphasis on business and investment
practices that increased the tolerance for risk and dramatically increased
the instability of the financial system.

In *The Death of Capital*, financialization is understood as the
process whereby the credit system makes increasing amounts of capital
available for speculative rather than for productive economic activity.
Financialization is supported by lax regulation and a belief in the ability
of the free market rather than government to make the correct choices
with respect to allocating capital. In 2008, the American economy led
the global economy into what one astute observer has described as

"a crisis of financialization . . . a crisis of that venturesome new world of leverage, deregulation, and financial innovation."[10]

The financialization of the U.S. economy was facilitated by two broad trends. First, as noted, regulatory and other business policies favored financial speculation over production. This took the form of accounting and tax laws that favored debt over equity and also permitted companies to disguise their true financial condition. As a formal matter, this favoring of speculation led to a system governed by formal rules that fictionalized the depiction of economic reality. These rules included:

- Accounting conventions that bore little relationship to reality (for example, the treatment of stock options).
- Accounting and tax rules that privileged debt capital over equity capital.[11]
- Tax rules that favored a small class of entrepreneurial capitalists so disproportionately that it created an American oligarchy to rival the Russian one that grew up in the shadow of the fall of the Soviet Union (including but not limited to favorable tax treatment of the earnings of the private equity and hedge fund industries).
- A proliferation of complex financial products that purported to reduce risk but actually increased it on a systemic basis (the first instance being portfolio insurance that contributed to the 1987 stock market crash and the last being credit insurance in the form of credit default swaps that pushed several large financial institutions into insolvency).

The denouement of the deregulatory orgy came in two parts: the 1999 repeal of The Glass-Steagall Act of 1933 that originally prevented commercial banks from entering businesses thought to be unduly risky; and the Securities and Exchange Commission's 2004 relaxation of net capital rules limiting the amount of leverage that the major investment banks could assume on their balance sheets.

Citigroup, Inc. was one of the main promoters of Glass-Steagall repeal under its former Chairman Sandy Weill; within a decade it was a ward of the state. The megabank spent the decade following Glass-Steagall repeal (under the chairmanship of former Treasury Secretary and proponent of Glass-Steagall repeal Robert Rubin, who joined the bank a wealthy and respected figure and departed a decade later much wealthier but far less respected) failing to combine its various businesses;

breaking securities and banking laws in the United States, Japan, and elsewhere; forming multibillion dollar off-balance-sheet entities to conceal liabilities from the prying eyes of regulators, credit rating agencies, and investors; playing a key role in championing the Internet bubble through the offices of, among others, the disgraced telecommunications analyst Jack Grubman; and losing tens of billions of dollars in ill-advised mortgage and corporate loans before being forced to come hat in hand in 2008 to the U.S. government for a bailout. It took less than four years for three of the firms that joined Citigroup in lobbying to be allowed to break the leverage barrier in 2004—Bear Stearns & Co., Inc., Lehman Brothers Holdings, Inc., and Merrill Lynch & Co., Inc.—to blow themselves up with their newfound powers. These rule changes were based on intellectually flawed rationalizations that were given establishment imprimaturs that included the Nobel Prize and a free-market ideology that gained a blind following after the collapse of a Soviet system that was doomed to failure based on its own flaws, not as a result of any genius in the American economic system.

The second facilitator of financialization was the U.S. legal system. One could fill the Library of Congress with books describing the flaws in the U.S. legal system. For the purposes of understanding the death of capital, however, there is one particular area of American jurisprudence that has been particularly damaging: the law governing fiduciary duty. Over the past century, the U.S. legal system has developed a body of law governing the conduct of fiduciaries that privileges the short-term economic interests of an individual company's shareholders over the long-term, noneconomic interests of society. This resulted from the adoption of what is referred to as the "agency approach" to the corporate governance challenge of aligning the interests of shareholders and management in public corporations. The agency approach promoted the view that the best way to align the interests of corporate managers and shareholders is to align their financial interests, and established that the primary or sole purpose of corporations is to maximize shareholder returns within the confines of the law.[12] As a result of this ideology—and it is nothing other than an ideology, because it is simply a human thought-construct—corporate managers and boards of directors are legally required to place the interests of shareholders ahead of those of debt holders, labor, the environment, and other parts of society that are arguably equally deserving of consideration.

One of the most pernicious consequences of the imposition of a narrow profit maximization motive on corporate boards of directors has been the flood of private equity transactions that consumed the public equity markets in the United States beginning in the 1980s and continued through the eve of the financial crisis. The concept of maximizing value for shareholders was used by so-called corporate raiders, leveraged buyout artists, and other private parties to wrest control of numerous public corporations from the hands of public shareholders. In the early days of the private equity movement, this arguably pressured public company managements to improve efficiency and productivity and contributed to better management and business practices. Unfortunately, by the mid-1990s and continuing up to the beginning of the 2008 financial crisis, this accomplished little more than substituting debt for equity on corporate balance sheets and diverting untold billions of dollars into private hands at the expense of public shareholders. Moreover, the going-private phenomenon likely imposed an enormous opportunity cost on the U.S. economy in terms of lost jobs, reduced research and development, and meaningfully lower productive investment in America's future. But it was sanctioned by the view that shareholders of public corporations were entitled to obtain the highest possible value for their stock (and the belief that the market for corporate control is the most effective way of delivering that result).

The narrow reading of fiduciary duty that was adopted by U.S. courts may seem to be consistent with the interests of traditional laissez-faire capitalism, but is, in fact, directly contrary to the teachings of Adam Smith and other theorists of capital, as the following pages explain. Moreover, the development of the law of fiduciaries has had a crippling effect on corporate creativity and social conduct. It has provided legal justification for short-sighted investment and business strategies that have diminished the productive capacity of the economy while encouraging speculative activity that has harmed businesses and communities. The nonshareholder interests that are deliberately pushed to the side by fiduciaries—the rights of workers, the health of the environment, the long-term contributions made by corporations to their communities in supporting social and educational programs—are at least as important in building a robust economy as maximizing value for shareholders in the short term. There is and never has been anything preordained in this interpretation of the law. Instead, this interpretation of the duties of corporate managers was an intellectual and moral choice, and a deeply flawed one that must be changed in order to develop a more just society and a healthier and more productive economy.

The Corruption of Moral Sentiments

There is another, crucially important reason why we need to question traditional economic and legal thinking to understand how the markets got things so terribly wrong both strategically and morally. In 2008, as in earlier crises, the markets were victims of a lowering of ethical standards and a thorough corruption of moral sentiments. This was hardly the first time such lapses occurred; this behavior followed a familiar pattern in which conduct that in earlier periods had been clearly considered illegal, immoral, or simply feckless somehow became accepted as conventional behavior that was widely known and acknowledged.

In the Internet bubble, one example of this type of conduct was the participation of research analysts in marketing initial public offerings of newly minted Internet companies that had few prospects for success. Securities laws were supposed to prevent such participation, yet even the largest and most reputable investment banks used their analysts in this manner. After the Internet bubble burst, high-tech companies engaged in a new set of shenanigans when they began repricing or resetting the dates on stock options for their top executives. Leading up to the 2008 crisis, questionable but widely known behavior was less a matter of breaking the law than violating common sense: the use of egregious amounts of leverage by virtually every participant in the financial markets (individuals, non-financial corporations, investment banks, hedge funds, private equity firms, commercial banks) in every financial activity imaginable from home ownership to the most arcane trading strategies.

These dangerous borrowing levels were in no way illegal; in fact, they were expressly sanctioned by the government. We have already noted the changes in net capital rules that were implemented in 2004 by the Securities and Exchange Commission that allowed five large investment banks to increase their borrowings, ultimately pushing the leverage ratios of some of the firms that failed from 12-to-1 to over 30-to-1 (meaning that a mere 3 percent drop in asset values could render them insolvent). This leverage was used to increase the profitability of these firms with little regard to the risks involved because the individuals managing these firms were compensated pursuant to asymmetric schemes whereby they not only profited greatly if their firms made money, but also remained obscenely wealthy even if their firms failed. As a result, firms like Bear Stearns and Lehman Brothers were left in the hands of modern-day Captain Ahabs like Richard Fuld and James Cayne who could afford to cling to their illusions and watch their ships sink while retaining enormous personal wealth. Everybody knew how leveraged these firms were in 2006 and 2007 but virtually nobody spoke up to warn of the possible dangers to the financial system posed by these highly leveraged firms. Markets are based on incentives. In the years leading up to the 2008 crisis, the incentive structures of Western financial markets became totally corrupted. The types of excesses seen in the last two bubbles dwarf those of the Gilded Age or the Reagan Years. America did not suffer simply an economic crisis; it suffered a moral crisis as well.

Low Rates and Lax Rules

It was within the context described above that the economic forces that had been building for years pushed the global financial system to the brink of insolvency in 2008. In an operative sense, the two most likely culprits were years of loose monetary policy and recklessly lax financial regulation, both of which were driven by free market ideologies that grew ascendant during the Reagan/Thatcher years.

Beginning in 1981, global interest rates began a long-term secular decline that continued through the financial crisis of 2008. These low rates pushed up asset values and financed higher debt-financed consumption funded by countries running current account surpluses and whose exchange rates were tied to the dollar. This process had to end sometime because interest rates could not fall forever. Moreover, debt and consumption growth came to exceed income growth, a situation that was unsustainable. At some point, people have to be able to pay for what they consume, and have to be able to repay their debts. As the United States recovers from the measures that were required to avoid a complete financial collapse of the global banking system, it is facing years of sustained high unemployment levels, below-trend economic growth (although perhaps we should begin questioning what the true trend was in view of the fact that much previous growth was debt-financed and government statistics are proving to be of dubious validity) and trillion-dollar deficits as far as the eye can see.

The financial world that almost collapsed in 2008 was far different from the world that was shocked by the U.S. stock market crash just two decades earlier in 1987. Financial markets were light years more technologically advanced this time around. Portfolio insurance, which contributed to the 1987 stock market crash, was primitive in comparison to the derivative weapons of mass destruction that brought the markets to their knees two decades later. Unfortunately, neither regulation nor traditional investment practices sufficiently adapted to this new regime. The explosive growth of the financial sector in the Western economies created a single, interlinked global market for money and credit that no longer operated according to the old rules. Instead of being governed by sovereigns, the world came to be ruled by currencies and interest rates that were no longer confined by national boundaries. Two closely linked manifestations of the emergence of finance as a dominant force led to tears. First, the invention of credit derivatives, so-called insurance products, facilitated speculation on an unprecedented scale. Second, the banking system became supplanted by its shadow, a parallel universe of financial institutions that operated outside the control of regulators while concealing their holdings and true financial condition from their own investors and lenders.[13]

Free market ideologies justified and reinforced the ascendancy of finance, but they failed to adequately account for the radical changes that technology and globalization wrought in the fabric of the markets. Supply-side economics, which called for lower taxes and less government involvement in the economy, failed to account for the procyclical nature of human behavior and the necessity to rein in the basic human instincts of greed and fear. Financial thinking on the part of investors as well as regulators failed to reflect the underlying changes in the markets and the economies whose goods they trade.

Western capitalism transformed over the past 30 years into its current form, one that is dominated like no time in previous history by the financial markets where goods and services are traded rather than manufacturing markets where goods are produced. In this phase of capitalism, every economic object is reduced to some type of marketable or tradable security or instrument. The accumulation of wealth is no longer based on the production of hard or tangible assets; today's wealth (at least in Western economies) is dominated by intangible forms that have been rendered interchangeable and tradable on the world's financial markets by financial technology. The result is a global economic system that is constantly shifting below our feet. Most of the time, those shifts are incremental and manageable. At other times, change speeds up, or changes that have been occurring over time suddenly accelerate and present a new set of economic conditions to which we have to adapt quickly. At these moments, the markets move in ways that suggest that the course of history is changing. Black Monday 1987 was one of those days. In 2008, we saw several such days when the stock market moved in 1,000-point arcs and credit markets froze up as though nobody would ever make or receive another loan. While changes in markets themselves affect the course of history, they importantly reflect changes occurring in the world outside the markets, the most important being those wrought by the minds of men.

By the time the crisis of 2008 materialized, finance, and the rules ostensibly designed to protect finance from itself, were woefully unprepared to manage a system that had changed profoundly from the world in which the rules that govern it were written. In a world of feedback loops that operate with exponential rather than linear force, and where discontinuities are woven into the fabric of market reality, traditional investment and regulatory theory had been rendered anachronistic. One explanation for what was happening is that a digital world was playing with analog rules. Another explanation is that a globalized world was operating according to local rules. The crisis revealed that time-honored modes of thinking about concepts such as risk need to be retrofitted to new realities. Most important, investors needed to start coming to terms with the fact that markets are not efficient and investors are not rational. And how could investors be presumed rational when they were not properly apprehending the world around them and when their thinking failed to reflect the radical changes that were occurring in markets and societies around the world?

The Global Liquidity Bubble

Abundant global liquidity gave investors a plethora of opportunities to invest based on these flawed beliefs. Beginning in the mid-1980s, the world became awash in capital as a result of a series of historic economic shifts that created enormous trade and capital imbalances throughout the global economy. These shifts were accompanied by advances—or what were widely hailed at the time as advances—in financial technology that facilitated the creation of new forms of money to soak up this global liquidity. After capital became untethered from gold in the early 1970s, there was literally no limit to how much capital could be created. As a result, too much capital killed capital.

Two broad economic phenomena illustrate the financial debacle that ensued. First, the growth of debt exceeded the growth of the underlying Western economies. Figure I.1 illustrates the inexorable growth in debt in the United States over the past several decades. In the United States, total debt as a percentage of GDP grew from 255.3 percent in 1997 to 352.6 percent in 2007.[14] It should also be noted that, for the first time, debt levels beginning in the early part of this decade began to constitute as great a percentage of GDP as they did during the Great Depression.[15]

This accumulation of debt was facilitated by the ability of financiers to literally create liquidity out of the air through financial innovations

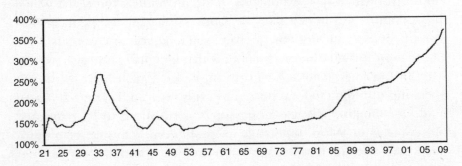

Figure I.1   United States Total Debt as Percent of GDP
SOURCE: Bridgewater Associates, Inc.

such as collateralized debt obligations (which packaged up trillions of dollars of individual mortgages, automobile loans, corporate bonds or bank loans, and other assets) and credit default swaps (a form of insurance on debt instruments such as bonds and mortgages). As new forms of capital were spawned, debt began to grow at an extremely rapid and ultimately unhealthy pace.

Second, an increasingly globalized financial system coupled excess savings in developing countries with a dearth of savings in developed countries. This devil's bargain of borrowing and lending created dependencies that ultimately grew into pacts of mutual financial destruction that, in terms of their threat to global stability, came to replace the Cold War nuclear weapons pacts of a generation earlier.[16] Neither of these phenomena—massive global liquidity and the links between developed and developing countries—could be maintained without the business of finance, whose transformation further increased instability. A world in which physicists made it possible for competing powers to blow each other into smithereens by splitting the atom was rendered even more unstable by one in which financial engineers deconstructed financial instruments into 1s and 0s and then recombined them into highly leveraged lethal weapons. With far more capital than could reasonably be put to productive use, the world's largest investors (which came to include not only large financial institutions but governments in the guise of sovereign wealth funds) began to direct these funds into highly speculative activities that were disguised in one of two ways. Some of these speculative activities were hidden in plain sight, like the equity and credit markets where asset prices exceeded all reason and new standards of valuation were cooked up by so-called experts to try to justify so-called new worlds.[17] Other activities were simply hidden in the previously mentioned "shadow banking system," a complex web of nonbanking institutions whose holdings and true financial condition were deliberately concealed by the largest financial institutions in the world from the eyes of regulators and investors.

The immediate result was the near collapse of the global economic system and the world's financial markets in 2008. The long-term result is likely to be prolonged and entrenched government involvement in previously lightly regulated capitalist economies and years of sluggish economic growth (once the bloom of government stimulus wears off).

Trillions of dollars of capital were directed to speculative activities such as derivatives trading, leveraged buyouts, and other investments that added little or nothing to the productive capacity of the economy. These funds were wasted, and they are lost forever. Even in a perfect world, much of this new capital would have undoubtedly found its way into unproductive uses. But a much better job could have been done to direct capital to areas that are both productive and life-enhancing, such as education, medical and scientific research, infrastructure improvement, and projects to improve the environment.

This less-than-optimal allocation of capital was the logical result of a series of policy choices that failed to direct money to productive uses. Monetary policy was strongly procyclical rather than countercyclical and tended to favored debt over equity, speculation over production. Other regulatory policies that governed the financial markets during this period—capital standards, accounting rules, tax laws—led the financial sector to conduct business in a manner that exacerbated rather than limited risk. Rather than leading financial institutions to ease credit during boom periods and tighten credit during downturns, policy led institutions to do just the opposite. This had the unintended and destabilizing effect of intensifying cyclical changes in the economy. Rather than leading individuals and institutions to save for a rainy day and create a cushion to permit them to survive economic downturns, these policies led them to spend when they should have been saving and borrow when they should have been reducing debt. The result was that capital was scarce when most needed and abundant when least needed and least able to be put to productive uses.

Too much money chasing too few goods is supposed to be inflationary, but the normal processes that cause inflation were moderated over the past three decades by technological changes and the entry of billions of low-cost workers from the developing world into the global economy. These changes kept labor costs low and gravitated against rising inflation during most of this period, although at some point these disinflationary forces will recede. By the same token, too much money chasing too few productive opportunities is bound to lead to speculation. Bad money supplants good money; debt supplants equity. This is the classic crisis of capitalism as Karl Marx first posed it, except that instead of products seeking out new markets, finance capital itself became the product looking for new outlets. Unfortunately it found all too many willing buyers of whatever new products Wall Street could cook up.

The credit crisis was the logical result of the proliferation of debt (and the substitution of debt for equity in virtually every kind of capital structure imaginable) that has been eating away at the stability of the United States' most important financial, legal, and social institutions for decades. The U.S. banking system finally collapsed in 2008 under the weight of trillions of dollars of bad loans that didn't have to be made. These loans were the deliberate result of decisions made by individuals who personally profited from them at a societal cost that will be calculated for decades to come. The collapse of America's financial markets was the outward sign of the potential beginning of the end of U.S. global hegemony and was as much the consequence of good decisions made in the developing world as the United States' own mistakes. The crisis in financial markets demands that policy makers engage in a radical rethinking of the mantras of free market ideology that have misguided U.S. economic and legal policy for the past several decades.

A Crisis of Confidence

In human terms, what triggered the credit crisis and resulting collapse in financial markets was a loss of confidence on the part of virtually every institution and investor of significance. The financial system is based on trust. Financial actors of all sorts—both individuals and institutions—lost trust in each other by the end of the summer in 2008. As a result, they stopped doing business with each other on the most basic level. Banks stopped making loans, and stock and bond traders refused to trade with each other. It took historic and unprecedented government actions to restore this trust. The kind of trust that allows markets to function builds up over many years, yet it is very fragile and can evaporate overnight. Once lost, it is very difficult to regain. The fact that markets began to stabilize in March 2009 should not be taken as a sign that the past can be forgotten.

Moreover, there are far more sinister long-term consequences of this crisis. The flawed financial products and investment strategies that were responsible for what happened originated in the hearts of Western capitalism—the towers of Wall Street and the City of London. The crisis of confidence that resulted from the failure of borrowers to meet their obligations can be laid directly at the feet of the largest financial institutions and gatekeepers in the world, and all of these are Western-based. As a result, confidence in the Western model of capitalism has suffered a body blow. The credit rating agencies and investment and commercial banks that promulgated the subprime mortgage debacle on the world have been completely discredited in an intellectual and moral sense by what transpired. The fact that this occurred during a period when U.S. foreign policy isolated the world's dominant economic power from its traditional allies and rightly or wrongly made it the target of hatred among large sectors of the world population may be a historical accident or may be suggestive of broader social and historical trends. Either way, however, the United States is exiting the first decade of the twenty-first century far weaker than it entered it. At the very least, the already battered U.S. dollar has been tarnished and will require Herculean efforts to be resuscitated. And rather than blaming others, the financially and militarily most powerful country in the world needs to look within and figure out how to do better.

By the time the total damage from the credit crisis is tallied, trillions of dollars of capital will have been destroyed. But it would be more correct to say that this capital was murdered. And as much as we would like to blame failures of human character and emotion (greed and fear), we must also blame failures of human intellect (stupidity). The most highly educated segment of our population—the PhDs, the MBAs, the JDs—made inexcusable errors of judgment, raising legitimate questions about the utility of such degrees when they fail to include a modicum of common sense and, more important, common decency in their curricula. As the holder of more than one of these degrees, this author is highly aware of their shortcomings.

While the world was going mad, nothing seemed amiss. In fact, these errors of intellect and judgment were endorsed by some of the most respected business and government leaders in the world. Alan Greenspan in particular repeatedly made public comments endorsing policies that in retrospect turned out to have been extremely reckless. At the time, however, these policies were part of an economic orthodoxy that few were willing to question. From an economic standpoint, this orthodoxy overlooked the important role that asset prices play in the economy; it also ignored the increasing role that debt was playing in the growth of the economy. It also failed to account for concepts such as discontinuity, path dependency, and feedback loops that can wreak havoc on an economy and markets. The failure to include these considerations in economic analysis led to fatal deficiencies in policy.

Lionized by some, Greenspan's reign as Federal Reserve chairman will likely be judged by history as an abject failure of policy and intellect. Greenspan himself felt compelled to admit that his worldview was flawed when, early in 2009, he told Congress that he had relied on his belief that financial actors would act in their own best interest while failing to understand that individual self-interest is often contrary to the public interest. In an exchange with Representative Henry Waxman, Greenspan admitted that "those of us who have looked to the self-interest of lending institutions to protect shareholders' equity—myself especially—are in a state of shocked disbelief." Waxman responded by saying, "In other words, you found that your view of the world, your ideology, was not right, it was not working." The former chairman responded, "Absolutely, precisely [perhaps the clearest answer Greenspan had ever given to Congress]. You know, that's precisely the reason I was shocked, because I have been going for 40 years or more with considerable evidence that it was working exceptionally well."[18] Had he been a student of Hyman Minsky instead of Ayn Rand, Greenspan would not have made such a fatal error.

In 1986, Minsky warned that, "the self-interest of bankers, leveraged investors, and investment producers can lead the economy to inflationary expansions and unemployment-creating contractions. Supply and demand analysis—in which market processes lead to an equilibrium—does not explain the behavior of a capitalist economy, for capitalist financial processes mean that the economy has endogenous destabilizing forces. Financial fragility, which is a prerequisite for financial instability, is, fundamentally, a result of internal market processes."[19] By ignoring the internal processes that led to an unsustainable buildup of low-cost debt, central bank policy under Greenspan fed a false prosperity. Coupled with tax and other economic policies that were aimed at rewarding speculative rather than productive investment, the result was a gutting of the United States' economic base and a mortgaging of its future.

Why Finance Matters

Students of history understand that the consequences of these errors are not merely theoretical. In *The War of the Worlds*, a history of the blood-soaked twentieth century, historian Niall Ferguson argues very persuasively that economic volatility coincides with social instability. He defines economic volatility as "the frequency and amplitude of changes in the rate of economic growth, prices, interest rates, and employment, with all the associated social stresses and strains."[20] Professor Ferguson makes a strong case that "ethnic conflict is correlated with economic *volatility*. A rapid growth in output and incomes can be just as destabilizing as a rapid contraction. A useful measure of economic conditions, too seldom referred to by historians, is volatility, by which is meant the standard deviation of the change in a given indicator over a particular period of time."[21] He explains, in words that now sound eerie written on the eve of the 2008 financial crisis and the controversial government bailouts that followed, that:

> Economic volatility matters because it tends to exacerbate social con-
> flict. It seems intuitively obvious that periods of economic crisis create
> incentives for politically dominant groups to pass the burdens of adjust-
> ment on to others. With the growth of state intervention in economic
> life, the opportunities for such discriminatory redistribution clearly
> proliferated. What could be easier in a time of general hardship than
> to exclude a particular group from the system of public benefits? What
> is perhaps less obvious is that social dislocation may also follow periods
> of rapid growth, since the benefits of growth are very seldom evenly
> distributed. Indeed, it may be precisely the minority of winners in an
> upswing who are targeted for retribution in a subsequent downswing.[22]

Even the least historically-minded among us need not be reminded that World War II and the Holocaust followed the Great Depression. The current race among China and other countries for scarce energy resources is just one area that could lead to potential armed conflict on a global scale, particularly in view of the permanent war raging above the oil fields in the Middle East.

The past has much to teach us about the consequences of ill-advised economic policies, but we needn't search very far to see the damage that has been wrought. Our mistakes have exacted an incalculable human cost on the citizens in this country and abroad. Millions of people have lost their homes and their jobs as a result of the subprime mortgage debacle. Toward the end of 2009, the official jobless rate in the United States was more than 10 percent and the number, when underemployed and discouraged workers were included, was over 17 percent. The real unemployment figure was probably in the vicinity of 20 percent. Economic hardship and the stresses unemployment causes have led families to break up and addiction and suicide rates to rise. At the end of 2009, one in eight Americans was receiving at least some of his or her nutrition from food stamps, including one in four children. Communities around the country have been destroyed by house foreclosures. Plant closures by the automobile industry have devastated the American heartland. The social fabric of an already fraying society has been badly damaged. A year after the crisis arguably reached its peak in the fourth quarter of 2008, the damage was still building in terms of lost jobs and abandoned hope. And the challenges facing Americans and the rest mankind are in no way diminishing.

Global Threats Require Systemic Stability

The world desperately needs a healthy financial system as it faces unprecedented strains on its resources and challenges to human survivability in the twenty-first century and beyond. Finance should not be treated like just another national pastime that can be followed through the media like baseball or cricket. And the financial markets are not the economy, even though they play one on television. The markets are the lifeblood of human civilization. They are the organizations that enable us to feed and clothe and heal our fellow humans, and abusing them is no different than abusing ourselves and risking our future. Like the capital that they shepherd, markets must be nurtured and protected, not abused and neglected and left to the offices of greed and fear.

Any serious book about markets today must be written with a consciousness of the significant challenges facing the human species as it enters the twenty-first century. There are many fine books on finance, but today's world calls for something more. Finance needs to be understood as the force driving most of the social, political, ecological and spiritual trends at work in the world. Unfortunately, many of these trends are highly noxious and pose long-term threats to our species. Fixing the global financial system is not only an economic imperative—it is arguably a requirement for the survival of mankind. One telling example will suffice to illustrate what is at stake.

The world is facing a growing trend toward aging populations. The costs of dealing with this unstoppable demographic phenomenon dwarf the trillions of dollars that were spent by governments to prevent a global depression in 2008. Table I.1, developed by the International Monetary Fund,[24] shows how much each country spent on the financial crisis as a percentage of its GDP, compared to how much each country is projected to spend as a percentage of its GDP to deal with the cost of its aging population. The latter so far exceeds the former as to render the amounts recently spent on the financial crisis almost trivial in present value terms. The column on the far right side of Table I.1 divides projected age-related spending by crisis spending to show how future

Table I.1 Net Present Value Impact on Fiscal Deficit of Crisis Compared to Age-Related Spending as a Percent of GDP

Country	Crisis	Aging	Age-Related Spending/Crisis Spending
Australia	26%	482%	18.5x
Canada	14	726	51.9
France	21	276	13.1
Germany	14	280	20.0
Italy	28	169	6.0
Japan	28	158	5.6
Korea	14	683	48.8
Mexico	6	261	43.5
Spain	35	652	18.6
Turkey	12	204	17.0
United Kingdom	29	335	11.6
United States	34	495	14.6
Advanced G-20 Countries	28%	409%	14.6x

Source: www.imf.org/external/np/pp/eng/2009/030609.pdf.

age-related spending is going to swamp recent crisis-related spending. For example, in the United States, aging-related spending will amount to 14.6 times the amount that was spent on the financial crisis! Coincidentally, in all of the G20 countries, average age-related spending will also amount to approximately 14.6 times the cost of the financial crisis.

What Table I.1 shows is that the United States and other G20 countries were facing forbidding financial challenges even before they had to step in with trillions of dollars of emergency funds in 2008. In other words, if we think we are facing fiscal challenges now, just wait until we get a few years down the road.

Moreover, beyond the example of aging populations and the cost of managing the financial crisis, there are other long-term threats to human survival, some of which require serious and immediate attention where a healthy global financial system will have to play an essential role. These threats, which are listed in Table I.2, are by their very nature unpredictable and have the potential to trigger extreme impacts—in short, they are the Black Swans that Nassim Nicholas Taleb has brought into popular consciousness that have been circling in the skies above us throughout history. They are among the threats that mankind must confront and overcome in order to preserve its future.

If one adds the costs for addressing these issues (which are enormous but currently incalculable) to those found in Table I.1, one doesn't know whether to laugh or cry. A bad outcome with respect to any of these potential crises could be a game-changer, resulting in exponential rather than linear damage: environmental catastrophe, a world war, a global health crisis, or a collapse of civil authority. These are precisely the type of discontinuities that today's investment strategies have been unable to master.

Table I.2   Future Black Swans?

Environmental degradation and climate change
Nuclear proliferation
Terrorism
Population imbalances
An increasing gulf between rich and poor
Ethnic conflict
A pandemic such as AIDS, SARS, or something worse
World hunger

The world is going to have to search high and wide for the resources to deal with these threats. But even if it can find the resources, it will not be able to deliver them if the global financial system remains an unstable house of cards. A strong and stable financial system will be the bare minimum required to deal with these threats, and we don't have such a system today. Moreover, such a system will have to be managed by men and women who possess raw intelligence, intellectual creativity, and moral courage. Our finance-driven world, unfortunately, has rewarded only the first two of these attributes, and its failure to recognize the third has been nothing short of catastrophic. People like Brooksley Born, the former chairperson of the Commodities Futures Trading Commission, whose advocacy for regulating the growing market for financial derivatives fell on deaf ears in the 1990s, are only now being recognized for their courage in speaking out. We need more Brooksley Borns and fewer Alan Greenspans. The most highly celebrated individuals in public life have repeatedly failed us. Individuals in privileged positions where they can make a difference in the world need to be smarter, wiser, and more courageous than their predecessors, very few of whom were willing to speak truth to power. Just as polities get the leaders they deserve, societies get the financial systems they deserve. We must look inward to examine the deeply embedded cultural values and intellectual assumptions that led economic actors of all types—investors, regulators, corporate executives—to conduct themselves in a manner that placed the stability of the financial system, and therefore of all of Western society, at risk.

The global economy and financial markets will also shortly be facing the disruptive challenge of unwinding the massive amounts of stimulus that the world's governments recently injected in order to prevent a global depression. It is very difficult to foresee how stimulus can be withdrawn without forcing the United States and other Western economies back into severe slowdowns. That is what happened in the 1930s, the last time the U.S. debt-to-GDP ratio was as high as it is today. If economic growth is insufficient to fund not just ongoing deficits but the repayment of the trillions of debt that has built up, withdrawal of stimulus can only lead to slower or negative growth. One alternative is that the stimulus simply won't be withdrawn in any meaningful way, creating a situation in which trillion dollar deficits will continue as far as the eye can see. The Obama administration is forecasting $9 trillion of deficits over the next decade, which would mean that the United States' budget deficit will be breaking through the $20 trillion level before 2020. A national debt of that size will cost more than $700 billion a year to service compared to the $202 billion cost of servicing the debt in 2009. To place this in context, the *New York Times* wrote that "an additional $500 billion a year in interest expense would total more than the combined federal budgets this year for education, energy, homeland security, and the wars in Iraq and Afghanistan."[24] Such a deficit, and the cost of servicing it, will drain away enormous resources from productive activities. The other alternatives for dealing with the swelling deficit are currency devaluation and inflation, both of which will adversely affect the U.S. economy in the years to come. If the dollar was not the global reserve currency, an objective observer would view the U.S. balance sheet as resembling that of a country heading for a sovereign debt default. Of course, other countries that have defaulted on their debt did not have the privilege of issuing debt in the global currency of choice, but eventually the United States will no longer enjoy that advantage unless it radically changes its ways.

The American political system—and that includes both politicians and voters—have shown little stomach to make the kinds of tough choices that would provide any alternative to a bleak future. The consequences of adding trillions of dollars of debt to America's balance sheet are certain to be profoundly negative. The resulting imbalances are likely to include a weaker currency and higher inflation, as well as unanticipated problems that will be disruptive to economic and social stability. Whatever course is chosen to deal with this debt, the ramifications are going to be highly disruptive to economic and social conditions as we know them today. For that reason, it is more urgent than ever that the proper systemic reforms be instituted as soon as possible to provide the necessary margins of safety before the inevitable instability lands on our doorstep.

A Few Words about This Book

The Death of Capital proceeds on the assumption that the closely linked disciplines of finance and economics are fields of thought that partake of the humanities even more than they do of the sciences. Accordingly, in order to better understand the causes and consequences of the 2008 financial crisis, one must delve into the key intellectual and moral underpinnings of the thinking and conduct that dominate modern markets. For that guidance, we will reread the work of four leading economic thinkers: Adam Smith, Karl Marx, John Maynard Keynes, and Hyman Minsky. These great thinkers share a profound understanding of how economies and markets should work (however their work, particularly in the case of Marx, has been distorted by later interpreters) because they were great philosophers of human nature. After reading their work, we should begin to understand why it is past time that we start to live the phrase "moral economy."

As the world has become increasingly interconnected and networked, the boundaries between finance and other disciplines have crumbled. The key mechanism that has facilitated this process is the digitalization of data. Digitalization has operated as a force that breaks down knowledge into its constituent parts and dissolves barriers between structures and disciplines to an extent unprecedented in history. When everything can be reduced to a 1 or a 0, as can be done today with computers, the barriers between different objects is much easier to overcome. This allows previously disparate areas to merge with one another. Modern economics is living proof of this, as the discipline has come to include thinking from mathematics and the hard sciences such as biology, physics, and chemistry (in quantitative finance) and psychology (in behavioral finance). The humanities also have a role to play in understanding markets, which the readings of Smith, Marx, Keynes, and Minsky are intended to demonstrate.

The forces that shape markets are essentially human, and great investors tend to be those individuals who think like great historians or cultural critics because they have learned to read humanity. Ultimately, human beings and not machines guide the economy. The most successful market navigators are those whose compasses allow them to pick up the subtle emotional breezes blowing through society that ultimately affect the way stock and bond prices float on the current. Great investors have the ability to read the current and the wind and form a coherent worldview (or investment thesis). Part of the problem with today's investment world is that too little of the world's money is driven by coxswain operating above deck while too much is guided by engineers trapped below deck enslaved by computer programs or other short-term oriented strategies that are completely divorced from the rhythms of the sea of humanity.

The Death of Capital proceeds as follows:

Chapter 1 attempts to develop a working definition of capital. The key quality that must be understood about capital is that it is a flexible process, not a fixed structure or category. As a process, it is inherently unstable. Capital died in the fall of 2008 because it was misunderstood and therefore mismanaged. In order to be sustained, it must first be understood.

Chapter 2 discusses the most important aspects of capital and capitalism through the prism of the work of four of the world's great economic thinkers: Adam Smith, Karl Marx, John Maynard Keynes, and Hyman Minsky. Despite manning two opposite ends of the ideological spectrum, Smith and Marx offer much-needed insights into the basic processes of economic behavior that are too often overlooked by those charged with overseeing the world's capital. Keynes and his best interpreter, Hyman Minsky, offer deep psychological insights into the processes by which capitalist systems involve instability. My reading of these thinkers is highly selective and may be deemed idiosyncratic by some readers, but at its core it seeks to bring out the common themes that each of them stress in trying to diagnose what ails the system that offers the last best hope on earth for sustained prosperity.

Chapter 3 discusses the death of the promise in modern finance. At its core, capitalism is a system built on promises. Capital died when economic actors stopped believing in each other's promises. Debt, which is the primary force that drives capitalist economies and distinguishes them from other forms of economy such as socialism, is a promissory structure. Lenders need to believe that their borrowers will keep their promises, and vice versa. Chapter 3 explores this complex relationship.

Chapter 4 discusses one of the most important economic phenomena of the last several decades, the "financialization" of the U.S. economy. Financialization is the process whereby speculation came to dominate productive investment and debt came to replace equity in capital structures large and small. While globalization has gotten all the press, financialization is every bit as important in understanding the changes that have occurred over the past two decades.

Chapter 5 describes one of the manifestations of the massive increase in indebtedness that has been one of the signposts of financialization: private equity. Private equity began as an innovative industry in the 1970s and 1980s, forcing large corporations to increase efficiency and maximize shareholder value. By the mid-1990s, unfortunately, private equity had outgrown this function and became primarily a speculative activity that generated enormous fees for private equity firms and their Wall Street sponsors while saddling Corporate America with loads of debt. Moreover, the key premise that underlies private equity investments—that investing in private firms inures management from the pressures of public ownership and provides a long-term perspective to grow businesses—has been completely belied by the industry's egregious fee structures, short-term oriented business practices and mediocre (at best) risk-adjusted returns. The long-term damage private equity has imposed on the U.S. and British economies will be felt for years to come.

Chapter 6 delves into derivatives with a special focus on credit derivatives, the financial instruments that were at the center of the 2008 financial crisis. Credit default swaps, the primary form of such derivatives, played a key role in the failures of Bear Stearns, Lehman Brothers, and AIG. Moreover, credit default swaps are truly what Warren Buffett terms "weapons of mass financial destruction" because of the perverse incentive structures they create that encourage creditors to force companies into bankruptcy. Derivatives have become, for the most part, a hotbed of speculation for wealthy institutions and should be strictly regulated.

Chapter 7 discusses how the legal system aided and abetted the financialization of the U.S. economy through establishment of a "fiduciary culture" that privileges short-term investment goals over long-term investment goals. This fiduciary culture acts as a smokescreen that enables society to place the wrong values on the wrong activities and outcomes. The result is a society turned upside down, in which value is consistently destroyed and dross treated as gold. This chapter also discusses how the professional investment industry has turned into a mechanism for destroying wealth rather than creating it. Enslaved by wrong-headed theories that markets are efficient and portfolios should be diversified into areas such as private equity, modern portfolio theory has turned out to be profoundly flawed. Moreover, modern portfolio theory fails to understand that divisions between debt and equity have been blurred by modern financial technology and clings to artificial distinctions that lead to liability mismatching and massive investment losses. It is time for these ideas to be cast aside.

Chapter 8 discusses financial regulation and the kind of changes in the current regulatory regime that are necessary to prevent a replay of the financial crisis. Sadly, there is a high likelihood that many of the abuses that led to the death of trillions of dollars of capital in 2008 will reoccur. As soon as the U.S. government stepped in and rescued Wall Street from itself, the so-called leaders of the financial industry immediately turned their attention to fighting against important regulatory changes that threatened their profits but were designed to protect society from speculation and risk-taking. Much more effort was spent trying to figure out how to avoid compensation restrictions than directing capital to needy borrowers and productive uses. The Obama administration and members of Congress came under intense lobbying pressure to back off on derivatives regulation although they stuck to their guns on compensation reform. Unfortunately, the failure to rein in credit derivatives could still render all other reforms moot. Chapter 8 offers an unexpurgated version of the types of regulation that are needed to address the two most important defects of the financial system that led to the crisis: the increasing opacity of modern financial practices; and the domination of speculation over productive investment. This is a tall order, but we should expect nothing less of ourselves and our leaders.

CHAPTER 1

The Death of Capital

C apital is a powerful and complex phenomenon that many thinkers have wrestled to define over the centuries. The statement that capital died in 2008 is intended to mean that after years of being misunderstood, abused, and wasted, capital stopped flowing around the world and became totally frozen in place. The manifestation of its death was the abrupt slowdown in economic activity that occurred in September 2008, around the time the U.S. investment banking firm Lehman Brothers declared bankruptcy and the U.S. government stepped in to prop up AIG with $85 billion of loans.

One of the most graphic illustrations of the cessation of economic activity that occurred in late 2008 is what happened to the Baltic Dry Index, a daily measure of global shipping activity.[1] (See Figure 1.1.)

Figure 1.1 shows this index falling off a cliff in September 2008, signaling the sudden collapse of global economic activity as capital flows came to a standstill. This index is considered to be a leading indicator of global economic activity and measures the price of moving the world's

Baltic Dry Index

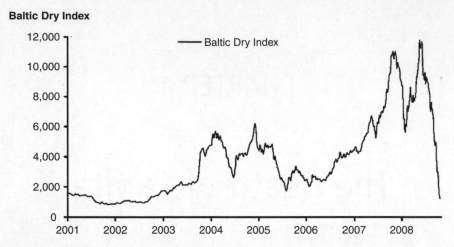

Figure 1.1   Capital RIP September 2008
SOURCE: Bloomberg.

raw materials around the globe. By the end of 2008, nothing was moving around the globe. Capital had indeed died.

One of the key characteristics of capital is that it is a process and not a structure or a category or a thing. Capital is a process because it is the embodiment of the human relationships that generate economic activity. That relationship can be one of equality or inequality (almost always the latter), but it is a relationship nonetheless. A relationship involves some type of connection in which the parties interact and affect the behavior of the other. In the autumn of 2008, the world saw a temporary but complete breakdown in this relationship.

In the first decade of the twenty-first century, capital had come to have virtually no connection with the underlying social relations that generate economic value. As the embodiment of the economic value created by human labor, capital has always maintained an indirect relationship with the actual act of wealth generation, so this is not a new phenomenon. But the distance between capital and wealth generation had been attenuated beyond all previous bounds by the changes wrought by modern finance. The very concept of capital—not to mention capital itself—had been devalued by modern financial practices. Rather than a precious resource that can be used to improve the human condition through the provision of jobs, health care, education, and the like, capital has become further alienated from these social purposes than in earlier historical periods.

The world experienced the death of capital that had been building up for decades due to a combination of counterproductive political and economic forces. In the autumn of 2008, in the wake of the bankruptcy of Lehman Brothers, capital froze, and with it the functioning of the global economy, when these forces coalesced into an overpowering wave of debt and disillusion. Capital was ultimately thawed out by the blowtorch of massive government stimulus and support, but its transformation into an object completely disembodied from its generative sources remained in place. Capital was placed on life support by emergency measures taken by the world's wealthiest governments and central banks; these entities threw trillions of dollars at the symptoms in order to temporarily restart the flow of capital around the globe. But the measures taken in late 2008 and early 2009 to keep the patient alive were only temporary and will have deleterious long-term effects, the most harmful ones likely being inflation and the devaluation of fiat currencies (in particular the U.S. dollar). In order to return capital to permanent health instead of merely the walking dead, proper long-term economic policies must be put into place. But those policies cannot be implemented without a thorough understanding of what capital is and how it functions. In order to be properly managed and regulated, capital must be understood in view of current market conditions. The very fact that capital died in the first decade of the twenty-first century suggests that those charged with shepherding it did not understand its true nature.

How did modern capitalism manage to place capital on the endangered species list? After all, modern society has developed far more advanced tools to manage risk—particularly man-made risk—than ever before in its history. Computer technology and mathematical ingenuity were ostensibly put to work to protect the financial system from precisely the disruptions that it suffered in 2008. Instead, in the ultimate irony, tools designed to reduce risk ended up increasing it—to reckless and systemically threatening levels. Students of capitalism have long known that there is something inherent in the nature of capital that renders it unstable. But what is it exactly that makes capital so difficult to manage?

The Four Essential Characteristics of Capital

Coming to a working definition of capital that reflects its real-world complexity is an imposing task. But avoiding it would be like performing an autopsy without touching the corpse. If the academics who have exercised such undue influence on markets have taught us anything, it is that markets work in theory but they do not work in practice. Accordingly, capital needs to be understood as it really is, not as we imagine it to be. That is why we cannot leave the definition to the professors. In order to define capital, we must combine theory and practice into a formulation that reflects the real world.

As noted previously, capital is a process. Because it is a process, it remains in constant motion. Below are the four characteristics of capital that are essential to a proper understanding of how it functions in the flesh-and-blood markets where money is made and lost every day.

Capital as It Is, Not as We Want It to Be
1. It is a process, not a structure or a category.
2. It is constantly changing form.
3. It is a construct of the human mind.
4. It is unstable.

The Oxford English Dictionary describes financial capital as "the accumulated wealth of an individual, company or community, used as a fund for carrying on fresh production; *wealth in any form used to help in producing more wealth*," (emphasis added).[2] "Wealth in any form used to help in producing more wealth" is the key to understanding capital because it describes a process, not an object or a structure or a category.

Capital Is a Process

First and foremost, capital is a living, breathing phenomenon. It is an expression of the human relationships that generate economic value. Just as these relationships are dynamic in nature, so is capital. Static capital is dead capital.

Without human labor producing it, capital cannot come into being. Both the creation of capital and the investment of capital originate in human relationships. For this reason, labor must be understood as another form of capital. Labor is exchanged for other forms of capital in the form of commodities (such as food, clothing and shelter) or for capital in the form of money. In today's knowledge economy, intellectual labor is the most valuable form of capital. The analysis of capital as the product of labor is well-rehearsed. What is less appreciated is the fact that invested capital is also representative of human relationships.

The world's financial markets are driven by investments made on behalf of institutions that represent charities, universities, labor unions, and municipalities. Their investments are made in order to support the basic human needs of their beneficiaries—education, health care, retirement funds, disability payments if individuals lose their ability to work. When we speak about the public utility function that certain parts of the financial system are designed to serve, such as banks, we are speaking about these institutions' function to provide for the betterment of human life. That function originates in the most basic economic act, the labor that creates capital. Capital is always one step removed from that labor, which was one of Karl Marx's great insights (as I will discuss in Chapter 2). But today capital has become so many steps removed from labor that it has lost its essential character as the motivating force behind improving human life. We cannot understand capital until we understand that it originates in human labor and that it has become more alienated from labor than perhaps ever before in history.

The most important attribute of capital as it functions in the real world is that because it is a process, it is a relationship and not a category or a structure. Capital is anything that can be exchanged for any other form of capital—money, property, labor. In the modern world, increasing amounts of capital are intangible in form such as patents, trademarks, copyrights, and other forms of intellectual property, as well as contract rights such as derivative financial instruments. Accordingly, the forms in which capital are represented have become increasingly complex. Finally, because capital is by its very nature a representation of something else, it is an indirect indication of the value of the underlying thing it represents.[3]

Capital Constantly Changes Form

Another essential characteristic of capital is that it has the potential to change form. Capital is chameleon-like. This is related to what is called its liquidity function. Illiquid capital is an oxymoron. In order for something to be considered capital, it has to have the potential to be turned into another form of capital, such as goods (food, clothing, housing), labor (which creates goods), or money (which purchases goods and labor). Turning one form of capital into another is perhaps the most important characteristic of capital; this characteristic is often taken for granted, always at an enormously painful, even financially fatal, cost. Many long-term investors learned this lesson about liquidity the hard way in 2008. People joke about John Maynard Keynes' remark that the market has the ability to remain irrational longer than an investor can remain solvent, but the great economist's point was a deadly serious one. Many institutions that view themselves as long-term investors and followed what came to be known as the "endowment model" of investing failed to realize that they also need liquidity in order to fund their operations.[4] Companies go bankrupt because they run out of liquidity and are unable to pay their bills even if the value of their assets exceeds the face amount of their liabilities (although they quickly discover that the value of their assets plunges if they file for bankruptcy). One of the keys to long-term investment survival is living to play another day, and liquidity crises are the single biggest threat to that ability.

Capital Is a Human Construct

Capital is also not something that is found in nature or subject to natural laws like physics and mathematics. Capital is a construct of the human mind. It is the tangible or intangible product of human labor, but as already noted it can also be human labor itself that can be exchanged for another form of capital (property or money, for example). As a human construct, it is a product of human perception. Capital only has value to the extent economic actors (human beings, or entities or organizations controlled by human beings) are prepared to place a value on it. This means that they are willing to exchange it for another form of capital that they believe to be of equal (or lesser) value. The concept of value introduces the psychological or subjective component of human nature into the mix. Value is a highly unstable concept that is constantly subject to changing human perceptions. While minions labor away in markets around the world each day purporting to place precise values on different types of securities and financial instruments, the only certainty about these values is that they are wrong. Values are changing constantly (the image of the blinking computer screen aptly captures this phenomenon) as the assumptions and circumstances used to determine value are adjusted. While this may seem an obvious point to make, the world's financial markets operate as though there is a Holy Grail of value that is constantly within reach. Nothing could be further from the truth. Chasing value is like chasing a mirage. Capital is the economic form of that mirage.

Capital Is Unstable

These three essential attributes of capital lead to one inevitable conclusion—capital tends toward instability rather than stability. A process that can change form and is subject to human perception is hardly a candidate for stability. And that is exactly what we find throughout history: Capital is a highly unstable concept. This quality remains poorly appreciated, and as a result, capital remains poorly regulated and managed. If we can come to a better understanding of capital, how it lives and how it dies, we can hope to corral it to better uses.

How Capital Dies

Once we understand what capital is, we can also understand how it ceases to exist. Capital's essential quality is change. When capital loses the ability to change, it dies. This is another way of saying what was said above: Capital must remain in motion at all times or retain the potential to be in motion. Static capital is dead capital. Unrelated, unconnected, or isolated capital is dead capital. When investors speak about "dead money" or "dead capital," they are speaking metaphorically about an investment that is neither generating a return nor likely to generate a return in the foreseeable future. The reasons for this are legion; the primary one is that it can't be turned into another kind of asset that can generate a return. When Western capitalism came to a grinding halt in the fourth quarter of 2008, capital stopped living and breathing. Capital literally and figuratively stopped moving and changing.

Because it is a relationship, capital requires at least two parties to bring it to life. This is where markets come into being. Capital requires some type of mechanism of exchange, initially of information about capital and ultimately of capital itself. Understanding market information requires market participants to share certain intellectual and moral assumptions. The parties do not have to like each other, they do not even have to trust each other, but they have to be able to agree on the value of something and believe that the system in which they are acting will enforce their bargain. There must be some kind of meeting of the minds, which is a human and social phenomenon. So we see again that at the all-important level of exchange, where capital creates value, capital is a social construct. Capital dies when it loses its human and social content. Inhuman capital is dead capital.

Capital is Misunderstood

It is apparent from observing the evolution of financial markets that too few people in positions of influence properly understand what financial capital is, how it functions, and how it should be managed and regulated. That is not to say that many of these same people have not figured out how to make money, in some cases enormous sums of it. But making money and understanding capital are two entirely different accomplishments. Society's confusion of wealth with talent and intelligence is only one of the illusions that needs to be dispelled in order to establish more stable markets and a more just society. But understanding capital is quite another matter. This lack of understanding is what led to capital's death and the economic and human chaos and suffering that ensued. It is also why capital virtually always provides less than optimal returns to its holders. The failure to understand capital is why all types of societies, whether they call themselves capitalist, socialist, communist, or some variation thereof, operate well below their full economic potential.[5] It is also why all economies, in particular those that call themselves capitalist, remain highly unstable even in the so-called age of advanced risk management.

Among other lessons, the financial collapse of 2008 demonstrated that the U.S. economic system was not built on stable and enduring intellectual and moral underpinnings. Instead, it was built on an ideological and intellectual house of cards on top of which was constructed an economic house of cards. Financial Armageddon finally arrived in 2008, as a number of market observers (myself included) had predicted, as a result of noxious regulatory and business trends that had gone unchecked for several decades. The external manifestations of these trends were excessive leverage at all levels of the financial system and a highly politicized and profoundly ineffective regulatory scheme governing financial markets. These were symptoms of a profound misunderstanding of capital, the basic building block of economies, and an equally deep failure to understand markets, the places where capital is exchanged. There was no appreciation of the fact that capital is an unstable social phenomenon, or that eradicating the relationship between capital and the labor that creates it would have serious (and potentially fatal) consequences. The nature of capital was badly misunderstood by its practitioners and guardians, and the result was a near-death experience for the Western banking system and the free markets themselves. *The Death of Capital* was written as a kind of post-mortem on a financial system that is now trying to be brought back to life. A healthy capitalist body still has a chance of being resurrected if those in positions of influence can come to understand how the *corpus economicus* really functions in a radically changing and unstable world.

The Failure of Risk Management

Ironically, the incessant march toward financial instability occurred in a world that had claimed to master risk. In 1992, the late Peter Bernstein wrote what is still rightly considered to be a modern classic on the subject of finance, *Capital Ideas*. Bernstein's book was widely admired for its insightful discussion of the academic theories that laid the groundwork for the revolution in finance that led to the development of derivative products, portfolio management techniques, and what many believed to be the advanced management of risk. In an early passage, Bernstein wrote the following:

> Today investors are more keenly aware of risk, and better able to deal
> with it, than at any time in the past. They have a more sophisticated

understanding of how financial markets behave and are capable of using
to advantage the vast array of new vehicles and new trading strategies
specifically tailored to their needs. Innovative techniques of corporate
finance have led to more careful evaluation of corporate wealth and
more effective allocation of capital. The financial restructuring of the
1980s created novel solutions to the problems arising from the separation of ownership and control and made corporate managers more
responsive to the interests of shareholders.[6]

Bernstein's endorsement of improved risk management techniques
exercised an immeasurably powerful influence on the financial markets
and society in general. Investors and regulators came to believe—falsely
as it turned out—that new products such as securitization and credit
derivatives were effectively dispersing risk throughout the global financial system where it could better be absorbed. Bernstein's imprimatur
regarding the ability of the new tools of finance carried a great deal of
weight, particularly within the financial industry; unfortunately it was
profoundly misplaced.

The risk management techniques praised by Bernstein relied on
advanced computer power to better capture relationships between the
prices of different securities and markets and to better measure the
correlation among different securities and asset classes. The intellectual
assumptions underlying such risk management approaches, however,
included reliance on two basis premises that were completely unfounded:
first, markets are efficient; and second, investors are rational. Beyond
these erroneous assumptions lay other flawed theories, such as the belief
that diversification of portfolios would protect investors from losses and
that relying on historical performance would serve as a valid means of
forecasting future price movements. Among other errors, all of these
assumptions failed to adequately account for small-probability high-
impact events (what have come to be known as "Black Swans" thanks to
the insights of Nassim Nicholas Taleb). Accordingly, risk management
models assumed normal distributions of events and did not stress test for
fat tail distributions that came to occur with increasing regularity during
the past 20 years. This turned out to be a fatal omission.

Another problem was that the models guiding investors failed to
evolve to reflect the increasingly networked nature of financial markets,
which created a situation in which the actions of a single large financial

institution could have a systemic impact. The technical term for such effects are "network externalities," which means that market developments will induce different firms to react in similar manners rather than act independently. Thus, the financial condition of an individual company proved to be an inadequate measure of systemic risk, and systemic disturbances increased the riskiness of individual companies that on their own may have looked stable. Finally, such risk management techniques sought to apply the laws of mathematics and physics to financial markets, which are socially and economically driven worlds that do not operate according to physical laws. Markets tend to be irrational; subjecting them to the rational laws of science is unlikely to lead to meaningful results. The damage wrought from such intellectual confusion has been extreme.

Four years later, in an enlightening 1996 book on the subject of risk, *Against the Gods*, Bernstein sounded a warning about undue reliance on some of the forecasting tools he had praised in *Capital Ideas*:

> Likeness to truth is not the same as truth. Without any theoretical structure to explain why patterns seem to repeat themselves across time or across systems, these innovations provide little assurance that today's signals will trigger tomorrow's events. We are left with only the subtle sequences of data that the enormous power of the computer can reveal. Thus forecasting tools based on nonlinear models or on computer gymnastics are subject to many of the same hurdles that stand in the way of conventional probability theory: the raw material of the model is the data of the past.[7]

And of course the history of financial markets since Bernstein wrote *Capital Ideas* and *Against the Gods* belies any rational observer's optimism about the ability of investors to properly utilize and profit from scientific, computer-driven risk management tools. In the last two decades alone, there have been five severe disruptions in the credit markets—four manageable ones in 1990–1991, 1994, 1998, 2001–2002 and the truly catastrophic collapse in 2007–2008 that required unprecedented global governmental intervention. Even though the financial system emerged basically intact from the first four of these debacles, it clearly gained little wisdom about the risks it was running. In fact, each succeeding market crisis revealed that the financial system had increased its risk profile after the previous one. The underlying causes of instability were being left unaddressed, and the imbalances bred by increasing global debt levels were increasing.

One clear lesson of episodes such as the junk bond/savings and loan scandal of 1990–1991, the Long Term Capital Management crisis of 1998, and the credit crisis of 2001–2002 was that neither investors nor regulators had learned very much from their mistakes. That, or they were too brainwashed with free market and risk management mantras to open their minds to the possibility that the conditions of underlying instability were worsening. In their blindness, they continued to cling to flawed assumptions and blatant misunderstandings about the basic ways in which markets work and the nature of capital itself. A system that is unwilling to question its assumptions is unlikely to be prepared for the adverse consequences that result from them.

The risk management ideology lauded in *Capital Ideas* exercised an enormous influence on the thinking of market practitioners, politicians, and regulators throughout the 1990s and early 2000s. This was extremely unfortunate because confidence in mankind's ability to master risk was profoundly misplaced. Moreover, the almost religious belief that computers and mathematical models could master risk and that regulation was increasingly unnecessary came at the worst possible time in history in terms of man's ability to inflict damage on the economic system, because radical changes in human economic and political arrangements were occurring.

At the beginning of the 1980s, Ronald Reagan and Margaret Thatcher entered office a year apart and led the ideological charge in favor of free markets. By the time Ronald Reagan left office in 1988, Soviet-style communism was coming apart and the Chinese version had been tossed aside by Deng Xiaoping in favor of a market-based economy. Less than a year after Ronald Reagan left the presidency, he watched the fall of the Berlin Wall that he had implored Mikhail Gorbachev to tear down. The victory of capitalism over communism that Reagan had led was complete.

It is all too rare when external events validate a political ideology, but this is what occurred when the Berlin Wall fell, the Soviet Union split apart, and China embraced capitalism. This historic endorsement of free markets validated capitalism throughout the world, overlooking the fact that communism collapsed due to its own flaws rather than the genius of capitalism. Nonetheless, the fall of communism was an unequivocally positive development for mankind. Billions of people around the world began to taste economic freedom for the first time. But the collapse of one flawed system was accompanied, particularly in the United States and the United Kingdom, by a virtually blind adoption of another flawed system: unfettered free market capitalism—a belief in the ability of the markets to cure all ills and to effectively manage all risks.

During this period, Alan Greenspan was anointed the high priest of free market capitalism as chairman of the Federal Reserve. Many books have already been written criticizing his ostensible adherence to free market dogma,[8] yet it should not be overlooked that Greenspan's own Federal Reserve was all too willing to bail out markets on numerous occasions. Greenspan was more than prepared to toss his free market principles out the window in the face of true systemic risk. The bailout of Mexico in 1994, the Asian financial crisis of 1997–1998, Russia's debt default in 1998, Long Term Capital Management's collapse in 1998, the Enron and WorldCom frauds in 2001, the 2001–2002 credit market collapse—in each of these cases, Greenspan's Federal Reserve intervened in the markets in one form or another. It did so either by radically and excessively lowering interest rates or directly or indirectly intervening in financial markets. Greenspan's frequent exercise of the central bank's lender of last resort function stood as a constant warning (for those who wanted to heed it) that the free market was not as free as it was cracked up to be, and that if allowed to continue functioning as it was, it would end up cracking up. Sadly, we came to discover in 2008 that the Soviet Union wasn't the only empire capable of being driven into insolvency and instability by the potency of the free market.

But despite the fact that the world's most esteemed central banker's actions did not live up to his free market reputation, the political and thinking classes continued to worship free markets (and Mr. Greenspan). The Glass-Steagall Act, which separated commercial and investment banking, fell by the wayside in 1999 under the lobbying of Citigroup, the now failed financial supermarket that spent the late 1990s and first decade of the 2000s engaged in a desperate attempt to combine its different businesses while engaging in a series of ethical, legal, and financial breaches that should have shamed its executives and board members rather than lifting them higher and higher in public esteem. Once the barrier between deposit-taking and risk-taking institutions had fallen, the next step was to eliminate regulations that limited the amount of leverage that these newly empowered investment banks could employ in their businesses. In 2004, the Securities and Exchange Commission, under heavy lobbying from the leaders of two firms that survived 2008 after agreeing to turn themselves back into commercial banks (Morgan Stanley and Goldman Sachs) and three that did not (Merrill Lynch, Lehman Brothers, and Bear Stearns), decided to lift the 12-to-1 limit on balance sheet leverage on the large Wall Street investment banks. Few questioned the wisdom of these moves and most praised the freeing of the financial industry from rules that were considered archaic and antigrowth. A few Cassandras suspected that the old rule was necessary to prevent Wall Street from destroying itself. But proponents of what turned out to be a suicide pact argued that Wall Street would lose business to London and other jurisdictions that permitted higher leverage, and the race to the bottom was on. By the time the walls came crashing down, several of the largest investment banks sported debt-to-equity ratios in excess of 30 to 1. When the public learned about how leveraged these firms had become, regulators and politicians began tripping over themselves to express their shock that gambling had been allowed at Rick's Cabaret. But by then it was too late—the chips were being called in, and the casino was no longer extending credit to even its best customers.

To the bitter end, however, free market acolytes continued to carry forward the belief that risk had been conquered and the markets could handle whatever came their way. In early 2007, shortly before the financial markets all but completely collapsed, Bernstein published a sequel to *Capital Ideas*, which he titled *Capital Ideas Evolving*. He should have named his new book *Capital Ideas Devolving,* for the net result of these ideas turned out to be the near obliteration of the Western financial system. On the eve of financial Armageddon, Bernstein wrote:

> It may sound ironic, but as investors increasingly draw on Capital Ideas to shape their strategies, to innovate new financial instruments, and to motivate the drive for higher returns in relation to risk, the real world itself is on a path toward an increasing resemblance to the

theoretical world described in *Capital Ideas*. Subsequent pages repeat that observation on more than a few occasions. Baloney those ideas were not.[9]

It is too late for Bernstein to retract that last sentence, but I will be presumptuous enough to do it for him. For if the financial world has come to resemble anything, it is the aftermath of the attack of the Martians in H.G. Wells' *The War of the Worlds*. Never have so many technically overeducated but morally undereducated people done so much damage to so many. The models and products that were developed to conquer risk instead turned on their inventors and destroyed them. The finance professors who concocted portfolio theory, the Black-Scholes model, credit default swaps, and collateralized default obligations have done little more than demonstrate the truth of the adage, "Markets work in theory but they don't work in practice."

Even worse, the post-World War II economic model that had served as the basis of so much apparent prosperity turned out to have been built on an edifice of debt and delusion. This model took a sharp turn for the worse in the 1980s, when debt assumed a much greater role in all levels of the U.S. economy. The ideological and intellectual assumptions that supported rampant debt incurrence, and the triumph of speculation over production, turned out to be profoundly flawed in their basic precepts.[10] As always happens in markets, which are primarily driven by emotion, the pendulum swung too far. Free markets required regulation, and computer technology and quantitative thinking cannot free the world from the demons of risk. In order to understand how the Western financial system destroyed itself, and to place this system back on a sound economic track, the post-World War II understanding of markets and capital must be revised. New answers are needed. The best place to start looking for them, as the next chapter suggests, is by rereading some great philosophers who happened to write about economics.

CHAPTER 2

Capital Ideas

One of the great ironies embedded inside the structure of all complex systems is that they sow the seeds of their own demise. Such is the case for complex economies. The collapse of the Western financial system in 2008 demonstrated beyond a shadow of a doubt that there are severe flaws in how modern capitalist societies have organized themselves. The free market mantras that permitted lightly regulated financial industries to conduct business in reckless and self-serving ways over the past three decades have been thoroughly discredited by the need for Western governments to bail out their largest financial institutions on an emergency basis.

The seeds of destruction were primarily ideological; they grew out of deeply embedded but flawed ways of thinking about capital, economic growth, and financial regulation. Instead of basing economic growth on a modified free market model that privileges concepts such as equity, transparency, production, and regulation, those in positions of influence chose a radical free market path of debt, opacity, speculation, and deregulation. This approach was based on the radical error of pretending that

49

markets are efficient and investors are rational when precisely the opposite is the case. The choices did not have to be as stark as that—there is a middle ground that can serve the interests of all of an economy's stakeholders. But the pendulum clearly swung too far in favor of the radical free market model. And the results now lie in ruins all around us: insolvent banks, disenfranchised workers, impoverished state, local and federal governments, a poisoned planet, embarrassed regulators, hypocritical legislators crying for retribution between visits to the campaign funding feeding trough on Wall Street, and a public that has lost trust in virtually all things economic. A capitalist system inherently prone to booms and busts became even more prone to disequilibrium. In order to understand what happened and rebuild a more resilient system, we must dig deeply into basic economic principles and reevaluate them.

There have been many influential economic thinkers whose work would greatly benefit market participants. In order to better understand the death of capital in 2008, four particular thinkers are worthy of extended discussion—Adam Smith, Karl Marx, John Maynard Keynes, and Hyman Minsky. But these thinkers need to be approached in a way that transcends economics. Three of the seminal works of economic theory that are examined in this chapter—*The Wealth of Nations* (1776); *Capital* (1867); and *The General Theory of Employment, Interest and Money* (1936)—are best considered intellectual performances that far exceed the discipline of economics and qualify as both great literature and great philosophy and have influenced intellectual debate in a variety of disciplines for generations. Each of these works has been analyzed and debated endlessly in academic and policy circles for years and continues to provide rich material for thinkers in a variety of disciplines. This is a tribute to the genius of their authors and to the fact that the issues discussed in these works are subject to multiple interpretations and misinterpretations. What follows is a highly selective if not idiosyncratic reading of the aspects of these seminal thinkers that ties together their interpretations of some of the key characteristics of capital, capitalism, and markets. It is my contention that these intellectual giants provide insights into the nature of capital that have in many cases been overlooked or misunderstood by investors, regulators and policymakers. The result has been that little progress has been made in managing effectively the boom and bust nature of free market capitalism, which in turn has caused capitalism to fall far short of reaching its potential to contribute to the growth and welfare of human society.

The first two thinkers, Adam Smith and Karl Marx, stand at opposite sides of the ideological spectrum yet share an enormous amount of common ground. These two philosophers remain two of the most insightful students of capitalism long after their work first came to light. Adam Smith saw capitalism as a force for good, while Marx saw it as a cause of conflict and abuse. Their work provides important insights into the characteristics that render capital inherently unstable and crisis-prone. What follows is not intended to be a complete discussion of these two complex thinkers; rather, it is an attempt to draw out some of their key ideas as they affect the modern understanding of financial markets. Smith and Marx speak to several of the key intellectual and moral underpinnings of our economic collapse. Both men describe markets that are governed by complex human relationships that at their basic level are strongly affected by people seeking social approbation. They also make powerful statements about the fact that human economic interactions, and the relationships between money and goods, are highly mediated. In discussing these two thinkers, I hope to illuminate some of the forces that have driven economic actors to behave in certain ways that have ultimately been very harmful to the long-term interests of society. By better understanding the profound truths that Smith and Marx described, we can hopefully address some of these flaws more effectively as we work to design a more effective economic system that serves the interests of all of us, not just the most privileged among us.

The last two thinkers wrote more recently and have been particularly prominent in recent discussions surrounding the financial crisis of 2008. John Maynard Keynes and his most important modern interpreter, Hyman Minsky, understood the psychological aspects of capitalism as well as anybody who has ever studied the system. In fact, Keynes may best be considered a great psychologist of economics, a role that Minsky assumed in warning of the dangers of financial stability. By focusing on the ways in which economic actors react to their environment, both men not only demonstrated great insight into human behavior but provided a road map for investors and regulators charged with navigating financial markets. Students of Minsky were undoubtedly the best prepared to recognize the unstable financing structures that led to the 2008 crisis, how these structures developed, and why such structures are endemic to the nature of capitalism and must be anticipated again.

The United States has spent the last three decades—the 1980s, 1990s, and 2000s—with a highly leveraged economic system whose primary occupation has been to conceal declining productivity and weakening profitability from the eyes of investors and regulators while enriching a small elite.[1] By the end of the Bush II administration, the United States faced the most serious economic downturn since the Great Depression of the 1930s as its banking system lay broken and major industries such as housing and automobile manufacturing were on the verge of total collapse. It is necessary to analyze the deep structures of capital and capitalism in order to understand what happened and chart a pathway to recovery. There is no better place to start such a study than the work of Adam Smith.

Adam Smith and the Tyranny of Crowds

When Adam Smith wrote about markets, he pictured in his mind the markets he used to walk through in the streets of the eighteenth century Scottish cities where he grew up (Kirkcaldy), attended school (Glasgow), and made his career (Edinburgh). These were smelly, bustling street markets filled with all sorts of physical goods and characters drawn out of a Charles Dickens novel. The historian Fernand Braudel gives us a vivid picture of the types of markets that Adam Smith experienced every day, filled with:

> [a] varied and active proletariat: pea-shellers, who had a reputation for being inveterate gossips; frog-skinners, . . . porters, sweepers, carters, unlicensed pedlars of both sexes, fussy controllers who passed on their derisory offices from father to son; secondhand dealers, peasants and peasant women recognizable by their dress, as were respectable townswomen looking for a bargain, servant-girls who had worked out, so their employers complained, how to make something out of the shopping-money (to shoe the mule, *ferrer la mule* as they said); bakers selling coarse bread on the marketplace, butchers whose displays of meat encumbered the streets and squares, wholesalers . . . selling fish, butter and cheese in large quantities; tax-collectors. And everywhere of course were the piles of produce, slabs of butter, heaps of vegetables,

pyramids of cheeses, fruit, wet fish, game, meat which the butcher cut up on the spot, unsold books whose pages were used to wrap up purchases. From the countryside there also came straw, hay, wood, wool, hemp, flax, and even fabrics woven on village looms.[2]

The overwhelming feature of these markets was the smells, the sounds of people and animals, the human movement, the interaction among butchers and bakers and tradesmen buying and selling their goods. Smith had a very specific conception of what markets looked like and how the people in them behaved. Such markets still exist today, primarily in less developed countries but also in some developed countries where they remain quaint reminders of how people used to live. They are colorful emblems of the basic human relationships that remain the foundation of all economic exchanges.

Of course, the markets that drive economic activity today look very different. Physical markets of the type that Adam Smith knew are largely a sideshow or curiosity in modern Western societies. The markets that fuel modern global economies do not involve the trading of physical goods. They are largely antiseptic, electronic arenas where the only strong odors arise from the excesses of the night before. The primary commodities exchanged in modern markets are electronic bytes that represent stocks, bonds, mortgages, corporate bank loans, and currencies or, increasingly, complex contracts that represent an interest in such financial instruments. To the extent there is a strong physical dimension to the proceedings, it is found in the impressive appearance that the technology that facilitates this trading assumes in the form of long rows of traders and their sleek computers and electronic computer screens. The sight is indeed impressive, but it has virtually no representational relationship with the underlying economic objects that are being traded. Unlike the street markets in eighteenth-century Glasgow or Edinburgh, the buyers and sellers rarely deal with each other face to face. Instead, they speak on the telephone or e-mail each other. Their communication is highly mediated; it is, to a large extent, impersonal and disembodied. This does not mean that their relationship is completely impersonal, but there is a great deal of truth to the concept that the age of gentlemanly capitalism has passed. The real question is whether the age of human capitalism has gone with it. The answer to that question is a resounding no.

Every day, on electronic trading floors around the globe, trillions of dollars of trades are effected on the basis of verbal agreements that are only later solidified into binding written contracts. A trader's word is literally his or her bond. A simple "you're done" is sufficient to signal that a trade is complete, whether that trade is for a million or a billion dollars of value. Despite the fact that the relationships between buyers and sellers as well as the goods they are trading are largely disembodied, a surprisingly small percentage of trades end up being seriously disputed. Part of the reason for this is that technology allows for discussions between traders to be recorded. Another reason is far more elemental—nobody will deal with a trader who doesn't keep his or her word, and word circulates very quickly about who is trustworthy and who is not in the tight-knit trading community. There are protocols that have been developed over time that must be followed by traders if they are going to be able to make a living in the business of trading. All of the computer terminals in the world can't erase the crucial human element that lies at the bottom of every single trade. This is one reason that Adam Smith has a great deal to teach us.

Adam Smith, of course, is best known as the author of what many people consider to be the bible of capitalism, *An Inquiry into the Nature and Causes of the Wealth of Nations* (1776). But two decades earlier, he wrote an arguably more important book, a treatise on moral philosophy, *The Theory of Moral Sentiments* (1759). In his earlier book, Smith sought to lay out the basis for moral conduct in human society and argued that peoples' concern for the opinions of others ultimately leads them to act in moral and civilized ways. In Smith's worldview, the process by which men develop a moral sense is very similar to the manner in which they develop markets. Both institutions—human society and human markets—are the result of human beings interacting with each other in ways that make them feel good about themselves by fulfilling their own needs. Just as the desire to fulfill material needs leads to the exchange of goods and hence the development of markets, the desire to fulfill emotional needs leads men and women to be sensitive to the views of others and thereby to develop a moral sense. Neither the markets nor the morals we develop are perfect; in fact, both are constant works-in-process that are flawed, subject to emotion, and unstable. Over time, Smith believes that the process of developing and refining our moral sense leads to the formation of order in morality and markets that is superior to other forms because it fulfills human needs better than other forms. In other words, Smith argues that such a system is not only a realistic description of how men and women behave, but it is a preferable system. That does not mean, however, that these systems can simply be allowed to operate without laws or institutions. Rather, Smith was searching for the optimal institutional framework in which people's innate qualities could be put to the best use. Taking people as they were (or, as he saw them, warts and all), Smith was trying to design a world that would make people the best they could be.[3]

In *The Wealth of Nations*, Smith famously wrote that "[i]t is not from the benevolence of the butcher, the brewer, or the baker, that we expect our dinner, but from their regard to their own interest."[4] Yet Smith's project was not to unconditionally praise an "invisible hand"[5] of self-interest guiding free-market behavior, but to identify those institutions and processes that could provide human beings with the best opportunity to act in constructive, decent, and moral ways. He believed that a free market in which men and women could demonstrate their worth by exchanging goods and services was among the most important of those institutions. The freedom to earn a living through exchange would, in Smith's view, give individuals the best opportunity to avoid the types of dependency on others that leads to immoral behavior.

Smith's view that people base their conduct on their concern for the opinion of others is wholly relativistic. As such, it provides both wisdom and a warning. The wisdom comes from Smith's recognition that human beings are strongly driven by social approbation. We desperately want to feel that we are part of a group. And the first step to accomplishing that is understanding how others feel about us. From the first words of *The Theory of Moral Sentiments*, Smith focuses on our concern for the feelings of others. "How selfish soever man may be supposed, there are evidently some principles in his nature, which interest him in the fortune of others, and render their happiness necessary to him, though he derives nothing from it, except the pleasure of seeing it." He continues, "[t]hat we often derive sorrow from the sorrow of others, is a matter of fact too obvious to require any instances to prove it." The way we try to understand how other people feel is to put ourselves in their place. "As we have no immediate experience of what other men feel, we can form no idea of the manner in which they are affected, but by conceiving what we ourselves should feel in the like situation." Continuing, Smith writes, "That this is the source of our fellow-feeling for the misery of others, that it is by changing places in fancy with the sufferer, that we come either to conceive or to be affected by what he feels."[6]

In order to judge the feelings of others, Smith tries to establish an objective standard (similar to the "prudent man" rule discussed later in this book) that he terms the "impartial spectator." It is from the standpoint of this impartial spectator that others should be judged:

> We conceive ourselves as acting in the presence of a person quite candid and equitable, of one who has no particular relation either to ourselves, or to those whose interests are affected by our conduct, who is neither father, nor brother, nor friend either to them or to us, but is merely a man in general, an impartial spectator who considers our conduct with the same indifference with which we regard that of other people.[7]

In Smith's world, all moral judgments rely on the judgment of this independent man.[8]

As the scholar Dennis Rasmussen has pointed out, Smith understood that undue concern with the opinions of others could "lead to a corruption of people's moral sentiments, selfishly motivated appeals to others' self-interest, and a good deal of ostentation."[9] Social approbation does not always bring out the best in people. Too often, people worship the wrong idols. Smith's statement that undue admiration for the rich is the source of the corruption of our moral sentiments, which is found on page xiii of this book, speaks an uncomfortable truth that should be posted on the entryway of every financial institution and government building in the world. Smith's philosophical project is aimed at fashioning a just society out of the fact that people are unduly concerned with the opinions of others, and that these opinions steer them to admire the wrong moral attributes in other people. But instead of simply identifying this as a flaw, Smith attempts to use worship of the rich as a basis for fashioning a more just society.

Smith believes that a commercial society is particularly well-suited to such a project. In a commercial society, people are dependent on one another to work together to meet their needs. They generally cannot meet their needs alone (even Thoreau ventured into Concord from Walden Pond from time to time to replenish his stores). For this reason, people have a strong incentive to work together and depend on each other. As Dennis Rasmussen writes, for this reason Smith believed that "commerce encourages traits like reliability, decency, honesty, cooperativeness, a commitment to keeping one's promises, and a strict adherence to society's norms of justice."[10] In Smith's view, it is incumbent upon people in a market society to conduct themselves in a moral way in order to be able to participate in and benefit from commercial activity.[11] It is in people's interest to engage in good behavior because that will better help them fill their needs.

Of course, Smith was striving for an ideal, and commercial life is not so simple. The warning concealed in Smith's words comes from his failure to identify any independent moral standard as the basis for human conduct. Instead of basing morality on natural law, religion, or reason, Smith argued that moral conduct originates entirely in human beings' feelings or sentiments. The rules of morality result from feelings, not vice versa. Smith writes:

> It is thus that the general rules of morality are formed. They are ultimately founded upon experience of what, in particular instances, our moral faculties, our natural sense of merit and propriety, approve or disapprove of. We do not originally approve or condemn particular actions, because, upon examination, they appear to be agreeable or inconsistent with a certain general rule. The general rule, on the contrary, is formed by finding from experience that all actions of a certain kind, or circumstanced in a certain manner, are approved or disapproved of....Those general rules...are all formed from the experience we have had of the effects which actions of all different kinds naturally produce upon us.[12]

These feelings are not only our own—they are what we imagine others would feel watching our conduct. "If we saw ourselves in the light in which others see us, or in which they would see us if they knew all, a reformation would generally be unavoidable. We could not otherwise endure the sight."[13] By making the opinions of others the standard by which we judge ourselves rather than some independent or objective moral standard, we risk surrendering ourselves to the madness of crowds. After all, history has demonstrated repeatedly that groups are particularly susceptible to flawed thinking.

There is a dark side to this concurrence-seeking ethos that has played itself out throughout history. It lies at the heart of the type of herd thinking that causes phenomena such as investment bubbles and, in its most pernicious form, genocide. In his classic study, *Groupthink*, Irving Janis identified strong consensus-seeking behavior as one of the main causes of defective decision-making in classic policy disasters such as the Kennedy and Johnson administration's actions with respect to the Vietnam War and the Bay of Pigs. (No doubt he could add the Bush administration's launch of the Iraq War to that list.[14]) The desire of members of a group to be accepted by others, which lies at the heart of Adam Smith's theory of moral sentiments, tends to silence dissenting voices, limit the airing of unpopular views, and lead to poor decision-making.

Permitting the opinions of others to govern important human activities is a highly problematic enterprise. It is another version of conceding all wisdom to the free market. But crowds, and markets, often get things terribly wrong; in point of fact, they often act irrationally. Smith's observed that human behavior and institutions evolve through the interaction of human beings attempting to satisfy their emotional or economic needs. However true this may be as a matter of fact, it need not be dispositive as a matter of prescription. Some human impulses are contrary to the health of the larger community, even deviant and dangerous. Greed and fear, two human drives that govern a great degree of market behavior, are directly contrary to the operation of healthy markets and a productive economy if they are not properly reined in. Adam Smith described how men and markets develop and believed that markets could be designed with the proper governing institutions to contain man's worst instincts. One of the purposes of *The Death of Capital* is to evaluate the failure to develop the right kinds of institutional structures to rein in the madness of crowds.

Smith wrote a long time ago, but the world has not passed him by. In many ways, the world is still trying to catch up to him. We are still trying to design the proper institutions and markets that will allow man's best attributes to flourish while governing the demons of his nature. Recent events demonstrate that the dark side of human nature—greed, fear, arrogance, stupidity—remains a formidable foe that places humankind's welfare at risk at regular intervals. The social approbation that Smith identified as the primary basis of man's moral sentiments still drives many peoples' behavior, especially their economic behavior. Sadly, free markets are all too imperfect governors of human behavior. The unfortunate truth is that financial crises, which are occurring with increasing, not decreasing, frequency are the result of deeply embedded traits of human nature and recurring failures to regulate our worst instincts. Two- and-a-half centuries after Adam Smith, mankind is still in need of protection from itself.

One of the frustrating lessons of markets is that investors continually ignore Groucho Marx's sage advice not to join any club that would accept them as members. Financial markets should often be avoided entirely, but investors cannot help themselves when they see everyone around them clamoring to participate. Today's markets are obviously far different from the more intimate ones that Smith walked in eighteenth-century Kirkcaldy, Glasgow, and Edinburgh. The products and economic actors he described—butchers and bakers, pin and woolen coat manufacturers—vividly captured his frame of reference. Smith had personal, first-hand interactions with the men and women hawking their wares in these teeming and chaotic markets that somehow organized themselves into institutions that made available food, clothing, and other goods to Scottish society.

Today, the trading of goods has been replaced by the trading of bytes and the personal relationships that defined mercantile relationships in the eighteenth century have been abraded by technology and radical changes in the forms that capital assumes. But at the heart of these markets still lie the personal and social relationships between human beings that Adam Smith identified as the central feature of all human institutions. It is incumbent upon us today to take his wisdom and apply it to the new outward forms that markets assume with the understanding that the inward forms that drive markets are still governed by human relationships.

The Fallacy of Composition

Another aspect of Adam Smith's view of how moral sentiments develop raises another set of challenges for promoters of free markets. Smith's description of men developing their moral senses in *The Theory of Moral Sentiments* tells a story of trial and error:

> In order to produce this concord [of sentiments], as nature teaches the spectators to assume the circumstances of the person principally concerned, so she teaches this last in some measure to assume those of the spectators. As they are continually placing themselves in his situation, and thence conceiving emotions similar to what he feels; so he is as constantly placing himself in theirs, and thence conceiving some degree of that coolness about his own fortune, with which he is sensible that they will view it. As they are constantly considering what they themselves would feel, if they actually were the sufferers, so he is constantly led to imagine in what manner he would be affected if he was only one of the spectators of his own situation. As their sympathy makes them look at it in some measure with his eyes, so his sympathy makes him look at it, in some measure, with theirs, especially when in their presence, and acting under their observation: and, as the reflected passion which he thus conceives is much weaker than the original one, it necessarily abates the violence of what he felt before he came into their presence, before he began to recollect in what manner they would be affected by it, and to view his situation in this candid and impartial light.[15]

Rather than beginning from a set of general rules, the rules of morality are developed from the experience of observing other people and accepting and rejecting the reactions to these observations. This is very similar to Smith's description of how markets develop in *The Wealth of Nations*, as Professor James R. Otteson argues very persuasively in *Adam Smith's Marketplace of Life*. Professor Otteson writes that Smith's view of human nature:

> [S]hows human morality to display four central substantive characteristics: it is a system that rises unintentionally from the actions of individuals, it displays an unconscious and slow development from informal to formal as needs and interests change and progress, it depends on regular exchange among freely associating people, and it receives its initial and ongoing impetus from the desires of the people who use it. But this account also adheres to a framework that . . . has the central elements of a system of unintended order modeled on an economic market.[16]

This process of observation and imitation leads human beings to adapt their behavior over time into modes that allow them to work together and build a functioning society. It is a process that is basic to many complex living systems.

In fact, Smith's view of the development of human morality is very similar to the process of self-organizing criticality described by Stuart Kauffman in his brilliant book on the organization of complex systems, *At Home in the Universe*. Kauffman argues that:

> Laws of complexity spontaneously generate much of the order of the natural world. . . . We have all known that simple physical systems exhibit spontaneous order: an oil droplet in water forms a sphere; snowflakes exhibit their evanescent sixfold symmetry. What is new is that the range of spontaneous order is enormously greater than we have supposed. Profound order is being discovered in large, complex, and apparently random systems. I believe that this emergent order underlies not only the origin of life itself, but much of the order seen in organisms today.[17]

Kauffman then describes some of the broad processes of natural life that he believes are echoed in economic systems.

> Life, then, unrolls in an unending procession of change, with small and large bursts of speciations, and small and large bursts of extinctions, ringing out the old, ringing in the new. If this view is correct, then the patterns of life's bursts and burials are caused by internal processes, endogenous and natural. These patterns of speciations and extinctions, avalanching across ecosystems and time, are somehow self-organized, somehow collective emergent phenomena, somehow natural expressions of the laws of complexity we seek. . . . No small matter these small and large avalanches of creativity and destruction, for the natural history of life for the past 550 million years has echoes of the same phenomena at all levels: from ecosystems to economic systems undergoing technological evolution, in which avalanches of new goods and technologies emerge and drive old ones extinct.[18]

His conclusion is that "the fate of all complex adapting systems in the biosphere—from single cells to economies—is to evolve to a natural state between order and chaos, a grand compromise between structure and surprise."[19] If this is, in fact, the way societies and markets evolve—and there is a great deal of evidence that such is the case—then these insights are extremely important for our understanding of financial crises, our approaches to managing them, and our hopes of preventing them or at least of mitigating the permanent damage they inflict.

Financial markets in a capitalist system are marked by constant change and adaptability at every level of operation. The creation of new financial products is often a response to a market inefficiency that can be exploited for profit. Sometimes that market inefficiency results from regulation, and other times from changes in the nonfinancial economy. But market changes begin with the actions of individual economic actors who are seeking to solve a problem and, in a capitalist system, earn a profit at the same time. Individual economic actors behave based on their view of their own self-interest. There is a strong procyclical, or path dependent, character to this activity. This is the essence of capitalism. Smith's and Kauffman's views of human processes and markets seem to describe the type of procyclical behavior that sows the seeds of financial crises.

The problem is that this regime runs into something known as the "fallacy of composition," which teaches us that the sum of individual decisions often does not add up to a beneficial result for the system as a whole. In fact, individual decisions that can be shown to be rational when considered individually often tend to lead to disastrous results when aggregated. Again, these results should not be surprising; in fact, they are predictable if you know where to look for the warning signs. In economic terms, this phenomenon is closely associated with procyclical behavior, which is a type of behavior that reinforces the existing direction of economic forces and markets. The classic example of the "fallacy of composition" was described by John Maynard Keynes in *The General Theory*, where he described how the rational behavior of individuals reducing their spending during an economic downturn will exacerbate that downturn and potentially lead to a depression (this is famously known as "the paradox of thrift"). In a market in which individuals are free to make their own decisions based on their self-interest, decisions based on rational individual profit motives (which are generally reasonably short-term in nature) ultimately tend to lead to instability rather than stability when they are aggregated. In certain respects this is also the great lesson of the economist Hyman Minsky, who taught that stability breeds instability. When the economy and the financial markets appear to be stable, it is perfectly rational for investors to feel that it is prudent to take more risk. The problem lies in the fact that everybody tends to increase their risk appetite at the same time, which raises overall systemic risk to dangerous levels. In fact, history has demonstrated repeatedly that risk at any time should only be increased cautiously because many other people are likely to be increasing theirs at the same time, magnifying the overall risk context in which the individual decisions are being made.

Investment contrarians fancy themselves capable of separating themselves from the crowd and investing in an anticyclical manner. In today's world, however, where investments are driven by computerized money flows and quantitative investment strategies, it has become more difficult than ever to separate oneself from the crowd logistically even if one can do so psychologically. Larger investment portfolios, in particular, are captive to market movements unless they exercise extraordinary vigilance in spotting procyclical market behavior and structure their investments in a manner that allows them to liquidate positions easily. As 2008 demonstrated, few large portfolios are capable of doing so, which explains the similarity in negative performance that occurred during that *annus horribilis*. Only investors who were able to spot the market excesses born of procyclical investment behavior that had been going on for years were able to defend themselves against the inevitable downward correlation of all asset classes that occurred when the markets could no longer sustain excessive valuations and leverage.

Karl Marx and the Origins of Opacity

There is a deep and bitter irony in the fact that another deep reader of man's economic nature—and arguably the most astute interpreter of capitalism despite the tragic misreadings that his work has engendered—sits at the opposite end of the ideological spectrum from Adam Smith. But a careful reading of Adam Smith and Karl Marx shows that these two thinkers share much more than is commonly believed. As we pick up the pieces of a world economy that was almost destroyed by the credit crisis of 2008, Marx's stinging comment about history repeating itself first as tragedy and then as farce mocks capitalism's compulsion to repeat the mistakes of the past. Marx's economic theories are highly complex and go far beyond the concept of class struggle for which he is best known. Indeed, it would be difficult to discuss the death of capital without addressing one of capital's most important critics. Despite the proclivity on the part of U.S. economic commentators to dismiss Marx as a crackpot, his writings offer profound insights into capitalism and capitalist processes. In fact, his work has been regaining its reputation in the wake of the financial crisis.[20]

For the purposes of understanding how Western capitalism came to consume itself at the dawn of the twenty-first century, there are few better places to retreat than the writings of Marx. Three of Marx's insights are particularly worthy of note.

1. Marx's conception of capital as a process and not a thing, which renders capitalism a system filled with contradictions that render it highly dynamic and unstable.
2. Marx's conceptualization of money and monetary forms as fetishes— indirect expressions of underlying social and economic relations whose meaning is obscured and distorted by their mediation through the form of money in its increasingly complex and derivative forms.
3. Marx's insight that value is a highly changeable and unstable concept.

All three of these concepts bear on the increasingly complex forms that money has assumed in the late twentieth and early twenty-first century. The more complex and opaque the forms of money became, the more unstable concepts of value (both economic and moral) became. And with unstable value came not only unstable markets but a highly unstable economy.

Capital Is a Process, Not a Thing

Marx's major work, *Capital*, is a tough go for most modern readers. Perhaps the best way to approach this monstrously large and convoluted work is as a major intellectual and literary achievement that happens to discuss economics. One of Marx's recent biographers, Francis Wheen, suggests why this is appropriate: "By the time he wrote *Das Kapital*, [Marx] was pushing out beyond conventional prose into radical literary collage—juxtaposing voices and quotations from mythology and literature, from factory inspectors' reports and fairy tales, in the manner of Ezra Pound's *Cantos* or Eliot's *The Waste Land*. *Das Kapital* is as discordant as Schoenberg, as nightmarish as Kafka."[21] He could have added that the book is as encyclopedic and apocalyptic as the American masterpiece,

Moby Dick. Just as Herman Melville's masterpiece swept away most of the American fiction that preceded it, *Capital* redefined most earlier economics treatises; after *Capital*, capitalism never looked the same. The image that most often comes to mind when one thinks about Marx's description of capitalism in *Capital* is the "dark Satanic mills" described by the iconoclastic English poet and artist William Blake in his poem of the early 1800s, "Jerusalem." In Marx's vision, capitalism is a dark and evil force capable of metamorphosing from one form into another. In fact, one of capitalism's greatest strengths (and instabilities) is its flexibility, its ability to adapt to changing circumstances of history, politics, or geography.

One of Marx's key economic insights is that capital is a process and not a thing.[22] He describes capital variously as "value in process," "money in process," and "money which begets money."[23] As such, capital is constantly moving, constantly changing form, and therefore unstable. Marx writes that "[i]t comes out of circulation, enters into it again, preserves and multiplies itself within its circuit, comes back out of it with expanded bulk, and begins the same round ever afresh."[24] In Marx's formulation, the key characteristic of capital is that it is both money and commodity. "It [capital] . . . always remains money and always commodity. It is in every moment both of the moments which disappear into one another in circulation. But it is this only because it itself is a constantly self-renewing circular course of exchanges."[25] Marx terms commodities a form of "use value" (because they can actually be used or consumed to meet human needs such as hunger), while money is considered a form of "exchange value" (because it can be exchanged for other things of value but cannot itself be consumed to meet human needs).

Because capital assumes both the form of money and the form of commodity in Marx's world, it is an extremely complex phenomenon. Capital spends its existence moving between these two forms—money and commodity—in order to play its multiple roles in the economy. (At one point, Marx writes, "Capital is money; capital is commodities."[26]) As money, it is used as a mechanism of exchange, while as a commodity it is used in its physical form. The transition between these two forms is what we can think of as the liquidity function, and the degree to which the liquidity function is operating smoothly is taken as one indication of the health of the economy.

Yet, as we saw from reading Adam Smith, liquidity can be a misleading sign of health. Just because economic actors are providing liquidity does not mean that the assumptions underlying their actions are justified. As individuals, they may be acting on assumptions that are perfectly reasonable with respect to their individual goals and aspirations. But when these atomized actions are combined, they alter the context in which those actions are taken and alter the original assumptions. Marx teaches us another way of understanding how the best laid plans of individuals can turn into the madness of crowds; he offers us a different angle into the "fallacy of composition." At times, the provision of liquidity is based on flawed understandings or assumptions about the relationship between capital's roles as money and commodity. Or, put another way, assumptions about the equivalence of the value of capital as money and capital as commodity are incorrect. Since most forms of exchange in an economy are mediated through the form of money, they are indirect and subject to distortion. This is what Keynes means when he says that "much can happen between the cup and the lip." Economic actors are dealing with inherently unstable referents precisely because they are referents and not the things themselves (that is, the underlying commodities). And there is no way to avoid this existential condition.

Those who approach the markets from a quantitative standpoint and attempt to model market moves would do well to keep Marx's fluid view of capital in mind. The value of any financial instrument stays fixed for only a theoretical moment in time (basically the moment at which another party buys it), and stock or bond prices are merely approximations of what the underlying economic referent is worth. This is why economics is better thought of as philosophy or art than science or mathematics, and why even a proper understanding of these latter two disciplines must include a healthy dose of the former two. The presumption of precision that market pundits bring to bear on their predictions of market behavior are highly misleading and render most market predictions mere palaver.

Our Fetish about Money

In Marx's formulation, money or exchange value (which again is just one form of capital) is itself a highly complex phenomenon. Man reduces different commodities to money in order to be able to exchange different commodities for each other. Money in this sense is a great equalizer or leveler of value. Money looks like a fixed object but represents something far more complex and dynamic. In Marx's world, money represents what he variously describes as "congealed labor" or "social hieroglyphics." What he means by this is that money is the tangible expression of the value that society places on the labor that created the commodity that is represented by money.[27] In this sense, labor is itself a form of capital, as noted in Chapter 1.

Marx developed the concept of the "fetishism of commodities" (*der Fetischcharakter der Ware*) to describe the manner in which commodities are transformed into money. Marx explains that "the products of labor become commodities, social things whose qualities are at once perceptible and imperceptible by the senses."[28] The relationships between human beings as economic actors exchanging goods assume the form of relations between physical objects. Marx continues.

> [T]he existence of the things *qua* commodities, and the value-relation between the products of labor which stamps them as commodities, have absolutely no connection with their physical properties and with the material relations arising therefrom. There it is a definite social relation between men, that assumes, in their eyes, the fantastic form of a relation between things. In order, therefore, to find an analogy, we must have recourse to the mist-enveloped regions of the religious world. In that world the productions of the human brain appear as independent beings endowed with life, and entering into relation both with one another and with the human race.[29]

Money, the form that all economic exchanges ultimately assumes, is opaque; rather than reveal the underlying social relations that create value, it obscures them.

David Harvey, one of Marx's best modern readers, writes that "the way things appear to us in daily life can conceal as much as it can reveal about their social meaning."[30] Elsewhere, Harvey writes, "[m]oney and market exchange draws a veil over, 'masks' social relationships between things. This condition Marx calls 'the fetishism of commodities.' It is one of Marx's most compelling insights, for it poses the problem of how to interpret the real but nevertheless superficial relationships that we can readily observe in the market place in appropriate social terms."[31] The late Polish philosopher Leszek Kolakowski elaborates, writing that "[t]his process whereby social relations masquerade as things or relations between things is the cause of human failure to understand the society in which we live. In exchanging goods for money men involuntarily accept the position that their own qualities, abilities, and efforts do not belong to them but somehow inhere in the objects they have created."[32] Fetishism, according to Kolakowski, describes "the inability of human beings to see their own products for what they are, and their unwitting consent to be enslaved by human power instead of wielding it."[33]

Marx was highly aware of the contradictory nature of the reality of economic life captured in the concept of fetishism. In *Capital*, he writes that "[i]t is . . . just this ultimate money-form of the world of commodities that actually conceals, instead of disclosing, the social character of private labor, and the social relations between the individual producers."[34] In other words, the relationships between the individuals who created the commodities are expressed in the form of the commodities themselves. As a result, the underlying relationships—their meaning, their value, both economic and social—are obscured.

In a financial world of increasing opacity, where money assumes increasingly complex and derivative forms, Marx's insight deserves special attention. The crisis of 2008, which buried the balance sheets of financial institutions in complex financial derivatives whose value turned out to be highly unstable if not completely indeterminable, was the ultimate lesson in the fetishism of commodities. Money, "the fetish character of commodities," the physical embodiment of the labor that goes into producing physical things, whether they be crops or widgets, is the primary way in which society comes to a common expression or understanding about the value of material things. Money is the common denominator to which all economic objects are reduced. But when money assumes indecipherable forms, the economic system becomes destabilized. Moreover, the stability or instability of money becomes a measure of the stability or instability of a society on other levels—social, political, and cultural.

There are two types of monetary stability that bear on this issue: the stability of the value of money and the stability of the form of

money. Modern markets have altered the character of both The forms
of money have grown increasingly complex, primarily though not exclusively through the growth of financial derivatives; this has both complicated and obscured the meaning of money. As a result, the stability
of money and its meaning have been shaken. Instead of simple expressions of debt such as bonds, we have complex expressions of value
such as credit default swaps and collateralized debt obligations. As noted
above and as discussed elsewhere in this book, these types of derivatives
are a striking example of the fetish of commodities. Even Marx could
not have dreamed of a form of money more alienated from labor than
these modern financial concoctions. Instead of simple legal tender, we
have complex legal contracts that in many cases impose contradictory or
poorly defined obligations on the parties and in which the lenders and
borrowers have for all intents and purposes no connection with each
other. Moreover, such financial constructs are the epitome of opacity;
their value is not immediately apparent but can be established only after a series of complex calculations. But even that determination is an
approximation, for those calculations are themselves subject to a series
of mathematical assumptions (not objective certainties) such as present
value, discount rate, correlation, and so forth. As a result, the ability
to reach general agreement on value is fragile and rather than being
scientific becomes highly susceptible to subjective judgment.

Trillions of dollars of financial instruments—stocks, bonds, loans,
currencies, and derivatives thereof—are traded daily based on verbal
agreements that are only later written down into enforceable legal contracts. It is a tribute to the strength of market customs and practices that
it took as long as it did for this system to break down under the weight
of new financial instruments whose novel formulations were sufficiently
complex to finally disrupt long-established norms of conduct.

The Instability of Value

It should be no surprise, then, that modern markets have the potential
to trade with far greater volatility than we have ever seen before. In a
world where financial instruments are almost ridiculously complex and
increasingly divorced from their underlying economic referents, the
concept of what a financial instrument is worth is thrown into question

to a greater degree than ever before. The advent of derivatives in particular has thrown the entire question of value into doubt, creating an opportunity for buyers and sellers to disagree to a wider extent than ever before on the clearing prices for trades. Just a few years before the 2008 financial crisis, Mark C. Taylor wrote a groundbreaking book, *Confidence Games: Money and Markets in a World without Redemption*, in which he predicted the nature of the crisis that would drive markets to the edge:

> As derivatives became more abstract and the mathematical formulas for the trading programs more complex, markets began to lose contact with anything resembling the real economy. To any rational investor, it should have been clear that markets were becoming a precarious Ponzi scheme. Contrary to expectation, products originally developed to manage risk increased market volatility and thus intensified the very uncertainty investors were trying to avoid.[35]

The condition described by Taylor is simply an extension, or exaggeration, of something Marx identified. There is an inherent contradiction in a system that uses money to express value at the same time that it conceals the underlying basis of that value. This creates the opportunity for the users of money to place an incorrect value on the underlying referent.

Marx understood that "[t]he possibility . . . of quantitative incongruity between price and magnitude of value, or the deviation of the former from the latter, is inherent in the price-form itself."[36] He argued that "[t]his is no defect, but, on the contrary, admirably adapts the price-form to a mode of production whose inherent laws can impose themselves as the means of apparently lawless irregularities that compensate one another."[37] Further, "[t]he price-form . . . is not only compatible with the possibility of a quantitative incongruity between magnitude of value and price, i.e., between the former and its expression in money, but it may also conceal a qualitative inconsistency, so much so, that, although money is nothing but the value-form of commodities, price ceases altogether to express value."[38] Marx's words are particularly apposite in markets where buyers and sellers are effectively on strike, such as the credit markets in 2008. The problem Marx describes—the incompatibility between value and its form of expression—is exacerbated when the form that money assumes is no longer simple stocks or bonds but far more complex derivative contracts such as credit default swaps or collateral debt obligations. Such instruments are by their very nature more difficult to value due to their inherent complexity. Their value is buffeted on a real-time basis by a variety of factors.

Take the example of a credit default swap: Its value is affected by changes in interest rates assumptions about the time value of money, changes in the financial condition of the underlying corporate credit, changes in the financial condition of similar corporations, supply and demand factors in the market for corporate credit, general economic conditions, and other factors. Moreover, the obligations of the two parties to the contract are defined in a contract that is theoretically standardized but is in practice bespoke. Accordingly, the ability to agree on the value of such complex instruments is highly compromised. This is one of the prices we pay—in some markets a very high price—for the benefits provided by instruments that are designed to reduce risk by carving it up in ways that dissipate it among different market participants. When one considers the complexity of such instruments within the context of what Marx teaches us about the instability of value, one might consider it a miracle that modern markets function at all. It is also a sign of the durability of Marx's thought that he still has so much to teach us today about capital and capitalism.

John Maynard Keynes

Reading *The General Theory of Employment, Interest and Money* (1936) should be sufficient to disabuse people of the dominant thought paradigms that have guided investors into serial investment disasters in recent years. The concepts of efficient markets or rational investors are rendered mincemeat in the hands of John Maynard Keynes, who writes with a flair that few before or after have been able to match. The irony is that his great wisdom about so many aspects of market behavior has also led to such grotesquely wrong conclusions about how to solve market crises and revive troubled economies. The Keynesian prescription for recovery involves doing more of what was done in the first place to create the crisis: governments spending, printing and borrowing more money. This may solve the immediate crisis, but it is bound to create long-term imbalances that must be resolved at some point in the future, either through currency devaluation, inflation, or other destabilizing economic and social processes. The problem is that nobody has come up with a viable short-term alternative to the Keynesian solution that does not involve swallowing some very distasteful short-term medicine: bank and business failures, high rates of unemployment, social upheaval, and similar distresses. In the midst of a crisis, Keynes' prescription makes sense as a means of preventing immediate economic calamity. But it leaves a much bigger mess to clean up in the long run.

Accordingly, Keynesianism is best limited to a prescription for crisis management. As Hyman Minsky stresses in his seminal study of the master, "[i]n 1936, when *The General Theory* appeared, the world was in the seventh year of the Great Depression."[39] The so-called classical school of economics had failed to predict the coming of the depression, and Keynes' work was an attempt to come up with both an explanation of the causes and proposed solutions. Keynes developed his economic insights within the context of a global collapse of unparalleled depth and duration. The real goal of economic policy should be to minimize the types of imbalances that lead to crisis in the first place, which requires a sophisticated understanding of the processes of capital and the behavior of capitalists.

A careful reading of *The General Theory* reveals that a book considered to be one of the great economic texts of all time is as much an economics treatise as a psychological primer on how investors behave and what this means for the market as a whole. While the book is filled with its fair share of economic jargon and mathematical formulas, it is primarily memorable for its passages describing human behavior. Perhaps this is what accounts for the fact that its lasting value lies more in its psychological insights into the markets and investor behavior than in its prescriptions for economic policy management. In fact, as noted earlier, its policy prescriptions tend to promulgate economic imbalances. The proper way to employ them proscriptively to reduce the boom and bust cycles of capitalism would be to apply them in a countercyclical manner outside of the crisis context for which they are primarily designed.

Keynes argues that emotion, not reason, is what dominates investment markets. The distinction he draws between speculation and productive investment is based on this view. Keynes defines "speculation" as "the activity of forecasting the psychology of the market" and "enterprise" as "the activity of forecasting the prospective yield of assets over their whole life."[40] Unfortunately, the more developed markets become, the more speculative they become because of the fact that market participants are primarily emotional animals. "As the organisation of investment markets improves," he writes, "the risk of the predominance of speculation . . . increase[s]."[41] Capitalism is highly unstable because it is inherently prone to the imbalances resulting from the fact that capitalists are driven by emotion rather than reason. "The social object of skilled investment should be to defeat the dark forces of time and ignorance which envelop our future. The actual, private object of the most skilled investment to-day is 'to beat the gun,' as the Americans so well express it, to outwit the crowd, and to pass the bad, or depreciating, half-crown to the other fellow."[42] In other words, the primary objective of investors is not to determine the fundamental value of an investment; rather, it is to determine what other investors think the value is.

In a famous passage, Keynes compares investing to a newspaper competition in which people have to choose the six prettiest faces out of a hundred photographs:

[P]rofessional investment may be likened to those newspaper competitions in which the competitors have to pick out the six prettiest faces from a hundred photographs, the prize being awarded to the competitor whose choice most nearly corresponds to the average preferences of the competitors as a whole; so that each competitor has to pick, not those faces which he himself finds prettiest, but those which he thinks likeliest to catch the fancy of the other competitors, all of whom are looking at the problem from the same point of view. It is not a case of choosing those which, to the best of one's judgment, are really the prettiest, nor even those which average opinion genuinely thinks the prettiest. We have reached the third degree where we devote our intelligences to anticipating what average opinion expects the average opinion to be. And there are some, I believe, who practice the fourth, fifth, and higher degrees.[43]

All financial instruments, not merely stocks and bonds, are subject to this type of beauty contest in which the goal is to pick the most average-looking girl. Keynes writes with respect to interest rates: "the rate of interest is a highly psychological phenomenon . . . the long-term market-rate of interest will depend, not only on the current policy of the monetary authority but also on market expectations concerning its future policy."[44] The problem arises when all the faces look pretty or ugly at the same time. At such times, all moors of value are lost and men are left to the vagaries of the crowd to guide their behavior. The outcome is rarely favorable for individual investors or for the market as a whole.

Keynes' famous description of the "animal spirits" that drive financial markets captures his emphasis on the emotional component that he views as central to the investment process. This famous passage is worth quoting in its entirety:

> Even apart from the instability due to speculation, there is the instability due to the characteristic of human nature that a large proportion of our positive activities depend on spontaneous optimism rather than on a mathematical expectation, whether moral or hedonistic or economic. Most, probably, of our decisions to do something positive, the full consequences of which will be drawn out over many days to come, can only be taken as a result of animal spirits—of a spontaneous urge to action rather than inaction, and not as the outcome of a weighted average of quantitative benefits multiplied by quantitative probabilities. Enterprise only pretends to itself to be mainly actuated by the statements in its own prospectus, however candid and sincere. Only a little more than an expedition to the South Pole, is it based on an exact calculation of benefits to come. Thus if the animal spirits are dimmed and the spontaneous optimism falters, leaving us to depend on nothing but a mathematical expectation, enterprise will fade and die—though fears of loss may have a basis no more reasonable than hopes of profit had before.[45]

Finally, he writes that "human decisions affecting the future, whether personal or political or economic, cannot depend on strict mathematical expectation, since the basis for making such calculations does not exist; and . . . it is our innate urge to activity which makes the wheels go round, our rational selves choosing between the alternatives as best we are able, calculating where we can, but often falling back for our motive on whim or sentiment or chance."[46] As insightful as these words are, we should also remember that were written by the man on whom modern policy makers are relying to revive the global economy. Policy makers need to understand the entirety of Keynes' message, not just the parts that they want to hear in a quest for politically expedient solutions to intractable economic problems.

Perhaps Keynes' most significant insight into human behavior involves what he termed the "paradox of thrift," the phenomenon that is a version of the "fallacy of composition" discussed earlier. Keynes did not originate this phenomenon; it appears to date back to the 1714 allegorical poem "The Fable of the Bees," which Keynes quotes from rather extensively in Chapter 23 of *The General Theory* (who says there is no place for literature in economics—even mediocre literature?). This characteristic of human behavior turns on its head all concepts of rational behavior. It also renders most market theories useless in practice. The paradox of thrift holds that if too many people seek to save rather than spend money at one time, the economy will be starved of investment and consumption and economic growth will suffer. The paradox comes from the fact that saving rather than spending is believed to be a constructive activity, yet it leads to economic harm when engaged in by too many people at the same time. This is also true with respect to investment activity. When market conditions lead too many investors to sell at the same time, markets tends to fall rapidly and in some cases collapse. Individual selling decisions may well be rational and designed to protect capital, but when too many investors make such decisions at the same time it leads to massive market losses. Few if any of the classic investment theories such as Harry Markowitz's modern portfolio theory or William Sharpe's capital asset pricing model or the Black-Scholes model effectively capture this reality (or other discontinuities, which are admittedly difficult to capture in mathematical language). Moreover, mass selling has the psychological effect of causing panic and leading to further selling, another phenomenon for which the classic investment theories fail to account.

Throughout *The General Theory*, Keynes stresses the importance of human expectations in economics. In fact, he writes that "the part played by expectations in economic analysis" was one of three "perplexities" that most impeded the writing of his great book.[47] For Keynes, expectations about the future are everything. "During a boom," he writes, "the popular estimation of the magnitude of both these risks, both borrower's risk and lender's risk, is apt to become unusually and imprudently low."[48] Human beings tend to believe that the current state of affairs will continue, although their belief is not based on anything to which they can point. "In abnormal times in particular, when the hypothesis of an indefinite continuance of the existing state of affairs is less plausible than usual even though there are no express grounds to anticipate a definite change, the market will be subject to waves of optimistic and pessimistic sentiment, which are unreasoning and yet in a sense legitimate where no solid basis exists for a reasonable calculation."[49] This leads to the uncomfortable reality that whatever the models purport to tell us, markets tend to seize up when large numbers of investors decide to sell at the same time because "there is no such thing as liquidity of investment for the community as a whole."[50]

One dramatic example of this phenomenon occurred in 1998 when the hedge fund Long Term Capital Management collapsed. Investors suddenly discovered correlations among different asset classes for which their models had failed to account. This was largely due to the fact that these correlations arose from factors such as overlapping ownership of assets by a concentrated group of institutions and hedge funds, the use of exorbitant amounts of leverage by these holders to own these assets, and other factors that even Nobel Prize winning economists failed to grasp (perhaps precisely because they were Nobel Prize winners!). These factors led investors to simultaneously sell positions that in theory should not have been correlated but in practice became instantly and highly correlated. One of Keynes' great strengths is that he didn't allow mathematical formulas to distract him from the human realities of investing. Hence, the famous adage that is attributed to him, "The market can stay irrational longer than you can stay solvent." In a world heading ever deeper into insolvency, such words should ring in our ears.

Hyman Minsky

The 2008 financial crisis did a great deal to revive the reputation of Hyman Minsky. The revival was long overdue. Minsky remains a grossly underappreciated thinker, but he understood and acknowledged the importance of those who preceded him. Minsky rightly considered

Keynes' *The General Theory* to be one of the most important works of modern thought: "[i]f Keynes, along with Marx, Darwin, Freud, and Einstein, belongs in the pantheon of seminal thinkers who triggered modern intellectual revolutions, it is because of the contribution to economics, both as a science and as a relevant guide to public policy, that is contained in his *General Theory of Employment Interest and Money*."[51] Minsky's work is based on his interpretation of Keynes, and it is difficult to read one today without reading the other.

Minsky is known for his "financial-instability hypothesis," which argues that stable economies sow the seeds of their own demise. Minsky traces this idea back to Keynes' thinking in *The General Theory*. Minsky explains that "implicit in [Keynes'] analysis is a view that a capitalist economy is fundamentally flawed." He continues:

> This flaw exists because the financial system necessary for capitalist vitality and vigor—which translates entrepreneurial animal spirits into effective demand for investment—contains the potential for runaway expansion, powered by an investment boom. This runaway expansion is brought to a halt because accumulated financial changes render the financial system fragile, so that not unusual changes can trigger serious financial difficulties. Because Keynes arrived at his views on how a capitalist economy operates by examining problems of decision-making under conditions of intractable uncertainty, in his system, stability, even if it is the result of policy, is destabilizing. Even if policy succeeds in eliminating the waste of great depressions, the fundamental financial attributes of capitalism mean that periodic difficulties in constraining and then sustaining demand will ensue.[52]

Minsky traced his financial instability hypothesis to Keynes, but there is an even deeper level that links these two men's thinking. Keynes' focus on the importance of human expectations in the face of uncertainty strongly influenced Minsky's view of how economic actors react to conditions of financial stability.

Implicit in Minsky's "financial-instability hypothesis" is the assumption that economic actors conduct themselves based on how they feel about their economic environment. When they experience a stable environment, they are emboldened to take risk; when they experience instability and hardship, they tend to act more conservatively. These are primarily psychological reactions to their experiences, an exercise of their "animal spirits" as Keynes described them. These two great economists understood that economic behavior was human behavior, and, as such, was influenced by the forces that govern human beings—feelings and emotion. This relates their work back to Adam Smith, who believed that human beings acted in a certain manner in order to gain the approval of other people. Acting in a manner that gained other peoples' approval, Smith believed, would reinforce certain types of behavior that were conducive to the development of a fair and just society. The essentially social nature of all economic behavior then calls us back to Marx's criticism of capitalism. Marx believed that capitalism would fail because it insufficiently acknowledged the social or human component of labor and instead reduced human relations through the process of fetishism to relationships between things in the form of money. These four thinkers believed that human relationships and emotions lie at the heart of all capitalist processes. As we have learned often enough over the past two decades, any system that fails to adequately account for the human element that lies at the heart of all economic activity is prone to instability and potential failure.

Hyman Minsky was largely unknown outside the world of economic professionals until the financial crisis, although some observers such as PIMCO's Paul McCulley, *The Credit Bubble Bulletin*'s Doug Noland, GMO LLC's Jeremy Grantham, and I were writing about him for several years before his work came all too vividly to life in the summer of 2007.[53] Today everybody is a Minsky disciple—or should be. Those who were familiar with Minsky's work before the crisis were in the best position to predict the credit cataclysm that occurred. Minsky should now take his place next to John Maynard Keynes as one of the twentieth century's most important economic thinkers. Like those in the pantheon he joins, his contributions were inspired by his keen insights into noneconomic topics such as human psychology.

The "financial-instability hypothesis" can be summarized as follows: The better things get, the better they are expected to continue to be. Human beings tend to extrapolate current conditions indefinitely into the future. Based on the assumption that positive economic conditions will continue, people let their guards down with respect to risk, which leads them to take more of it. As each individual takes more risk, the overall riskiness of the system increases. This is not an insight into economics; it is an insight into human behavior. Minsky did not require a degree in mathematics or physics to come up with his financial instability theory—what he needed was a keen insight into human nature and human psychology.

Minsky expounded on his theory at greatest length in his seminal work, *Stabilizing an Unstable Economy* (1986). Minsky divided the process of risk absorption into three phases. In the first phase, which he called "hedge finance," economic actors expect cash flows from their business operations to be sufficient to meet their obligations now and in the future. In the second phase, termed "speculative finance," economic actors do not expect cash flows from operations to be sufficient to meet all of their cash payment obligations, particularly their short-term obligations. In this phase, actors must roll over existing debt in order to remain solvent. The third phase, which was given the colorful and somewhat controversial name of "Ponzi finance," involves a situation in which economic actors know that they will not be able to meet their cash obligations through operations and will have to borrow to meet them. In this phase, additional debt must be raised in order to retain solvency.[54] Ponzi finance is the dominant characteristic of the United States and other Western economies today. It is a decidedly unhealthy state of affairs.

The stability of an economy is determined by the mix of these three types of financing structures within it. Hedge finance structures are subject to the risk that business operations will not generate sufficient cash flows to meet future obligations. Speculative and Ponzi finance structures are not only subject to that risk but are vulnerable to a much more significant risk that is outside the control of individual businessmen—the risk that financial markets will become inhospitable and render it difficult to roll over existing debt or raise additional debt to meet future obligations. As Minsky writes, "[s]peculative and Ponzi units must issue debt in order to meet payments and commitments. This means that they must always meet the market. Furthermore, they are vulnerable to any disruption, in the form of transitory unfavorable financing terms, that may occur in financial markets."[55] For this reason, speculative and Ponzi finance structures are far riskier than hedge finance structures, and an economy whose composition is weighted more toward Ponzi financing rather than hedge financing is prone to instability.

Large Western economies had become Ponzi economies by the mid-1990s. By the mid-2000s, conditions were so Ponzi-like that it was only a question of "when," not "if" the system would succumb to internal instability. From homebuyers who borrowed more than their homes were worth based on the belief that home prices would continue rising, to private equity firms that purchased companies at exorbitant prices using debt structures that enabled them to pay interest in additional debt rather than cash, the entire financial system was engaged in one massive Ponzi scheme in the sense that Hyman Minsky used the term. This does not mean that such financing schemes were fraudulent or illegal (although in the case of the mortgage market many reportedly were). It does mean, however, that in most cases they were imprudently or even recklessly constructed.

Minsky's use of the term Ponzi should not be glossed over. Minsky responded to harsh criticism of his use of the term in a long footnote to his seminal article titled, "The financial-instability hypothesis" (1982): "[t]he type of financial relations that I label Ponzi finance is a quite general and not necessarily fraudulent characteristic of a capitalist financial structure. Financial relations the validation of which depends on the selling out of positions are a normal functioning part of the capitalist process. Furthermore, every 'bubble' or stock-market speculation in which profitability depends on the timing of entry and exit is of the nature of a 'Ponzi scheme.'"[56] Recent commentators who have brought Minsky's work back to the prominence that it deserves have devoted little attention to Minsky's terminology, but it deserves further emphasis than it has received.

Minsky's use of the term "Ponzi" in describing the type of financial structure that grew predominant in the late twentieth and early twenty-first century should not be considered disingenuous. Ponzi is not a morally neutral word. It refers to Charles Ponzi, an infamous swindler who, for a short period in 1920, employed the technique of using money raised from later investors to repay earlier investors. He was not the first and certainly not the last crook to employ such a scheme, but his name stuck to it (although Bernie Madoff has offered himself as an alternative, with the new term "being Madoff'd" starting to sneak into modern vernacular). Minsky was making a point in using such a value-laden term, and despite his seemingly innocent disclaimer about his intent, there can be no question of his disapproval:

> However, the label attached to the financing relations I identify as Ponzi is not important. What is important is whether or not such structures exist and what effect such financing has on system behavior. In particular, if Ponzi financing exists, if the extent of Ponzi financing determines the domain of instability of the economy, and if Ponzi financing is a normal adjunct of investment production, then there are normally functioning endogenous factors that make for significant instabilities.[57]

Minsky's insight about Ponzi structures is of crucial importance in understanding modern capitalism. Ponzi finance is highly unstable; it is vulnerable not only to changes in conditions of borrowers, but to deterioration in market conditions. Ponzi finance is closely associated with financial instability. Describing such a state of affairs with a term associated with a swindler should not be understood as value neutral; it is a way of suggesting that such financing structures are irresponsible and immoral, even if they are not illegal. The fact that they lead to financial instability that causes social unrest, higher unemployment, a widening of the gap between rich and poor, and other adverse consequences suggests that such financing structures should be viewed as reckless and socially damaging. In his own deadpan way, this is what Minsky was trying to tell us.

Government policies that permit Ponzi finance to flourish end up imposing an enormous burden on society. This is why an increasing number of economists take issue with former Federal Reserve Chairman Alan Greenspan's view that a central bank should not take action with respect to a sharp increase in asset prices. In fact, Minsky teaches that it is not rising asset prices per se that should trigger countercyclical policy by central banks so much as the reasons behind the rise. If Ponzi finance structures are responsible for pushing prices higher, central banks should begin tightening policy and taking other steps to counter the process. Failing to take any action in the face of sharply rising asset prices that were being fed by an orgy of leverage in the form of Ponzi finance turned out to be a catastrophic error on Greenspan's part during his term, a mistake that was repeated by his successor Ben Bernanke during the first two years of his term. Minsky's "financial-instability hypothesis" also renders highly dubious concepts such as "the great moderation" that Bernanke endorsed in advocating that the economy had reached a new era of stability in the mid-2000s. Bernanke promulgated this view in a widely noted speech in 2004 and again in a 2006 speech and clung to it until 2007. A careful reading of Minsky, however, would have led Bernanke to reach just the opposite conclusion—that benign economic conditions would lead, not to further benignity, but to instability. This turned out to be a profound intellectual error as it led the Federal Reserve to follow a lax monetary policy for far too long.

It is one thing when manufacturing firms collapse under the weight of their debts and other obligations; their balance sheets can be restructured and their assets sold or liquidated in the process Joseph Schumpeter described as "creative destruction." The presumption is that more productive businesses will take their place in the economy. But when financial firms run into trouble because they cannot pay their debts, a larger societal interest is harmed because of the public utility function that financial institutions play in the economy. This is particularly true in regulated industries where the government has provided an explicit or implicit guarantee. The collapse of a financial firm leads to deflationary debt destruction as capital is wiped out. This leads to a loss in confidence among economic actors that leads to the death of capital. When that occurs, governments must act through their central banks and fulfill their functions as lenders of last resort. In 2008, conditions became so desperate that the world saw its central banks and governments perform this function in previously unimagined ways.

Lessons on Capital from the Masters

Smith, Marx, Keynes, and Minsky are deserving of a much more thorough examination than they have received here. The point of this discussion of their work has been to draw out some common insights that these intellectual giants offered with respect to capital and capitalist processes. First, all of them consider capital and capitalism to be highly unstable phenomena that are subject to the emotions of economic actors in the marketplace. This renders markets themselves extremely unstable and subject to cycles of boom and bust. Second, the unavoidable conclusion that reading these men's work leads to is that understanding capital, capitalism, and markets requires a deep understanding of human nature, in particular the irrational and emotional side of human nature. Mathematical understanding is of extremely limited utility when it comes to navigating financial markets because the forces that drive these markets are not mathematical or rational in nature. Third, these four thinkers believe that capitalist processes bear within themselves the seeds of their own instability and potential destruction. The innate nature of capital and capitalism involves contradictions and conflicts that lead to instability.

Reading these seminal thinkers then raises the question about what one should think about the fact that so much of modern finance theory and market dogma is guided by belief in concepts such as efficient markets, quantitative finance, and other rational constructs that are repeatedly belied by the real world experience of investors. Why do investors ignore not only the best that has been thought about markets but their own experiences, and as a result repeatedly subject themselves to catastrophic losses? The answer lies in the fact that investors, who also happen to be human beings, cannot escape their essential nature. Emotion is such a powerful phenomenon precisely because it trumps reason. Men are made to believe that the future will resemble the past, and in some respects it does. But they tend to be extremely selective in choosing which past they remember.

As with so many complex systems, markets discovered in 2007 and 2008 that the tools designed to reduce risk introduced new risks that hadn't been contemplated. Even worse, these risks were hidden by the complex and opaque nature of the new financial instruments that were sold as risk management tools. These products contained within them the seeds of their own demise because they were not in fact new creations but just another form of capital and subject to the same laws that have always governed capital. If we are to contain the madness of crowds, we need to help them understand what is driving them insane. In uncovering the answer to this question, we learn that the fault lies not in the stars but in ourselves. For while every individual rationally pursues economic goals that he believes will enrich him, the aggregation of those individual desires tends to lead to instability. It is no accident, therefore, that each of the four thinkers discussed in this chapter emphasized the important role played in the markets by the "fallacy of composition." Cycles of boom and bust will remain with us as long as we remain human. Try as we might to remove the human element from economics, the dismal science remains in its essence trapped by who we are.

CHAPTER 3

Empty Promises

At the heart of Adam Smith's admonition that society should strive to be just is the concept of debt: debt, not in a purely financial sense, but in a philosophical and moral sense. Every economic transaction involves an exchange of value between two parties. But it also involves an exchange of promises. Two parties undertake obligations to each other. One party offers something to another party, and this gives rise to an obligation by the other party to give something back. Smith was seeking to outline the types of institutional arrangements that would ensure that such exchanges would be fair to both parties, or as fair as possible within the exigencies of human society. He was asking the question: What do human beings owe each other? What is a debt? What is an obligation? How do we balance the scales between people as evenly as possible?

Promises Aren't What They Used to Be

Any discussion of the modern financial system and the disarray into which it was thrown in 2008 must confront the overwhelming role that debt plays in virtually all financial arrangements. Among the most significant changes in the global economy—particularly in the United States and other Western economies—over the past three decades was the incredible increase in indebtedness at all levels of society. Between 1980 and 2008, the share of household and consumer debt alone increased from 100 percent of the U.S. GDP to 173 percent, an increase of approximately $6 trillion.[1] The debt balloon expanded until it literally burst. The growth of debt financing and the increasing substitution of debt for equity in institutional capital structures and personal balance sheets has been the gravamen of our age. We cannot understand what happened to our economy or to our society until we understand debt in both its economic and cultural senses. In order to properly discuss debt, we need to understand the essential role that promissory arrangements play in every financial instrument or transaction known to man.

Every financial instrument involves some type of promise. Whether it is called a stock or a bond, equity or debt, an insurance policy or a pension trust, an option or a futures contract, every financial instrument involves an immediate payment of money in exchange for a promise of future receipts. Sometimes that promise of future payment is contingent, as in the case of an equity security. In other cases, the promise is certain, as in the case of a debt obligation like a bond or a bank loan, or in the unhappy case of a life insurance contract. The primary difference between debt and equity is the degree of certainty and the time horizon (fixed or uncertain) over which that the promise will be kept.

Any type of promise implies a belief in the future. Promises are by their nature a sign of optimism. Equity promises are more contingent than debt promises, so perhaps they denote the greatest degree of optimism of all financial instruments. In a leveraged capital structure, all of the debt is effectively a form of equity since there is a significant risk that it will not be repaid. Equity demands a higher return than debt because of this high degree of uncertainty regarding repayment. The forms that our financial promises assume say a great deal about our expectations about the future, not only economically, but philosophically and culturally. In recent years, the traditional differences between debt and equity have become blurred. This is due to the fact that leverage has become an increasingly dominant component of the economy's capital and of the capital structure of companies. Financial innovation has created new forms of capital such as new types of preferred stock and convertible debt that combine the attributes of debt and equity. Many derivative instruments also combine debt and equity features. High yield bonds (corporate debt obligations rated less than investment grade by the major rating agencies) are another type of security that combines the attributes of debt and equity. The high yield bond market has exploded in size since its founding in the 1980s. Today, these bonds constitute a significant component of the capital structures of many U.S. and European corporations. While they are considered debt, however, they are not really debt at all. Instead, they are in reality a hybrid debt/equity security that is best described as "equity with a coupon" that poses a high risk of default.

This conflation of debt and equity is one reason why traditional correlations between asset classes have broken down. While traditional portfolio theory teaches that the returns on bonds and stocks should not correlate in certain types of economic environments, recent experience has demonstrated that the returns on these different asset classes in fact correlate very strongly, particularly in extreme market conditions. This should not be surprising in view of the fact that these asset classes have increasingly come to resemble each other in their constituent parts. The different debt and equity layers of a leveraged capital structure—which now describes the vast majority of corporations in the United States and Europe—should logically trade in tandem as the financial condition of the underlying business improves or deteriorates. There is no rational reason why a leveraged company's debt and equity should react any differently to positive or negative news about the business's prospects. The fact that the stock prices of bankrupt companies trade above zero while its debt trades at a sharp discount remains one of the abiding anomalies of the financial markets, one that is best explained by the adage that markets don't work in theory but have no choice but to work in practice.

As the forms of debt and equity have changed, so have the guises in which financial promises travel. First, as noted above, debt rather than equity has become the predominant form of capital in circulation. Second, the structures in which debt appears have become increasingly complex and opaque and organized in a manner that has ruptured the relationship between borrowers and lenders. These changes have radically transformed the economy on both a local and global level and have served as both cause and consequence of profound changes in our values and expectations.

The fact that debt has come to play such a dominant role in our economy says a great deal about our values and beliefs as a society. By choosing to use debt as the dominant medium of exchange, we are telling each other that we trust each other. We are saying that we will keep our promises. We are confirming that our words have common meanings, that we speak a common language, and that we follow a common set of rules. More than anything, we are also affirming our belief in the future. We are telling each other that the world will continue to prosper and grow and that we will do everything reasonably necessary to ensure that happens. Most important, we are counting on the fact that future conditions will be sufficiently robust to allow this debt to be repaid.

At the heart of every debt obligation lie two promises: a lender promises to lend money to a borrower, and a borrower promises to repay that money (with interest) to the lender. In today's highly complex economy, modern debt obligations such as bonds or bank loans include an additional web of subsidiary promises known as "covenants" that govern the behavior of the borrower and the lender. These covenants provide that the borrower will promise to conduct its business in a certain way as consideration for accepting the loan. For example, the borrower will agree not to incur additional debt, or not to pay dividends to its shareholders, or will agree to make financial reports to the borrower on a certain schedule. As long as the borrower keeps these subsidiary promises, the lender promises to stand aside and allow the borrower to manage its affairs as it sees fit.

Martin Wolf, the chief economic commentator for the *Financial Times*, writes that "the central feature of the financial system . . . [is that] it is a pyramid of promises—often promises of long or even indefinite duration. This makes it remarkable that sophisticated financial systems exist. . . . Promises may not be kept."[2] Continuing, Wolf describes the trillions of dollars of outstanding financial assets as "promises of future, of often contingent, receipts in return for current payment. . . . As the financial system grows more complex, it piles promises upon promises."[3] Promises are by their very nature uncertain in their fulfillment. Promises also contain a temporal element—they are executory in nature. As such, they are subject to the contingencies of time and human nature.

When we make a promise to another person, that person is depending on the fact that nothing will change (or change sufficiently) in the intervening time to alter our commitment and ability to keep our word. Yet the world is filled with changing circumstances that may affect our ability or willingness to keep our promises. As all of us know, the only certainty in life is change. So promises are, by their nature, highly contingent. In many respects, making a promise or accepting a promise is a great leap of faith. It denotes a commitment by the person making the promise, and trust by the person receiving the promise. In the global economy, millions (probably billions and perhaps trillions) of promises big and small are made every day. While these promises are being made, circumstances both internal and external to the parties to the promise are changing, sometimes radically. Few of these changing circumstances make it easier for promises to be kept. Most of the time, reality is working to give people reasons or excuses to break, or amend, their promises. It is no small miracle that so many promises are ultimately kept. Large and complex financial transactions involve such a large number of complicated promises (both internal, such as the commitments of the parties, and external, such as the multifarious laws and regulations that must be satisfied) that it is often a miracle that these transactions get consummated at all.

The Digitalization of Promises

In recent years, the form of debt, and therefore the character of our promises, has been drastically altered by the application of computer technology and advanced mathematics to traditional financial instruments such as bonds, mortgage loans, and corporate loans. The digitalization of financial information that was made possible by the computer chip ushered in a revolution in finance that profoundly altered the relationship between lenders and borrowers. The primary change it wrought was severing the personal connection that traditionally existed between the parties to a loan. Instead of going down to the local bank and obtaining a mortgage from a banker with whom he has a personal relationship, today's homeowner enters a transaction with a faceless corporation. This impersonal corporate entity will finance the most important financial transaction the borrower will likely enter into in his lifetime and will be granted enormous power over the borrower's financial future. In effect, this regime creates a system of debts without promises, which in many respects is an oxymoron, or a system of impersonal promises, which is also a contradiction in terms. A better understanding that many of the obligations created by modern finance are empty promises helps us to appreciate the nature of the promises economic actors are now expected to keep, why they are harder to keep (or easier to break) than earlier promises, and why this renders the financial sector increasingly unstable and vulnerable to periodic crises.

Today, all financial data is capable of being digitalized. When data is digitalized, it is reduced to 1s and 0s. This means that every financial instrument is reduced to the same basic constituent parts. The differences between various types of debt obligations, such as mortgages, automobile loans, or bank loans, are effectively erased by this process. The ramifications of this transformation of different things into the same thing have been truly revolutionary. On a practical level, it became possible to analyze, manipulate and stress-test voluminous amounts of financial data in relatively short periods of time. Lending decisions that used to be based, at least in part, on a personal relationship between a lender and a borrower instead came to rely on computer-based underwriting systems that substituted credit scores for human judgment. Among other things, this led to profound intellectual errors involving the use of financial models that failed to consider whether the data was being tested against proper benchmarks.

The digitalization of information made possible the phenomenon that came to be known as "securitization." This process involved the bundling of hundreds or thousands of individual mortgages into special purpose entities that could then be sold to institutional investors. Securitization dramatically increased the distance between individual borrowers and their lenders. Securitizations were effected through the formation of special purpose investment vehicles (that is, corporations or

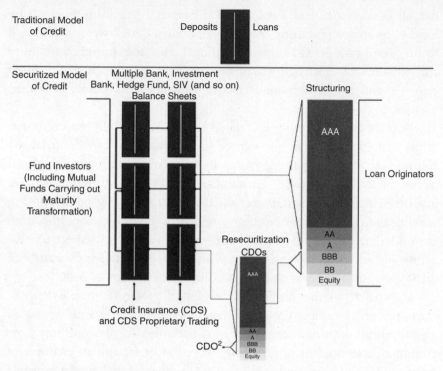

Figure 3.1 Increasing Complexity of Securitized Credit Model

limited liabilities companies) that were normally formed in a tax-favored jurisdiction like the Cayman Islands. The capital structures of these entities were divided into different pieces (Wall Street adopted the French word *tranche* to describe these different pieces) that were piled on top of each other and given descending credit ratings from AAA to BB with an unrated bottom tranche of equity.

Figure 3.1 compares that traditional model of credit (on the top of the figure) with the much more complex securitized model of credit (on the bottom of the figure). By the time the financial engineers were done, we sure weren't in Kansas anymore.

Collateralized Mortgage Obligations

In the case of mortgages, these products were called collateralized mortgage obligations (CMOs). The theory behind CMOs was that a geographically diversified pool of mortgages would have a low risk of default because real estate is local in nature and heavily influenced by local economic conditions. Moreover, these entities were considered to be overcollateralized in the sense that there was believed to be more collateral (more mortgages) than necessary to repay each of the rated tranches and to produce an attractive return to the equity (bottom) tranche.

Both of these assumptions turned out to be woefully wrong. First, while real estate is local, the sale of the ultimate debt to financial institutions that are linked together in global markets eradicated the local nature of the underlying investment. Creators of CMOs should have been looking at the capital sources, not the underlying borrowers, in seeking the protection ostensibly provided by diversification.[4] Second, the underlying mortgages turned out—particularly with respect to sub-prime and Alt-A borrowers—to be worth far less than their face amount during the historic housing market collapse that began in 2006.

Compared to the traditional model of credit (a simple lender/borrower relationship), the securitized model of credit introduced an enormous amount of complexity into the mix. To illustrate just how complex these concoctions became, we will first look at an example of a basic CMO and then jump to a more complicated real-world example that should make readers' heads spin.

Figure 3.2 shows the structure of a basic CMO. Very few if any such structures exist in the real world today, although in the early years of the market deals generally had a limited number of tranches like the one in the figure. CMOs are generally designed so that payments on the underlying mortgages are applied sequentially from the top tranche to the bottom tranche through the life of the deal. The bottom tranche is

Tranche	Par Amount
A	$ 194,500,000
B	36,000,000
C	96,000,000
Z–accrual	73,000,000
	$ 400,000,000

Figure 3.2   Basic CMO Structure
Source: Frank S. Fabozzi, *Fixed Income Analysis*, Second Edition (Hoboken, NJ: John Wiley & Sons, 2007), 278.

unrated and considered equity because it assumes the first risk of loss when mortgages in the pool default.

One of Wall Street's basic business principles is to introduce complexity into its products so it can obscure what it is really selling. CMOs, however, set new standards for complexity (topped only when credit default swaps came along and began to be used to provide insurance on the different tranches of CMOs, a topic discussed in Chapter 6). From the perspective of the manager of a CMO, these products often function like Rubik's Cubes due to the complex web of covenants with which they must comply. Every time the manager wants to buy or sell a new mortgage, he must run that mortgage through a complex model to insure that all of the multiple covenants governing the CMO remain in compliance.

To give readers a flavor of how complex these instruments became, Figure 3.3 shows the structure of an actual CMO issued in 1994 that issued 17 different tranches of debt.

In view of the fact that this was typical of the actual types of instruments that regulators were trying to decipher in the midst of the financial crisis, it is a miracle that the system survived at all. This complexity also raises questions about the ability of even the most sophisticated regulators to even begin to understand these types of investments before being able to determine whether they might cause systemic threats.

One issue with respect to all of these increasingly complex derivative concoctions is the degree of separation between the underlying borrower and the ultimate lender. As the forms of these contracts become increasingly convoluted, the relationship between borrower and lender becomes increasingly attenuated. Promisor and promisee basically have no relationship with each other but are instead connected through a chain of contracts that remove any real sense of a promissory connection from the relationship. In really exotic structures, like the ones that brought insurance giant AIG to its knees, credit default swaps can be tied to individual tranches of collateralized debt obligations (CDOs) that themselves consist of pools of underlying obligations in other CDOs (these are known as CDO-squareds). In such structures, the distance between the lender and ultimate borrower is so attenuated that they might as well reside in different galaxies.

Total Issue: $300,000,000   **Original Settlement Date: 3/30/94**
Issue Date: 2/18/94

Tranche	Original Balance ($)	Coupon (%)	Average Life (years)
A(PAC Bond)	24,600,000	4.50	1.3
B(PAC Bond)	11,100,000	5.00	2.5
C(PAC Bond)	25,500,000	5.25	3.5
D(PAC Bond)	9,150,000	5.65	4.5
E(PAC Bond)	31,650,000	6.00	5.8
G(PAC Bond)	30,750,000	6.25	7.9
H(PAC Bond)	27,450,000	6.50	10.9
J(PAC Bond)	5,220,000	6.50	14.4
K(PAC Bond)	7,612,000	7.00	18.4
LA(SCH Bond)	26,673,000	7.00	3.5
LB(SCH Bond)	36,087,000	7.00	3.5
M(SCH Bond)	18,738,000	7.00	11.2
O(TAC Bond)	13,348,000	7.00	2.5
OA(TAC Bond)	3,600,000	7.00	7.2
IA(IO, PAC Bond)	30,246,000	7.00	7.1
PF(FLTR, Support Bond)	21,016,000	6.75*	17.5
PS(INV FLTR, Support Bond)	7,506,000	7.70*	17.5

Figure 3.3   Summary of Federal Home Loan Mortgage Corporataion   Multi-class Mortgage Participation Certificates
*Coupon at issuance.
Structural Features
Cash Flow Allocation: Commencing on the first principal payment date of the Class A Bonds, principal equal to the amount specified in the Prospectus will be applied to the Class A, B, C, D, E, G, H, , J, K, LB, M, O, OA, PF and PS Bonds. After all other Classes have been retired, any remaining principal will be used to retire the Class O, OA, IA,IB, M, A, B, C, D, G, H, J and K Bonds. The notional Class IA Bond will have its notional principal amount retired along with the PAC Bonds. *Other:* The PAC Range is 95 percent to 300 percent PSA for the A-K Bonds, 190 percent to 250 percent PSA for the LA, LB and M Bonds, and 225 percent PSA for the O and OA Bonds.
SOURCE: Frank S. Fabozzi, *Fixed Income Analysis*, Second Edition (Hoboken, NJ: John Wiley & Sons, 2007), 278.

The distance between the individual mortgage borrower and the ultimate investor in a CMO is illustrated in Figure 3.4.

Figure 3.4 is intended to show the structure of a typical transaction. The process begins when a group of mortgages are packaged together, which occurs on the far left hand side of the diagram. Individual borrowers are aggregated into a pool of borrowers by the originator, who then sells this portfolio to a special purpose vehicle, which is the CMO itself. The CMO then sells rated tranches of debt to investors in order to fund the purchase of these assets. In the real world, these two steps basically occur simultaneously. The original borrower is found all the way on the far left-hand side of the diagram, and the ultimate lender is found all the way on the right side. We are a long way from going to the local bank to get a loan from your friendly neighborhood banker. Figure 3.4 illustrates why CMOs and other types of CDOs are the ultimate fetish instrument. The actual CDO tranches that are sold to investors are completely untethered from the underlying human and economic obligations on which they are based, and create an enormous distance between the ultimate lenders and the actual borrowers who must repay the loans.

This raises important questions about how to determine the value of these instruments, because one of the key points about fetish instruments is that they obscure rather than reveal the relationships that underlie them. As discussed in Chapter 2, money is already one step removed from the commodities whose value it represents. As money assumes increasingly complex forms, its relationship with these commodities becomes increasingly complicated and obscured. The value of a stock or bond, which are just two of the virtually unlimited forms of capital in circulation today, is determined by a complex group of factors because these securities are representations of complex underlying economic relationships. As the forms of money grow increasingly complex, it becomes more and more difficult to determine their value. By the time we reach complex derivative instruments, which are sophisticated legal contracts with many moving parts, the determination of value is almost forbiddingly difficult and requires as much art as mathematics. The liquidity function, which is the ultimate arbiter of value in market economies, is strongly influenced by the form that money assumes. For this reason, complex derivatives are necessarily far less liquid than more simple forms of money like stocks and bonds.

CMOs were constructed using several assumptions that might have worked in theory but failed miserably in practice. The first assumption was that diversification of the underlying portfolio by property type and location would minimize losses based on the belief that these varying

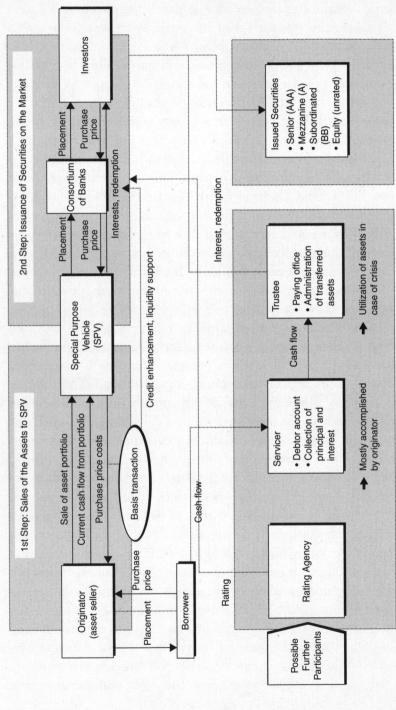

Figure 3.4 Degrees of Separation

SOURCE: Andreas A. Jobst, *Collateralized Loan Obligations (CLOs): A Primer*, London School of Economics and Political Science, Financial Markets Group, 2003.

property types would not behave the same way (in terms of price) in an economic downturn. In point of fact, virtually all real estate prices correlated downward—sharply downward—when the real estate bubble burst beginning in 2006. Why did this happen? This is where things got interesting. As noted earlier, the very fact that so many properties became securitized rendered obsolete the age-old real estate adage that "all real estate is local." Securitization rendered all real estate global, not local, because its ultimate ownership became vested in CMO debt tranches owned by institutional investors. These investors were spread throughout the global financial system rather than located inside local banks whose financial fortunes were closely tied to the local communities near the properties. The money that made it possible to bid up real estate prices in local markets in states like Florida, Arizona, and California no longer originated in those states but instead came from financial centers in Europe and Asia (and even Iceland) where the rated tranches of CMOs were sold. The globalization of the real estate market was the logical outcome of the sundering of the promissory relationship between lender and borrower, but the ramifications were far more profound than a borrower's inability to maintain a personal relationship with his or her lender. Rather than spreading risk, securitization concentrated it among a group of electronically linked investors subject to herd-like behavior.

The second erroneous assumption used to promote CMOs was the belief that a man's house is his castle, that he will do anything to defend it (in modern times this has come to mean he will do anything to prevent being kicked out of it by his lender), and it is therefore a sound credit risk. In fact, just the opposite was true. As the economist Robert Shiller points out, "[a] home represents a highly leveraged exposure to a single, stationary plot of real estate—about the riskiest asset one can imagine."[5] Moreover, the riskiness of this asset was increased when lending standards were thrown out the window by subprime lenders who engaged in some of the most reckless lending practices one can imagine. For example, NINJA loans were extended to borrowers with no jobs, no income and no assets; other loans were extended in amounts that exceeded the value of the underlying properties. The thought that combining hundreds or thousands of risks into a single pool would somehow reduce overall risk actually should have been highly counterintuitive. Yet this was precisely the conclusion that was reached by teams of highly educated mathematicians who apparently were so caught up in their theories and equations that they forgot to apply any common sense to their work. One can concede, for the sake of argument, that it is a rare individual who possesses both the advanced mathematical talents required to design and analyze complex financial instruments and deep knowledge of the financial markets in which those instruments will be traded. But the firms that sold hundreds of billions of dollars of these products certainly possessed inside their walls the combination of talents that should have been brought to bear on the validity of the basic assumptions underlying the CMO financial models. But instead of acting as a series of checks and balances, the different parts of these firms appeared to reinforce reckless behavior rather than rein it in.

A third flawed assumption involved the wholesale dependence on FICO scores to measure the creditworthiness of borrowers. Moody's Investors Service and Standard & Poor's, the two agencies whose ratings were required for the CMO to sell debt to investors, used FICO scores to evaluate the creditworthiness of the underlying borrowers in these CMOs. FICO scores are credit rating scores that are generated by Fair Isaac Corp. of Minneapolis, Minnesota, that evaluate a person's credit-worthiness. The rating agencies (as well as the underwriters and investors in these deals) failed to take into account the fact that FICO scores had not been in existence during previous recessions. As a result, these scores were incapable of providing accurate predictions of consumer behavior during a sharp housing downturn. Rating agencies read data without any reference to historical context. By accepting past data at its face value and failing to adjust it for changes in economic conditions, the rating agencies ended up issuing the wrong ratings on hundreds of billions of dollars of CMOs.

HSBC Drinks the Mortgage Kool-Aid

The folly of this type of thinking is illustrated by what happened when London-based HSBC Holdings PLC, one of the world's largest banks with operations in 76 countries and territories, joined the subprime party with its 2003 acquisition of Household International, Inc. Household was a large subprime lender based in Prospect Heights, Illinois, the heart of the United States. Less than four years later, in February 2007, the 142-year old British giant announced that it was adding $1.7 billion to its loan reserves to account for losses in its subprime mortgage portfolio. But that was only the beginning. Before the subprime crisis was over, HSBC would suffer many more billions of dollars of losses from the work of its clever doctorates.

The business that HSBC had acquired from Household focused on second lien loans, sometimes known as "piggyback loans." These loans allow a buyer to combine a bigger mortgage from a first mortgagor with a second lien from a second lender that often amounts to 100 percent of the purchase price of a home. In the event of default, the second lien holder is only paid off after the first mortgage is satisfied. For this reason, second liens pay higher interest rates than first liens and are ostensibly more attractive to some lenders who believe that they are capable of evaluating the risk. HSBC believed it was one such lender. It was wrong.

Shortly after its purchase of Household, HSBC's then Chief Executive William Aldinger (in a comment he surely came to regret) bragged that the bank employed 150 PhDs skilled at modeling credit risk. He didn't define what he meant by "risk," and clearly neither did his hard-working PhDs, because it turned out that they clearly lacked the expertise necessary to properly analyze subprime credit and default probabilities. By the end of the first quarter of 2009, HSBC's subprime losses had reached $8.3 billion and were still running. Management admitted that the write-downs were not over either. At that point, it did not require a degree in higher mathematics to calculate the loss at an astonishing $55.3 million per PhD (assuming any of the original 150 were still around and had not been fired).

The HSBC saga illustrates the risk of undue reliance on financial models. Among the problems involved in analyzing HSBC's portfolio, according to the *Wall Street Journal*, was an absence of data on loans to subprime borrowers making small or nonexistent down payments (i.e., borrowers with no equity in their homes who would find it relatively easy to walk away from their loans). It turns out that HSBC was relying heavily on FICO scores. Prior to this, FICO scores had never been tested against a downturn in the housing market or against second lien loans, rendering them of limited predictive utility. Douglas Flint, HSBC's finance director, told investors that "what is clear now is that FICO scores are less effective or ineffective" when lenders are granting loans in an unusually low interest rate environment. It turns out that using FICO scores in such an environment is akin to using peak earnings to calculate and then project a corporation's future earnings, or applying the decade's lowest default rates to project future corporate bond default rates (all errors that were made by major financial industry players at various times). Actually, if you think about it, it shouldn't have required a single doctorate, not to mention 150 of them, to figure out that different credit tools were needed to build and monitor subprime loan portfolios. As Peter Bernstein noted in his book on risk, "Likeness to truth is not the same as truth. Without any theoretical structure to explain why patterns seem to repeat themselves across time or across systems, these innovations provide little assurance that today's signals will trigger tomorrow's events. We are left with only the subtle sequences of data that the enormous power of the computer can reveal. Thus, forecasting tools based on nonlinear models or on computer gymnastics are subject to many of the same hurdles that stand in the way of conventional probability theory: the raw material of the model is the data of the past."[6] The markets would see this error repeated many times over the next couple of years or, to be more precise, they would see the consequences of an error that was being committed incessantly in the financial world throughout the 1990s and 2000s materialize in frightening dimensions in the 2007–2008 time frame.

A Fetish Is Not a Promise

Securitization eradicated the individual identity of borrowers and substituted a broad-based credit rating that investors came to rely upon in determining whether to purchase CDOs. It no longer mattered whether a borrower was an individual purchasing a home or a car, a corporation using the money to build a new plant or to finance the acquisition of a competitor, or a private equity firm paying too much to buy a company in order to generate transaction fees for its general partners. The individual borrower came to have absolutely no meaning to the ultimate lender. There was absolutely no relationship between borrower and lender.

The securitization of financial assets such as mortgages or bank loans represents the latest modern manifestation of what Karl Marx termed the fetish character of commodities, the commodity in this case being the mortgage or bank loan itself. Marx's description of the lack of relationship between the underlying economic commodity and the form in which it is traded in the marketplace (which was discussed in more detail in Chapter 2) perfectly describes a collateralized debt obligation. Any relationship between lender and borrower in such a product has been completely eradicated. A collateralized debt obligation is the ultimate fetish instrument. The distance between the individual mortgage holder, the economic actor generating cash flows in the form of mortgage payments, and the lender, is about as attenuated as possible. This effectively obliterates the promissory character of the original mortgage and leaves room for all kinds of mischief that can interrupt the flow of funds and repayment of the underlying debt. In more blatant situations, courts in the United States have prevented loans from being foreclosed due to an inability of the collateralized loan obligation to prove ownership of the underlying loans. In other words, the entity lost track of the deed to the home![7] Instruments that were designed to reduce risk by slicing and dicing it and reallocating it among parties who could pick and choose their favorite flavor instead ended up creating a poisonous buffet.

Parties that have no relationship are in no position to make promises to each other. Financial instruments, even the debts packaged into large pools and then resold to investors in securitized form, still involve formal but depersonalized promises between the parties that created them. Adam Smith's view that the regard for the opinion of others keeps people in line can play no role in a system in which personal relationships have been sundered. Changing the form of these instruments devalued the promises that stand behind them. It also left the global economy holding sacks of empty promises.

CHAPTER 4

Financialization

One of the key economic phenomena of the last three decades has been the United States' transition from a manufacturer and exporter of goods to a manufacturer and exporter of dollars and other financial products such as derivatives. This could not have been achieved without the complicity of the nation's trading partners, particularly Japan, China, and Middle Eastern countries that needed to invest huge oil surpluses. But the phenomenal growth of finance capital that has come to define capitalism over the past 30 years was accompanied by policies that favored financial market deregulation, a diminution of workers' rights and organized labor power, weakened antitrust enforcement, and corporate governance rules that placed the rights of shareholders ahead of those of all other corporate and societal constituencies. The growing dominance of finance in the world economy was an essential factor in the displacement of productive investment by speculation that culminated in the financial crisis of 2008. Finance became its own *raison d'etre*, and instead of providing credit to fund capital expansion and economic growth, the financial sector's function became to expand itself.

Money Begetting Money

The term that has been used to describe this phenomenon is "financialization." It is the process of money begetting money, or more broadly of capital begetting capital. Financialization, along with globalization, is arguably the defining economic force of our time. Surprisingly little has been written about this phenomenon while barrels of ink have been spilled (and continue to be spilled) on the topic of globalization.[1] The term is broadly defined as increasing the role that finance plays in virtually every facet of modern life and culture. Perhaps the most useful definition has been provided by the late Peter Gowan, who defined "financialization" as "the total subordination of the credit system's public functions to the self-expansion of money capital. Indeed, the entire spectrum of capitalist activity is drawn under the sway of money capital, in that the latter absorbs an expanding share of the profits generated across all other sectors."[2] Gowan's definition certainly captures the increasingly dominant role that finance has assumed not merely in modern market economies in which the exchange of physical goods has been increasingly supplanted by the exchange of different intangible forms of capital, but in modern culture where areas such as media, architecture, and art have become increasingly permeated by monetary forms and influences.[3]

Financialization has also been nourished by remarkable advances in computer technology that have turned the world into a vast network of interconnected markets. Commodities are now traded around the clock through these global networks, and it is the very ability to trade these economic objects 24/7/365 that has had an enormous effect on their value, as well as on the stability of their value and of the values that they represent. In the 1950s, President Dwight Eisenhower warned of the dangers of the military-industrial complex. Today, the world is threatened by a financial-political complex. While we still have superpowers (as well as rogue actors) staring each other down with nuclear weapons of mass destruction, today we also have highly leveraged financial institutions deemed too big to fail staring each other down with complex financial instruments that are capable of unleashing incalculable economic losses and global instability.

Most important, all of these institutions are linked through a global computer network. As Professor Mark C. Taylor points out, "*the distinctive characteristic of our age is not simply the spread of computers but the impact of connecting them.* When computers are networked *everything* changes. What has occurred in the past four decades is the emergence of a new network economy that is inseparable from a new network culture."[4] Instead of the leaders of sovereign nations holding the keys to complex launch codes, young men and women sit in front of blinking computer screens with no conception of the power they wield over the financial fate of the world. As Taylor notes, "[t]he constantly changing networks that increasingly govern our lives have a distinct logic that we are only beginning to understand."[5] The same can be said of the logic with which these networks govern the markets. Without really understanding what was happening, the world surrendered its sovereignty to those who neither appreciated nor understood or even cared about the responsibility with which they had been vested. This is the real meaning of financialization in global financial markets.

The term financialization began to gain traction in the 1990s in the work of the political scientist Kevin Phillips. Phillips used the term in his 1993 book *Boiling Point* and then devoted an entire chapter to the subject in his follow-up work, *Arrogant Capital*, which appeared the following year. In *Boiling Point*, Phillips described financialization as "the cumulating influence of finance, government debt, unearned income, *rentiers,* overseas investment, domestic economic polarization, and social stratification."[6] He also made the point (which had been made by earlier economic historians, most notably the eminent Frenchmen Fernand Braudel) that "excessive preoccupation with finance and tolerance of debt are apparently typical of great economic powers in their late stages. They foreshadow economic decline, but often accompany new heights of cultural sophistication, in part because the hurly-burly expansion of the middle class and its values are receding. Yet these slow transitions involve real economic cost to the average person or family, and political restiveness reflects that."[7] In *Arrogant Capital*, Phillips expanded on his definition of financialization to tie it to government's decreasing control over capital flows and the economy. He wrote, "finance has not simply been spreading into every nook and cranny of economic life; a sizeable portion of the financial sector, electronically liberated from past constraints, has put aside old concerns with funding the nation's long-range industrial future, has divorced itself from the precarious prospects of Americans who toil in factories, fields, or even suburban shopping malls and is simply feeding wherever it can."[8] The result of this process is a "split between the divergent real and financial economies."[9] In populist terms, financialization stands for the triumph of Wall Street over Main Street. In economic terms, it denotes a far more complex shift in the composition of economic growth in favor of financial rather than industrial capital.

An important component of Phillips' populist view of financialization is the significant political power that financial institutions exercise over U.S. society, which allows them to block reforms aimed at reining in excessive leverage and other potential systemic risks. These institutions and the individuals who manage and work in them have been able to influence economic policies and structures to serve their interests. The most significant manifestation of this power in recent decades has been an incessant push toward financial deregulation, which created more opportunities for financial firms to earn profits through activities that involved greater risks such as increasing balance sheet leverage and reducing systemic transparency. In fact, much of the efforts of powerful financial institutions have been directed at ensuring that their actions are concealed from the eyes of regulators and investors. This has had the effect of ensuring that the risks they were taking were kept beyond the reach of government control.

The concealment of risk has become such a priority for Wall Street that even huge scandals and enormous financial losses and market disruptions resulting from such activities have failed to stop such activity. In 2001, Enron Corporation was revealed to be an empty shell that had shuffled many of its most valuable assets off of its balance sheets with the assistance of some of the largest financial institutions in the world, including Citigroup and J.P. Morgan. Politicians and regulators screamed in outrage as Enron's investment grade rating was shown to be a complete sham and the company was forced to file for bankruptcy protection. But at precisely the same time this was occurring, those very same financial institutions were sponsoring even larger off-balance-sheet entities known as structured investment vehicles or SIVs to hold hundreds of billions of dollars of mortgages, loans, and other financial assets that they wanted to conceal from the eyes of their investors and regulators. This sham only came to an end in 2007 when these entities, which were recklessly financing the purchase of long-dated, illiquid, complex securities with short-term commercial paper, suffered a loss of confidence and were no longer able to roll over their short-term financing facilities. They were forced into liquidation at great cost to their sponsoring banks and equity investors.

But even this couldn't convince Wall Street to come out into the open. At the same time these SIVs were collapsing at great reputational and financial expense to the largest financial institutions in the world, these same firms were actively building and sponsoring secretive trading platforms known as "dark pools." These were designed to facilitate trading strategies such as flash trading that were not only unavailable to the general public but gave these firms the ability to front run (trade ahead of) their own clients, an obviously illegal and immoral activity that was further debased by its very secrecy. Only in the summer of 2009 did the regulatory authorities begin to step in to prevent this latest version of Wall Street's obsession with hiding its activities from the eyes of the world, and even then financial firms were fighting tooth-and-nail through their lobbyists to prevent these extremely profitable activities from being shut down. The financialization of the markets had finally merged into a kind of sanctioned criminality.

When risk is hidden, risk-taking tends to become excessive because economic actors come to ignore the consequences of their actions. A key, and until recently often overlooked, aspect of financialization is a financial industry that has devoted much of its high-priced intellectual capital not only to mispricing risk but to deliberately concealing it. This has permitted these institutions to sell complex products such as derivatives for more than they are worth to parties who are deprived of the information to price them properly. This could only occur because politically powerful institutions were able to muscle regulators into maintaining a hands-off attitude toward their activities.

Power Begetting Power

In the years between the publication of Phillips' books in the early 1990s and the collapse of the financial system in 2008, the largest financial institutions in the United States worked assiduously to limit the ability of regulators to control their business activities. These were the years of prosperity during President Bill Clinton's two terms in office through the time of the first Iraq War, and then the period after the 2001–2002 credit crisis that saw an explosion of debt and complacency that will prove to have few parallels in history. The financial-political complex was successful in, among other things, repealing the Glass-Steagall Act in 1999 (which had limited the ability of deposit-taking institutions to take risks) and lowering the net capital requirements of the five largest investment banks in 2004, two landmark regulatory changes that significantly heightened the systemic risks that led to the 2008 financial crisis. These risks materialized in two primary areas: derivatives and balance sheet leverage for investment banks. The time-honored complicity between K Street and Wall Street to feed the beast of speculation blew up in everybody's faces. Efforts to limit leverage at financial institutions and regulate derivatives in the aftermath of the crisis—measures that could have prevented the crisis in the first place—were actively combatted by an expensive lobbying effort by the largest financial industry firms.

The industry's attempts to block regulatory reform are as old as the industry itself. A case in point, which preceded the 1987 stock market crash, is recounted by former Federal Reserve Chairman Paul Volcker. Volcker told of his failed attempts to alter the rules governing margin requirements in 1986 in order to slow down the flood of leveraged buyouts that were worrying the central bank chairman and other policy makers. Leveraged buyers of corporations were using the target company's shares as collateral for the debt used to purchase these shares, so one obvious way to limit these transactions would have been to limit the amount of borrowing that could be incurred in such situations. When Volcker made such a proposal, he ran into strong resistance from none other than former Merrill Lynch Chairman, and then–Secretary of the Treasury Donald Regan. Volcker explained how Regan mobilized the Wall Street powers to defeat his proposal:

> [W]e played around with making a ruling to apply the margin requirement to the extent we could. Don Regan, then the Secretary of the Treasury, got practically every agency in the government to write to us saying that such a ruling would destroy America. Even

the State Department wrote to us. And what the hell did the State Department have to do with it? The administration didn't want to interrupt the M&A boom. That was partly ideology, partly whatever. We circulated the proposed ruling for comment, and suddenly this very technical question was a highly distorted front-page story in *The New York Times*. As a sheer political matter, I think it [the regulation of leveraged acquisitions] would have been almost impossible, even if you had had more conviction than I had. The intensity of the political pressure sometimes startled me.[10]

This incident was an eerie precursor to what occurred two decades later when, as previously noted, Henry Paulson, the then chairman of Goldman Sachs and soon-to-be treasury secretary, led the lobbying effort to relax the net capital rules that were limiting the investment banks' ability to leverage their balance sheets more than 12 to 1. Henry "Hank" Paulson, along with his colleagues from Morgan Stanley and three firms that would not survive 2008—Bear Stearns, Lehman Brothers, and Merrill Lynch—argued for this relief from balance sheet constraint on the basis that it was creating a competitive disadvantage for U.S.-based investment banks vis-à-vis U.S. commercial banks and foreign institutions. Ironically, it was the regulatory change these men sought, not the *status quo,* that came close to destroying U.S. capitalism.

The failure of three of the five firms that lobbied for net capital relief in 2004 did nothing to change the financial industry's *modus operandi.* According to the *New York Times,* on November 13, 2008—a mere month after receiving Troubled Asset Relief Program (TARP) funds—the nine largest participants in the derivatives market (including Citigroup which was generally acknowledged to be insolvent at the time, and Bank of America, which was about to set off a political maelstrom by allowing its newly acquired Merrill Lynch to pay out billions of dollars of bonuses after reporting an unexpected multibillion dollar loss) created a lobbying organization, the CDS Dealers Consortium. The group hired a prominent Washington lobbyist and attorney, Edward J. Rosen, who drafted a confidential memorandum that was shared with the Treasury Department and congressional leaders and played a key role in shaping the debate over derivatives legislation. Apparently, the fact that Bear Stearns and Lehman Brothers were largely driven out of business through the credit derivatives market, and that Goldman Sachs and Morgan Stanley were placed in jeopardy by credit default swap traders, was quickly forgotten. There was nothing unusual about this; it was business as usual. But business as usual was what pushed the financial system to the brink in the fall of 2008, and there is little reason to think that continuing to permit the parties that benefit the most from relaxing financial regulation should be permitted such a significant role in shaping it.

Another area in which the financial industry has been active in pushing its agenda even after the crisis demonstrated beyond a shadow of a doubt that its agenda poses a danger to the financial system involves the so-called "shadow banking system" and the off-balance-sheet vehicles known as SIVs that caused hundreds of billions of dollars of losses in 2007–2008. These SIVs were deliberately designed as special purpose entities that were hidden from the prying eyes of investors and regulators. Moreover, they used enormous amounts of leverage to enhance their returns. The flaw in their business model was that they used short-term borrowings to invest in illiquid long-term obligations, and when the credit markets froze up beginning in 2007, they found they were unable to roll over their borrowings, resulting in massive defaults and losses.

Despite the obvious idiocy of such structures, the banks and other financial institutions that sponsored them are going down fighting. On June 4, 2009, the *Wall Street Journal* reported[11] that a group funded by these institutions that included the Chamber of Commerce, the Mortgage Bankers Association, and the American Council of Life Insurers, sent Treasury Secretary Timothy Geithner a letter urging the delay of a new rule requiring SIVs to be brought back on the balance sheets of their sponsoring institutions. This group spent millions of dollars lobbying members of Congress on the issue as well. Their concern was that the rule will require the sponsoring institutions to set aside more capital to hold these entities on their balance sheet, which is exactly what these institutions should be doing! Next to the failure to regulate the credit default swap market, permitting SIVs to grow to the point where they threatened the stability of the financial system ranks as the most serious failure of regulation that led to the 2008 crisis. Again, there is nothing surprising about these lobbying efforts other than the fact that they once again demonstrate that key financial players and their congressional sponsors have learned little from the worst crisis of capitalism in the last century.

Theories of Financialization

It is abundantly clear that financialization does not come about by accident; rather, it is the deliberate result of policy actions designed to lead an economy in a direction that favors certain interests over others. Perhaps this is why Marxist-oriented critics have been the most interested in discussing the subject and the most astute in dissecting its implications. Observers who are opposed to the governing ideology of the system tend to be far more willing to look at complex issues with an eye toward genuine reform.

A far more theoretically sophisticated discussion of financialization than Kevin Phillips' can be found in Giovanni Arrighi's books, *The Long Twentieth Century* (1994) and *Adam Smith in Peking* (2007). In *The Long Twentieth Century*, Professor Arrighi, a Marxist-oriented professor of sociology who passed away in 2009, defines financialization as a pattern of economic accumulation in which profit-making occurs increasingly through financial channels rather than through trade and commodity production.[12] Professor Arrighi based his articulation of financialization on the work of another Marxist professor, Professor David Harvey. Both Professor Arrighi and Professor Harvey are astute interpreters of Karl Marx (something Kevin Phillips certainly has never aspired to be) and interpret the shift in global economic activity from production to speculation as a process involving dramatic changes in the way that capital is accumulated and the new forms that capital began to assume in the 1970s. The advent of new financial instruments and markets, such as those for derivative products, was evidence of the inherent flexibility of capitalism and capital accumulation. Indeed, as we defined capital in the last chapter, we saw that one of its key attributes is that it is highly flexible and can assume many different guises.

Harvey argued that capitalism began a historic transition in the late 1960s to a system of "flexible accumulation."[13] This was a response to the rigidities of a form of capitalism Harvey calls "Fordism," which is characterized as "rigidity of long-term and large-scale fixed capital investments in mass-production systems that precluded much flexibility of design and presumed stable growth in invariant consumer markets."[14] Flexible accumulation "rests on flexibility with respect to labor processes, labor markets, products, and patterns of consumption. It is characterized by the emergence of entirely new sectors of production, new ways of providing financial services, new markets, and above all, greatly intensified rates of commercial, technological, and organizational innovation. . . . It has also entailed a new round of . . . 'time-space compression' . . . in the capitalist world—the time horizons of both private and public decision-making have shrunk, while satellite communication and declining transport costs have made it increasingly possible to spread those decisions immediately over an ever wider and variegated space."[15] These changes are reflected in the dramatic evolution in financial markets:

> There have been phases of capitalist history—from 1890 to 1920, for example—when "finance capital" (however defined) seemed to occupy a position of paramount importance within capitalism, only to lose that position in the speculative crashes that followed. In the present phase, however, it is not so much the concentration of power in financial institutions that matters, as the explosion in new financial instruments and markets, coupled with the rise of sophisticated systems of financial coordination on a global scale. It is through this financial system that much of the geographical and temporal flexibility of capital accumulation has been achieved.[16]

New financial products and new trading systems that link markets around the world have enabled the financial industry to expand (in Harvey's words, to achieve "geographical and temporal flexibility"), but they also contribute to instability. Harvey writes that "the financial system has achieved a degree of autonomy from real production unprecedented in capitalism's history, carrying capitalism into an era of equally unprecedented financial dangers."[17] To some degree, finance capitalism has always played a dual role, serving the industrial economy as well as serving itself. The question is the balance between these two roles. A healthy and productive economy is one in which finance capitalism is supporting economic activity that adds to the productive capacity of an economy to a meaningful degree. That contribution will differ at various times and in various contexts, but it is clear that the two decades leading up to 2008 saw too much of finance capitalism's intellectual and capital energies focused on speculative rather than productive activities. While significant sums of money were spent on productive activities such as scientific research and business innovation, even greater sums were expended on speculative trading of securities and the pointless debt-financed buying and selling of businesses. These activities diverted much needed capital from productive uses that could have enhanced the underlying capacity of the economy to grow.

Arrighi builds on Harvey's work in developing the concept of financialization. He writes that "finance capital is not a particular stage of world capitalism, let alone its latest and highest stage. Rather, it is a recurrent phenomenon which has marked the capitalist era from its earliest beginnings in late medieval and early modern Europe. Throughout the capitalist era financial expansions have signaled the transition from one regime of accumulation on a world scale to another."[18] Specifically, he argues that financialization is "the predominant capitalist response to the joint crisis of profitability and hegemony."[19] In other words, financialization is capitalism's response to the persistent problem of finding new markets in which to earn profits. When manufacturing no longer is capable of generating sufficient profits, capital flows toward speculative activities in the financial realm. As Professor Arrighi describes the phenomenon, "financial expansions are taken to be symptomatic of a situation in which the investment of money in the expansion of trade and production no longer serves the purpose of increasing the cash flow to the capitalist stratum as effectively as pure financial deals can. In such a situation, capital invested in trade and production tends to revert to its money form and accumulate more directly."[20] In other words, when financialization has taken hold of an economy, finance-driven deals (transactions that do not add to the capital stock) are necessary to keep capital from dying.

The current situation of the United States economy, in which manufacturing has declined and finance dominates, is an illustration of this process. In *Adam Smith in Peking*, Professor Arrighi describes financialization as the last (and perhaps terminal) stage in the search for profitability. He writes:

> The logic of the product cycle for the leading capitalist organizations of a given epoch is to shift resources ceaselessly through one kind

or another of innovation from market niches that have become over-crowded (and therefore less profitable) to those that are less crowded (and therefore more profitable). When escalating competition reduces the availability of relatively empty, profitable niches in the commodity markets, the leading capitalist organizations have one last refuge, to which they can retreat and shift competitive pressures onto others. This final refuge is Schumpeter's headquarters of the capitalist system—the money market.[21]

By the "money market," Professor Arrighi means the markets in which money is the primary product, not money market funds and other short-term investment instruments. The post–World War II United States economy has experienced this process. Since the late 1940s, the share of national income coming from manufacturing has declined by approximately two-thirds while the share attributable to FIRE (finance, insurance, and real estate) has doubled. See Figure 4.1.

The "money market" is a very broad category that in the period leading up to the 2008 financial crisis was typified in Corporate America by the boom in leveraged buyouts (see Chapter 5), where debt was incurred not to build new plants, purchase new equipment, or to fund research and development projects, but simply to effect a change of ownership in which equity is purchased with debt. Arrighi bases his analysis in great part on the detailed statistical analysis of UCLA Professor

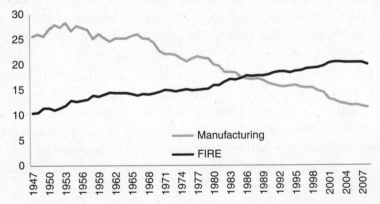

Figure 4.1 Rising Post-World War II Dominance of Finance Industry and Decline of Manufacturing 1971–2008
Source: Bureau of Economic Analysis

Robert Brenner, who describes this activity very clearly in a passage worth quoting at length:

> In the end, there was no escaping the fact that the explosion of investment and consumption that drove the last phase of the U.S. expansion—as well as the major uptick in productivity growth to which it gave rise—was heavily dependent upon a historic increase in borrowing, which was itself made possible by a record equity price run-up that was powered by speculation in defiance of actual corporate returns.[22]

In the mid-2000s, many of these transactions took the even more egregiously speculative form of transactions in which one private equity firm sold a company to another private equity firm, or financings in which private equity firms loaded companies with more debt in order to pay cash dividends to themselves. Not only did these transactions add nothing to the productive capacity of the economy, but by increasing financial commitments without improving companies' ability to meet them, they rendered the financial system more unstable. As Brenner describes it:

> Rather than discovering and funding the most promising fields for expansion . . . the deregulated U.S. financial sector ignored the paucity of underlying corporate profits and drove an epoch-making *misallocation* of funds into high-tech paper assets and, in turn, as a consequence, a parallel, and equally titanic, *misdirection* of new plant, equipment, and software into oversubscribed manufacturing and related lines, especially information technology. The logic behind this behavior lay in the peculiar constraints under which financial markets operate, which could not be further from the fantasies of orthodox economic theory.[23]

The last sentence is Professor Brenner's way of describing the fee incentives that drove many of these nonproductive transactions to be made. Moreover, these transactions were laden with large up-front fees payable to the investment bankers and private equity sponsors in order to ensure that these parties could extract their pound of flesh before the companies involved could succumb to the heavy debts thrust upon them. The rising failure rate of private equity transactions beginning in 2008 was all too predictable in view of the incentives that drove these deals to be done in the first place.

Professor Arrighi also argued, following on the work of the French historian Fernando Braudel, that financialization is "a symptom of maturity of a particular capitalist development."[24] While it is too soon to determine whether the particular brand of Western capitalism that gave birth to the boom and bust has reached its zenith, it is certainly beyond dispute that the cycle that came to a resounding thud in 2008 showed its age in the dominance of finance capital in the economy through the mid-2000s. Every boom and bust cycle ends when certain features grow out of balance, and the use of leverage, derivatives, and securitization had undoubtedly grown to unsustainable levels by 2007.

The financialization of the U.S. economy also coincided with a consumption boom that began in the early 1980s. Both phenomena were induced by extremely lax monetary policy on the part of the Federal Reserve, which created a worldwide liquidity boom. Since all of this liquidity could not be put to use in truly productive activities, much of it found its way into financial speculation and the consumer version of speculation—consumption. Consumption, particularly when it involves goods that are believed to increase in value, such as houses, collectibles, and art, should be considered another form of speculation. The increasing size of the average U.S. home, as well as the growing number of second homes and vacation properties and the purchase of multiple automobiles and other vehicles, were further manifestations of the speculative aspect of consumption. Consumption grew to a record percentage of U.S. GDP during this period from the 40-year average of approximately 66 percent to 71 percent by late 2007 (see Figure 4.2).[25]

The increasing dependence of the U.S. economy on both financialization and consumption, rather than on the expansion of production, is what haunts the U.S. economy today.

Where financialization has taken hold, the financial economy drives the real economy rather than vice versa. The result has been a world replete with too much debt, too much unused capacity, too much labor, and central banks continuing to produce too much money as they attempt to keep the entire system afloat. This regime is unsustainable and unhealthy for long-term economic growth. History is replete with examples of financialized economies that came crashing down on the heads of their financiers and government enablers, forcing governments to resort to radical policy actions that were designed to prop up short-term

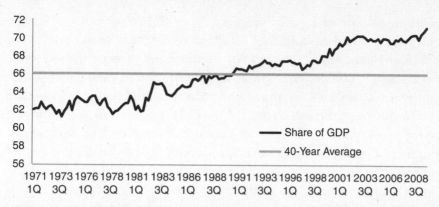

Figure 4.2 Consumption as a Growing Percentage of U.S. GDP, 1971–2008
SOURCE: Bureau of Economic Analysis

growth but failed to create the proper foundations for long-term growth. Financialization is a sign that economic policies have failed to create the conditions for robust organic growth—instead, an economy that is dominated by finance capital is characterized by a dependence on debt rather than equity finance and speculative rather than productive investments. These activities result from highly distorted incentives written into the law by politicians who are directly or indirectly beholden to the agents of financialization while they are in government and after they retire into private sector sinecures. Financialization creates an insidious cycle of unproductive economic activity that must feed on itself because, creating nothing productive itself, it has nothing else to feed on.

The Monetization of Values

It is in cultural terms, perhaps, that financialization may be having its greatest impact on the world. Culture is what ultimately shapes behavior. It tells people what types of conduct is acceptable. Financialization involves a process in which boundaries are broken down between the economy and other parts of society such as art, education, and the media. As boundaries between the economy and culture broke down through the processes of financialization, cultural and behavioral standards lapsed as well. In some respects, financialization taught some of us that anything goes. It is undeniable that regulators, legislators, and senior executives came to tolerate and even encourage types of behavior that in earlier eras were deemed unacceptable. Standards of judgment and conduct that became normalized in the marketplace during the Internet bubble and the mortgage bubble were symptoms of profound cultural changes that were inseparable from the process of financialization itself.

In this sense, financialization also can be understood as the "monetization of values" whereby all conduct is measured by whether it produces a profit, not whether it is economically or socially productive or consistent with traditional laws or morality. Conduct such as Wall Street analysts touting stocks that they were privately trashing during the Internet bubble, or mortgage lenders extending credit to borrowers whom they knew could not repay it during the housing bubble, were tolerated and even encouraged by their supervisors, who stood to earn enormous profits from this unethical behavior. Moreover, this conduct was an open secret in business and regulatory circles, creating a culture of tolerance of illegality and immorality. Even worse, this culture was further encouraged by the public statements of business and government leaders such as Alan Greenspan, who publicly praised the wonders of computer technology and adjustable rate mortgages (the latter comment being sufficiently loony to prompt the question whether there should be age limits for certain federal employees). Complicity was rampant at every level of the financial and political system.

In economic terms, financialization was the stage that capitalism reached at the end of the twentieth century and the beginning of the twenty-first century when commodity production became merged with aesthetic production. The collapse of the gold standard was the first step in setting loose radically destabilizing measures of value in the global economy.[26] These forces would not have become destabilizing had prudent and nonpoliticized regulation been put in place to govern them. But unsurprisingly, the interests that served to profit from the new regime, what I have been calling the financial-political complex, used their power and influence to manipulate legislation and regulation to serve their short-term goals at the expense of the longer term interests of the system. This is an age-old story, and as the world digs out from the ruins of the economic crisis of 2008, these forces are back at work, trying to gain advantages regardless of the longer term health of the system. Active lobbying against financial industry reforms such as the regulation of credit default swaps and pay caps on egregiously overpaid and socially unproductive investment bankers and traders are the latest examples of the embedded moneyed powers clinging to their advantages. Proper resolution of the debate—reasonable reforms that place the interests of the system ahead of those of self-serving individuals—will need to take into account the pernicious influence of financialization on the hearts and minds of virtually every member of society.

CHAPTER 5

From Innovators to Undertakers

The financialization of the U.S. economy has been characterized by an enormous increase in indebtedness among corporations and consumers. Among the leading contributors to the increase in corporate indebtedness has been the leveraged buyout boom. At the peak of the debt bubble that led to the 2008 crisis, private equity was the motivating force behind the leveraging of Corporate America. From 2003 through 2007, annual leveraged buyout debt issuance skyrocketed from $71 billion to $669 billion.[1] In 1980, $5 billion of capital was committed to private equity funds; by 2004, this figure had increased to $300 billion.[2] And by 2008, this number was approaching $1 trillion.[3] As with all things on Wall Street, investors and promoters took a decent idea and replicated it into oblivion.

Promoters of private equity make two primary arguments. First, they argue that private ownership obviates the so-called "agency problem," which refers to the issues that arise when the management of a public company has only a small ownership stake in the business. Harvard Business School Professor Michael C. Jensen sounded this cry in his 1989 apologia for leveraged buyouts, "Eclipse of the Public Corporation." In that article, Professor Jensen wrote: "By resolving the central weakness of the public corporation—the conflict between owners and managers over the control and use of corporate resources—these new organizations [private equity-owned businesses] are making remarkable gains in operating efficiency, employee productivity, and shareholder value."[4] In the early years of the private industry, these claims were supportable. Unfortunately, as the industry grew and became commoditized, such claims lost their validity.

Second, private equity proponents argue that private owners of corporations are in a position to take a long-term view of these businesses and make decisions free of the short-term demands of the public markets. Like many aspects of the financial markets, these arguments work in theory but fail in practice. In particular, these arguments made sense when a few pioneers were engaging in these activities but became devalued when crowds rushed in to imitate them. To the extent that the agency problem is solvable (which is questionable), public companies have solved it by granting their managers generous equity participation through stock options and other performance-based compensation schemes. These forms of executive compensation have not only opened the door to a panoply of new abuses, but have also undermined one of the justifications for private equity. Public company executives can be incentivized in very similar ways to private company managers. Moreover, private equity funds have turned out to be as riven with conflicts of interest as public corporations and as short-term oriented as their public company brethren.[5]

The History of Private Equity Funds

In the 1970s, private equity funds did serve an important systemic purpose by pressuring public company management teams to improve productivity and better align their interests with those of their shareholders. Private equity arguably played an important role in the 1980s in forcing large conglomerates to rationalize their holdings and maximize shareholder value. Unfortunately, the price of this activism was a growing love affair with debt as a means of enriching shareholders in the short run. Moreover, the evidence suggests that, over time, private equity's original goal (in addition to generating profits for its partners) fell by the wayside as more entrants joined the industry. Instead of becoming an engine of innovation and change, private equity became little more than a fee vomitorium for Wall Street and a disposal site for businesses that had outlived their usefulness as public companies, components of large conglomerates, or productive contributors to the broader economy. By the mid-1990s, private equity was no longer focused on squeezing efficiencies out of stodgy businesses through superior management techniques; instead, it became focused on taking advantage of the low cost of capital to take dying businesses off the hands of owners who no longer wanted to provide them with decent burials. Private equity became the place where capital went to die.

In 1990, Hyman Minsky foretold the situation that came to pass with respect to the disproportionately influential (and negative) role played by private equity in the economy in the first decade of the twenty-first century:

> A peculiar regime emerged in which the main business in the financial markets became far removed from the financing of the capital development of the country. Furthermore, the main purpose of those who controlled corporations was no longer making profits from production and trade but rather to assure that the liabilities of the corporations were fully priced in the financial market, to give value to shareholders. The giving of value to shareholders took the form of pledging a very high proportion of prospective cash flows to satisfy debt liabilities. This prior commitment of cash meant that there was little in the way of internal finance left for the capital development of the economy. . . . The question of whether a financial structure that commits a large part of cash flows to debt validation leads to a debacle such as took place between 1929 and 1933 is now an open question.[6]

In 2008, a little more than a decade after Minsky's death, we learned the painful answer to that question. In the corporate sector, the 2008 financial crisis was the culmination of years of investment activity that consisted of little more than working to ensure that, in Minsky's words, "the liabilities of the corporations were fully priced in the financial market, to give value to shareholders." In other words, speculation trumped productive investment as debt was substituted for equity on corporate balance sheets in transactions whose primary purpose was not to add to the productive capacity of the economy but to generate fees for private equity firms and their Wall Street underwriters and advisers. Only secondarily were these transactions designed to generate profits that the firms could share with their limited partners after skimming their generous share off the top. And the primary use to which those returns were put was to raise more money from the same institutions to start the process all over again.

As Professor Jensen wrote in 1989, "the public corporation is not suitable in industries where long-term growth is slow, where internally generated funds outstrip the opportunities to invest them profitably, or where downsizing is the most productive long-term strategy. . . . In . . . cash-rich, low-growth or declining sectors, the pressure on management to waste cash flow through organizational slack or investments in unsound projects is often irresistible. It is in precisely these sectors that the publicly held corporation has declined most rapidly."[7] This was true in the 1980s, when large, profitable conglomerates like Chicago-based Beatrice Cos., which owned such well-known branded consumer product names as Avis, Tropicana, Playtex, Hunt-Wesson, and Samsonite, were disassembled through leveraged buyouts. Jensen's observation continued to be true 20 years later, when faltering auto giant Chrysler Corp. and auto and consumer finance giant General Motors Acceptance Corp. (GMAC) were sold to the private equity firm Cerberus Capital Management LLC by their ailing parents who had nowhere to bury these businesses other than bankruptcy court. The difference between these two types of companies, however, could not be starker.

Beatrice was an $11 billion conglomerate whose individual businesses were viable but undervalued by the public stock market. Chrysler was a dying business in a restructuring industry suffering from deep structural problems that needed to be liquidated.[8] GMAC, on the other hand, was providing consumer financing to an overburdened consumer purchasing products from two crippled industries: autos and housing. Cerberus Capital Management's investment in Chrysler and GMAC was a vivid illustration of how businesses that were too infirm to be sold to strategic buyers could still be unloaded on so-called sophisticated financial buyers due to the availability of inexpensive debt capital and the ability of private equity firms to charge huge (and completely unjustified) fees for simply completing transactions regardless of their investment merit or prospects for profitability. Cerberus was no fool, however; rather than make the entire multibillion dollar investment itself, it managed to convince other buyout firms not only to participate alongside it in a type of investment syndicate but to pay it a portion of any future profits if the investment worked out. (While investors in Cerberus's funds had a right to be unhappy with these two investments, investors in funds that couldn't come up with enough investment ideas on their own for their capital and decided to let Cerberus promote them should be apoplectic.) But when firms are motivated (and compensated) on the quantity rather than the quality of their investments, as private equity firms came to be in the 1990s and 2000s, such seemingly irrational arrangements are tolerated in the money-driven logic of Wall Street.

From Boom to Bust

Due to the fact that the early entrants in private equity were able to enjoy little competition and therefore monopoly profits, the business gained the veneer of wealth, power, and legitimacy that allowed it to grow into a major financial force. But its growing size and scale quickly erased its so-called advantages—immunity from the agency problem, for example. A careful analysis of the private equity industry over the last 30 years—which basically spans its entire modern history—demonstrates that private equity funds and the executives who run them create little value either for the economy at large or for their investors. A number of individual transactions have undoubtedly created value, but on the whole the industry has been a bust from a macroeconomic and societal standpoint. What these investors have mastered is the art of enriching themselves at the expense of virtually everybody else with whom they come into contact. Private equity is a form of financial vampirism, sucking the blood out of corporate corpses and leaving them empty.

The primary economic act that a leveraged buyout or leveraged recapitalization (which is best understood as a partial leveraged buyout) accomplishes is to substitute debt for equity on a company's balance sheet. It rarely creates new products. It rarely builds new plants. It rarely funds new research and development. And it rarely leads to the creation of new jobs or new industries. Every aspect of corporate existence is sublimated to the need to service the company's indebtedness. As economist Robert W. Parenteau has written: "With LBOs came a surge in corporate debt that was unrelated to the expansion of the capital stock. Firms were borrowing without building much in the way of new plants and equipment. Debt obligations were being piled onto an existing capital stock that was not much more productive than prior to the LBO boom."[9]

The substitution of debt for equity was one of the leading contributors to the 2008 financial crisis due to the fact that it increased the volume of financial commitments that companies were facing as the financial markets ceased to function and the economy came to a grinding halt in the final quarter of 2008. This was a classic illustration of the "financial-instability hypothesis" outlined by Hyman Minsky, who, as we saw in Chapter 4, argued that years of economic stability would breed instability as economic actors grew increasingly complacent during calm periods and increased their risks by taking on more debt obligations. As. Parenteau points out, "[e]ventually, the weight of an accelerating pace of financial commitments against little improvement in the means to increase corporate sector incomes would insure a state of rising financial fragility."[10] The private equity industry and the investors who provided it with equity and debt capital were a living example of Minsky's "financial-instability hypothesis" as they continued to build up Ponzi finance structures in the years leading up to the 2008 crisis through the use of financing strategies and instruments that allowed them to stretch balance sheets to the furthest possible limits. (These included covenant-lite bank loans, second lien bank loans, so-called toggle notes that could pay interest in cash or in additional notes, and so on.[11]) This incessant buildup of debt, led by the private equity industry, rendered corporations increasingly reliant on functioning capital markets and their ability to access additional capital at low cost. This could only continue if lenders maintained confidence in their borrowers' promises to repay them. In other words, the entire financial system was relying on lenders remaining as complacent about repayment in the future as they had been during the period when excesses were building. As we saw in Chapter 3, the death of the promise rendered this an extremely dubious proposition.

The private equity business began with a small number of firms and outsized returns. It is difficult to imagine today, in a world filled with multibillion dollar private equity funds, that the pioneers of the industry, Kohlberg Kravis & Roberts, started out raising money on an ad hoc basis in 1976 after Bear Stearns, the firm at which its principals were working, turned down a proposal to set up a separate unit to do leveraged buyouts. In 1978, KKR raised the first known private equity fund with a specific mandate to sponsor public-to-private transactions; the fund was all of $30 million in size. Initial investors included Allstate Insurance Co., Teachers Insurance and Citicorp's venture capital fund. KKR's 1979 acquisition of Houdaille Industries for $355 million marked the first sizeable modern public-to-private buyout of a public company. It employed 13 percent equity and 87 percent debt. The pace of public-to-private takeovers picked up steadily after that. Between 1979 and 1982, the number of these transactions increased from 16 to 31, and the average value of deals rose from $64.9 million to $112.2 million. In the late 1970s and early 1980s, leveraged buyouts of public companies made sense because many public companies were trading below replacement value (i.e., it was less expensive to purchase the company's stock than to try to rebuild the assets from the ground up).

Wall Street is a funny place. It touts originality but flourishes by copying the ideas of others. In the case of leveraged buyouts, it took one spectacular deal to open the floodgates for the private equity business. In 1982, a small buyout firm in New Jersey run by former Treasury Secretary William Simon and his partner Ray Chambers, Wesray Capital Corporation, purchased Gibson Greeting Cards from RCA Corporation for $80 million. The firm invested a mere $1 million of its own money in the deal and borrowed the other $79 million. A year later, Wesray sold 30 percent of the company in an initial public offering that valued Gibson Greetings at an extraordinary $330 million. This was better than the alchemists had done turning dross to gold in the Middle Ages. This transaction attracted hordes of copycats to the business. New private equity funds sprung up overnight around the United States. New commitments to these funds grew from a mere $0.5 billion in 1982 to $1.9 billion in 1983 and $14.7 billion in 1987. A new industry was born.

Anybody who had studied business history would have known that the result would be an all-too-predictable crowding-out effect whereby too much capital would depress returns for all but a few firms.

By the time 2000 rolled around, the industry was grossly overpopulated with too many firms chasing too few targets, many of which had already been through one or more cycles of private ownership. Like many things on Wall Street, a good idea had been taken to such extremes that it had become a very, very bad idea. Private equity claimed that its *raison d'etre* was the failure of public company management teams and boards of directors to maximize value for their shareholders while doing little else of value for society. In the early days of the private equity industry, the targets of going private transactions were typically inefficiently run public corporations whose top executives were doing little to maximize the value or efficiency of their companies' assets. Many large conglomerates that were constructed in the 1960s and 1970s were disassembled in the 1980s and 1990s by private equity firms that were able to wring efficiencies out of bloated overhead structures and inefficient managements. But soon the hunter came to resemble the prey. Early returns among the pioneers of private equity were high largely because there was little competition in the industry. The early industry leaders—KKR; Forstmann, Little & Co.; Wesray; Gibbons, Green, van Amerongen & Co.; and others—were able to generate returns of 30 percent or better in part due to the fact that they did not have many competitors when they were buying companies in the 1980s and early 1990s. By the mid-1990s, however, the market was populated by hundreds of private equity firms that were attracted to the high returns earned by these early industry leaders. The entrance of multiple competitors turned a once extremely profitable industry into a much less profitable industry, if not for private equity firms than certainly for their limited partners. It also turned into an enormous source of profits for Wall Street, which cheered on the growth of the private industry with all of its financial and political might.

As the business became overcrowded, Wall Street adopted the auction process as the most efficient way in which to sell corporate properties. This was extremely positive for sellers and disastrous for buyers because it drove the prices of corporate assets through the roof. In an auction, the winner quickly became the loser as it immediately became the owner of a property for which it had likely overpaid by a considerable margin, particularly in periods when debt capital was cheap (which covered most of the 1990s and 2000s). Moreover, winning an auction required very little acumen on the part of private equity firms; it does not take any special skill to pay more than the next guy for a company. Accordingly, as the years progressed, acquisition multiples continued to climb to uneconomic levels. The race to the bottom was being run by professionals whose skills were untested by adverse market conditions and whose qualifications as stewards of corporate assets were based primarily on their academic achievements and their ability to navigate benign fundraising markets (both with investors and lenders). Few boasted track records of managing businesses through difficult business cycles. The table was being set for Armageddon.

Private Equity Fees: The New Agency Problem

Just as some pundits have described hedge funds as a compensation scheme rather than an asset class, the same could be said about private equity. Private equity firms have mastered the art of charging fees with respect to virtually every activity in which they engage. In fact, private equity firms charge their investors for practically everything they do short of going to their gold-plated bathrooms (high-priced attorneys have reserved that right for themselves). Private equity firms charge fees on the money they raise, on each transaction they complete, on each portfolio company they monitor, on each financing or merger and acquisition transaction their portfolio companies complete, and on each portfolio company they sell. One would think that the management fees they charge on the money they manage would cover these activities, but apparently those fees (which until recently were routinely a generous 1.5 to 2 percent per year) are simply for the privilege of being allowed entrance to the club.

A simple example will suffice to demonstrate the egregiousness of these fees. When Dollar General Corp., the chain of discount stores taken private by KKR and Goldman Sachs, filed for a $750 million initial public offering of stock in 2009, it was required to disclose the fees the company had been paying its two private equity sponsors. It turned out that Dollar

General had paid KKR and Goldman Sachs a "success fee" of $75 million for buying it in 2007; $13 million in additional "monitoring fees" over the next two years; and would be paying them a final $64 million upon completion of the offering to terminate the monitoring relationship. In other words, KKR and Goldman Sachs soaked Dollar General for $152 million in fees in addition to the management fees (presumably 1.5 to 2 percent per annum) and performance fees (presumably 20 percent above some hurdle rate) they were earning from their funds. Some portion of these fees may have been shared with these firms' limited partners, but that information was not disclosed. Nonetheless, this $152 million didn't come out of nowhere; whatever portion (if any) that was not rebated to limited partners came out of the pockets of the same investors who were already paying management and performance fees. Moreover, Dollar General happened to be one of the very few large, private equity transactions of the 2005–2007 vintage that flourished sufficiently to be able to issue public stock in 2009. Most other large deals were struggling, yet involved the payment of similarly large success fees, monitoring fees, and whatever other fees could be cooked up to their private equity sponsors. In every case, these large fees contributed to the weakening of balance sheets and enriched private equity sponsors at the expense of creditors and limited partners. In view of the fact that private equity returns are far less attractive than advertised even before adjusting them downward for liquidity and leverage (see the next section), it would seem that it is long past the time when limited partners should be closing down this particular feeding trough. The real question: What are these private equity managers doing to earn these fees (especially since they are already earning hefty management fees)? The answer is that they do nothing other than what they are being paid to do in the first place: manage their limited partners' investments.

The inappropriateness of these fees is demonstrated by a simple comparison with another group of managers that is hardly shy about charging fees: hedge fund managers. A hedge fund charges a management fee (normally between 1 and 2 percent) plus a performance fee (normally 15 or 20 percent of the profits). If, in addition, the hedge fund were to charge an additional fee on every stock or bond transaction into which it entered, that would be considered egregiously unfair to investors. Yet that is analogous to the additional fees that private equity firms charge with respect to monitoring their portfolio companies, or arranging financing or merger transactions involving their portfolio companies. For some reason, private equity limited partners have been convinced that they should pay these additional fees, but it strains credulity to come up with a reasonable basis to justify this practice when they are already being charged hefty fees on their funds. This is why it is not surprising that one study has found that the actual fees paid to private equity firms amount to as much as 6 percent per year.[12] These fees are *prima facie* evidence that these firms have abused the special position of trust that they hold as fiduciaries to their limited partners. These fees amount to tens if not hundreds of millions of dollars that reduce the value of portfolio companies and represent a direct shift of wealth out of the pockets of their investors and into the pockets of the private equity firms' principals. Another study concluded that two-thirds of expected income for private equity firms comes from fixed revenue components that are not sensitive to investment performance.[13] In other words, private equity firms have structured their businesses to reward themselves handsomely regardless of the outcome of their investments, which directly contradicts the private equity mantra that the interests of shareholders and management should be aligned. So much for solving the agency problem!

One further word should also be said about the industry's high management fees. A 1.5 to 2 percent fee on the large sums of money that the private industry raised became a deeply corrupting influence on general partners because it amounted to so much money that it rendered performance-based fees far less important. Private equity firms managing multibillion dollar funds were assured of gargantuan compensation regardless of whether or not their deals were successful, creating a clear conflict of interest between themselves and their limited partners. The payment of additional success fees upon completion of acquisitions of individual portfolio companies further exacerbated this conflict. A much more equitable arrangement would involve much lower fixed management fees, no additional fees for carrying out the necessary tasks of managing the portfolio companies, and a 20 percent performance fee with high water marks and clawbacks. Such a fee structure would not only appropriately incentivize private equity firms to perform but also properly reflect their limited contribution to economic growth.

Accordingly, instead of solving the agency problems inherent in public companies, the typical private equity fee structure introduced a slew of new problems. It didn't have to be that way. But human nature being what it is—and Wall Street being the kind of place it is—it was perhaps inevitable that the abuses that private equity was designed to cure would sneak back in through the back door. The combination of high management fees on invested and committed capital, additional fees for managing portfolio companies, and a significant share of the profits from selling portfolio companies established a strong incentive for private equity firms to raise as much money as possible, put it to work as quickly as possible by buying companies, and then pay themselves a dividend or sell these companies at a profit as quickly as possible. Most significantly, even if the third part of this triad is not accomplished, the private equity firm profits handsomely merely from raising a fund and investing the money quickly regardless of the quality of those investments. The behavior of the largest private equity firms in the period leading up to the 2008 crisis conformed to this pattern as these firms raised the largest possible funds and put their capital to work as quickly as possible in some of the largest and most questionable private equity deals on record. Examples include: the $29.9 billion buyout of casino giant Harrah's Entertainment, Inc., by a private equity group led by Apollo Management LP and Texas Pacific Group; the $17.6 billion purchase of Freescale Semiconductor Inc. by a group of private equity firms that included The Blackstone Group, The Carlyle Group, Pereira Funds and Texas Pacific Group; KKR's and Clayton Dubliner's purchase of U.S. Foodservice at an actual multiple of EBITDA of more than 18 times (despite intellectually insulting attempts to convince investors that the multiple was much lower). While private equity firms used to take years to invest their funds, some of the largest funds raised by Bain & Company and The Blackstone Group in recent years spent as much as half of their funds (which amounted to billions of dollars) within the first year of raising them.

In late 2009, a large group of institutional investors began organizing to fight back against the egregious fees being charged by private equity firms. A group of 220 investors with about $1 trillion invested in this asset class joined together to demand that private equity firms adopt a framework of best practices and align their interests more squarely with their investors. The new group is called the Institutional Limited Partners

Association and is particularly focused on the panoply of fees that they are charged in addition to the basic management and performance fees. Better late than never, although the private equity industry is not going to give up these fees without a fight.

The irony of such a demand should not go unremarked. Private equity transactions—leveraged buyouts—are based on the rationale that public corporations inadequately align the interests of managers and shareholders. Leveraged buyouts are designed to better align those interests as well as improve operational efficiencies in the business. One would think that the private equity firms pursuing such strategies (or giving them lip service since few leveraged buyouts in recent years were done to improve productivity) would apply the same principles to their own businesses. Instead, they do the opposite. They disenfranchise their limited partners by providing them with limited transparency and liquidity and extract huge fees from them that are unjustified by the risk-adjusted returns they offer (as well as basic standards of fairness and decency). Of course, nobody is putting a gun to the head of the largest pension funds and endowments in the world to invest in these funds, but these institutions are placed under enormous peer pressure by the propaganda machine that has been built up by the private equity industry and the investment banks that feed off the fees paid by the industry. A better educated investor community would not tolerate the abusive treatment that private equity firms have doled out to their investors.

The Myth of Private Equity Returns

The quality of private equity returns is a topic that deserves more public attention than it has received. Like all investment returns (and statistics generally), private equity returns are subject to manipulation and interpretation. They are significantly affected by the timing of when investments are made and when they are sold, which is not always entirely within the control of the private equity general partner and therefore not necessarily a fair measure of performance. Moreover, public market conditions play an enormous role in determining the success or failure of private equity investments since the outcome of these investments is usually dependent on conditions in the public markets. Accordingly, measuring private equity performance must take into account timing and coincident market conditions as well as factors such as liquidity, leverage, and fees to come to a meaningful conclusion. Unfortunately, there is little evidence that any of these considerations are taken into account when investors evaluate these returns and render their decisions about whether to invest in this asset class.

If private equity returns were, in fact, subject to the type of scrutiny that all investment returns should be subject, it is highly questionable whether any but a small portion of them would prove to be particularly attractive. Any type of investment return must be risk-adjusted in order to be properly evaluated. In the case of private equity returns, risk adjustment means reflecting the fact that these investment funds are highly concentrated, highly leveraged, extremely illiquid, and subject to inordinately high fees. If one is to compare them to other types of returns in a fair manner, one has to make sure that these characteristics of private equity are fully adjusted-for in the return calculation. In the case of private equity returns, there is little evidence that this is done. Instead, investors tend to look at unadjusted numbers and leave with the impression that private equity outperforms many other asset classes. This simply isn't the case.

A similar argument was made in an important comprehensive study of corporate capital structures in the United States in the 1980s and 1990s: "The investors in LBO funds might be thought smart money, but this identification is not self-evident. Returns of 30 percent sound good until one recognizes that a bet on the S&P 500 consisting of one part equity and five or ten parts debt would have done better, given the trend of equity prices. Institutional investors who are prepared to sell their shareholdings in the market to LBO organizers who then reap substantial fees from the same institutions for underperforming a (leveraged) benchmark does not meet a minimal test of smart money."[14] In an age when consultants and investors throw around terms like "Sharpe ratios" (which measure the excess return generated per unit of risk taken), it would seem a fairly elementary proposition that returns from private equity should be risk-adjusted. A typical leveraged buyout fund suffers from a number of risks that fiduciaries are taught to frown upon—concentration risk (funds are generally invested in a limited number of portfolio companies compared to a public equity fund); liquidity risk (portfolio companies must be sold in private corporate transactions or in initial public offerings of stock rather than in public markets); and leverage risk (portfolio companies are purchased using significant degrees of leverage, particularly in the years approaching the 2008 financial crisis). Accordingly, when a private equity firm advertises that it has earned compounded annual return of 25 percent over its lifetime, that number needs to be understood (and adjusted downward) in the context of the concentration, liquidity, and leverage risks that were taken to obtain that return.[15]

A simple illustration drawn from a 2005 study of private equity returns by Steve Kaplan of the University of Chicago Graduate School of Business and Antoinette Schorr of MIT's Sloan School of Management will suffice to demonstrate the complexity of the task.[16] Between March 1997 and March 2000, an investment of $50 million in the S&P 500 would have grown to $103.5 million, a return of 26.8 percent. A private equity fund investing $50 million and realizing $100 million after fees during that same period would have generated an internal rate of return (IRR) of 26 percent. The three-year period immediately following paints a completely different picture. A private equity fund investing $50 million in March 2000 and realizing $50 million in March 2003 would have returned 0 percent, but would have grossly outperformed the S&P 500 during that period, in which a $50 million investment would have shrunk to $29.5 million. This lesson in absolute versus relative returns should be kept in mind when evaluating all money managers, including private equity firms. But the analysis is even more complex than that, because a truly accurate analysis of returns would have to dissect the specific investments that a private equity firm makes, the amounts of leverage it employs in each investment, the manner in which it treats its limited partners with respect to transparency and fees, and other factors. Investing in the public markets is much simpler and more transparent, even in hedge funds that also suffer from agency problems due to their similarly egregious fee arrangements.

Even with these qualifications, it is highly questionable whether any but a very few private equity firms have earned their keep. Most of the studies of private equity returns have concluded that private equity returns are no better than the returns that an investor could obtain from investing in the public stock market using similar amounts of leverage. Investors in private equity funds pay a high price in terms of liquidity and fees for the right to become members of the private equity club. But a closer look at this club suggests that membership does not have its privileges. In fact, after 2008, investors in private equity may do well to recall the old Groucho Marx joke that says that a person should be wary of joining any club that would invite him or her to become a member. Private equity clubs share some of the attributes of roach motels (once you enter, it takes years to exit) and high-end luxury vacation home clubs (the exit fees may be painful, they require a lot of upkeep, you are partners with a lot of difficult people, and there may be little money left at the end).

The most damning broad-based study of private equity returns was performed in 2008 by two European professors, Ludovic Phalippou of the University of Amsterdam Business School and Oliver Gottschalg of HEC Paris.[17] Professors Phalippou and Gottschalg evaluated 1,328 mature private equity funds and found that performance estimates identified in previous research and used as industry benchmarks are overstated. They summarize their conclusions as follows: "We find an average net-of-fees performance of 3 percent per year below that of the S&P 500. Adjusting for risk brings the underperformance to 6 percent per year. We estimate fees to be 6 percent per year." With respect to benchmarks, the authors find that "it is basically impossible for investors to benchmark the past performance of funds with information reported in prospectuses. These documents contain only multiples and IRRs. . . . We show . . . that average IRRs give upward biased performance estimates. In addition, IRRs cannot be directly compared to the performance of, say, the S&P 500 over the same period." They also point out that while many investors told them they were satisfied with private equity returns because they had "doubled their money," the average fund duration was 75 months (6.25 years); in comparison, the average public stock market portfolio returned on average 1 percent per month between 1980 and 2003, which would have produced a better return than a doubling of an investor's money over that period. The authors also offer possible reasons for private equity underperformance (and investors' acceptance of it), including the possibility that investors "might attribute too much weight to the performance of a few successful investments"; and the possibility that "investors have a biased view of performance because performance is generally reported gross of fees and . . . fees [are] larger than for other asset classes." Finally, the authors point out that some investors such as pension funds and government-related entities may have noneconomic motives for investing in private equity such as stimulating local economies. Unfortunately, in view of pending pay-for-play scandals in California, New York and other states, it is turning out that the non-economic motives for investing in certain private equity funds were hardly benign.

About the only independent study (that is, a study not financed by the private equity industry itself) that argues in favor of private equity outperformance was one conducted by Professor Gottschalg and Professor Alexander P. Groh of the Montpelier Business School in France in 2006.[18] This study, however, is narrowly based and focuses on only 133 U.S. buyouts between 1984 and 2004 and compares this limited universe to a mimicked portfolio of equally leveraged investments in the S&P index. This study claims that the 133 buyouts outperformed the public market by 12.6 percent per annum gross of all fees. Based on the fact that this study only looks at a very small number of the buyouts done during the 20-year period in question and compares them to a simulated selection of S&P 500 companies, it is difficult to conclude very much from it. Moreover, this study says very little about the returns of private equity funds since it focuses on individual private equity transactions. It is a theoretical exercise that has little application to the real world where investments are made and money is earned and lost.

The 2008 financial crisis demonstrated several of the inherent flaws of the private equity industry. This is unfortunate because an industry that is designed to be sheltered from the vagaries of the public markets should have been better positioned to survive such a market downturn. The fact that the private equity industry fared so poorly during the crisis reveals the fact that its original character as an asset class that was designed to be a superior form of long-term ownership of capital assets has failed. The losses generated by firms in 2008 wiped out years of positive returns and strongly suggested that previous years' returns, to the extent they were based on unrealized gains and subjective valuations of portfolio companies, were unjustified. The industry has wanted to have it both ways; it wants to be judged on long-term performance but be compensated on short-term performance. Those goals are at odds with each other. Now, most firms (even the elite performers) are far under water in terms of earning their performance fees and some are facing large cash clawback liabilities resulting from recent losses that have eaten up profits from performance fees earned on companies that were bought and sold at a profit in early years of their partnerships. The results from 2008 will further damage the long-term track records of virtually every private equity firm in existence, making it harder for them to conceal the true mediocrity of the industry's returns and more difficult to justify its very existence.

Men Behaving Badly

The behavior of private equity firms is usually a reliable indicator of the stage a credit cycle has reached. The less productive their behavior, the more likely the cycle is reaching its late stages. Two types of transactions in which private equity firms have engaged in recent years have been clear indications that credit is cheap, that the credit cycle is far advanced, and that debt investors in particular should be running in the other direction from offerings involving private equity-owned borrowers.

The first type of transaction that investors should avoid is the infamous "dividend deal," in which a private equity-owned firm borrows money to pay a dividend distribution to its private equity owners. The debt raised in these transactions is not used to enhance the business of the borrower in any way, for example, by building additional facilities, funding research and development, creating new products, or hiring new workers. The money instead is paid out to the private equity sponsor in order to reduce the capital it originally invested in the business. This practice is contrary to the *raison d'etre* of private equity, which is supposed to be based on overcoming an important aspect of the agency problem, specifically, the problems raised when the owners and management of the company have only a small ownership stake in the enterprise. While the private equity firm generally maintains a significant ownership position after a dividend transaction, the amount of money it has at risk in the business is significantly reduced if not eliminated.

Dividend transactions are particularly noxious to the health of lenders, who are left lending money to a company whose owners are in possession of a free "call option" on any appreciation in the value of the business but are also free to walk away without any personal liability if the business begins to falter under the weight of its new debt. The only potential limitation on these dividend deals is the law governing fraudulent transfers, but these are relatively easily avoided.[19] Many companies that have paid dividends to their private equity sponsors over the years have subsequently gone bankrupt, leaving their lenders with large losses and their private equity sponsors feeling no pain.[20]

The second practice that indicates that the credit cycle is entering its terminal stages is the phenomenon of private equity-owned companies being sold by one buyout firm to another. Some firms, like Simmons Company (the mattress manufacturer) or General Nutrition Companies, have been sold numerous times among buyout firms. Simmons Company, in fact, is a company that fell into bankruptcy after paying a large dividend to one of its private equity owners during the course of being bought and sold seven different times by buyout firms over a period of two decades.[21] One of the purposes of a leveraged buyout is supposed to be to wring efficiencies out of a business that was previously held publicly. Accordingly, there is little rationale for a private equity firm purchasing a company that has already been retooled by another private equity firm since there should theoretically be few efficiencies left to capture. The real reason such deals are done, of course, is to generate fees for private equity firms. The selling firm is able to generate a "realization event" that triggers a "transaction" fee and allows it to return capital to investors, while the buying firm is able to pay itself a transaction fee on the purchase. The wonder is that high-yield bond investors and leveraged bank loan lenders continue to finance such transactions, which obviously contribute nothing to economic growth other than to keep investment bankers and private equity personnel employed. The question investors and lenders should be asking when they see such deals is why no strategic buyer is interested in buying these companies at a higher price than another private equity firm. The answer to that question is the reason why investors should avoid lending to these companies and be asking their private equity firms why they can't find something better to purchase than somebody else's used merchandise.

Private Equity and Cheap Debt:
Birds of a Feather Flop Together

The private equity industry could not have flourished without access to investors willing to pay its egregious fees. But there is another group of investors who have been more than willing over the years to lend their capital to this industry at rates that offer nothing close to an appropriate return for the risk: junk bond investors in the 1980s and 1990s and leveraged loan investors in the 2000s. Without investors willing to grossly underprice risk, the private equity business never would have reached the size and scope it did early in the twenty-first century.

The story of Michael Milken and Drexel Burnham Lambert, Inc., has been told many times (mostly inaccurately), and this is not the place to repeat it. Suffice it to say that Milken never intended the market he founded to be used to finance the types of change-of-control transactions that private equity came to represent. In the early days of the junk bond market, Drexel Burnham financed new businesses and new technologies such as Turner Broadcasting System, Inc. (CNN), McCaw Cellular Communications (cellular telephones), Circus Circus Enterprises and other gaming companies that now comprise modern Las Vegas, and many other productive projects that did contribute to the growth of the economy. By the time Milken was forced to leave Drexel Burnham to fight highly politicized government charges against him (that pale in comparison to the wrongdoing that has occurred in the succeeding two decades), private equity was beginning to become an unproductive force in the financial markets and Milken was advising companies to issue equity, not debt. But the many copycats on Wall Street that saw the profits that Drexel Burnham had generated from the junk bond business had no interest in listening to Milken's message. The leveraging of the United States had started apace.

KKR became the dominant private equity firm of the 1980s on the back of Drexel Burnham's junk bond financing engine. The relationship culminated in the ill-advised buyout of RJR Nabisco (completed without Milken's involvement), which boasted a novel security called "increasing rate notes" that ultimately threatened to blow up the tobacco maker. KKR and its investors were able to escape (barely) from this transaction with their capital intact, and KKR was able to console itself with the enormous fees it paid itself while taking a reputational beating in the press from which it never fully recovered. The RJR Nabisco deal showed Wall Street at its egotistical, greedy worst, and the years that followed did little to dispel the view that private equity dealmakers and their Wall Street amanuenses were interested in little but lining their own pockets at the expense of everyone else.

Drexel Burnham was not so fortunate and ultimately succumbed in February 1990 to the pressures of a government investigation that had begun in 1986 (extremely poor management of the firm didn't help either). But the rest of Wall Street took up the mantle of junk bonds and continued to feed the private equity monster. In the wake of Drexel's bankruptcy, LBO transactions plunged from $75.8 billion in 1989 to $17.9 billion in 1990 and $8 billion in 1992 as the savings and loan crisis and a deep recession slowed deal activity to a halt. But soon merger activity reignited, with M&A activity increasing from $100 billion in 1992 to almost $600 billion in 1996. During that period, the number of completed deals increased from 3,500 to 6,100. This increase in transactional volume was part of the deconstruction of American conglomerates, a process that many view as having contributed to productivity improvements and operating efficiencies in U.S. business.

There is another view, however. There is a great deal of evidence that shows that most mergers do not lead to efficiencies and enhanced productivity but basically lead to job cuts and are admissions that companies can't generate growth on their own. Moreover, there is very little strategic impetus or justification for most private equity transactions. As noted above, private equity became a dumping ground for businesses that no longer fit within conglomerates and can find no strategic purchaser or partner. The high cost of capital involved in leveraged buyouts suggests that they are an extremely inefficient way for an economy to recycle its garbage, although outright liquidation or downsizing may be no more efficient. Accordingly—and this is borne out by the depressed condition of American industry today—it might be more appropriate to view the statistics describing the merger boom of the 1990s as an augur of negative economic things to come.

In the early twenty-first century, a new kind of cheap financing became the main facilitator of leveraged buyouts—leveraged loans purchased by collateralized loan obligations (CLO). While leveraged loans

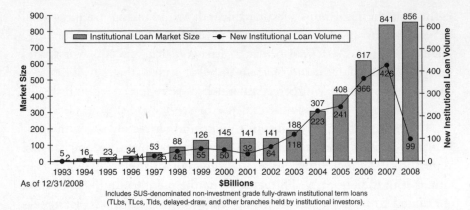

Figure 5.1 Institutional Leveraged Loan Market Size
SOURCE: Credit Suisse, LPC.

had been around since the 1980s, they only developed into a tradable security in the 1990s with the introduction of prime rate mutual funds and hedge funds that were willing to invest in them. Figure 5.1 shows the growth of this market through the 2000s.

The market exploded, however, with the advent of collateralized loan obligations, a type of collateralized debt obligation that was focused on holding leveraged loans as its primary form of collateral. Banks began to shape loans to these borrowers to conform to their specific structural needs, and a marriage made in heaven was born. Figure 5.2 shows the

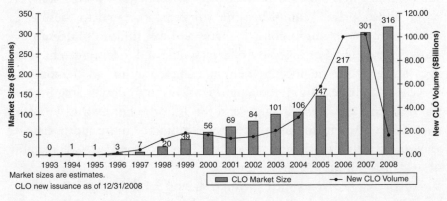

Figure 5.2 Historical Growth of the CLO Market
SOURCE: Credit Suisse, Moody's, S&P, Fitch, Intex.

explosion in the CLO market and how it almost perfectly tracked the growth in the leveraged loan market.

By the mid-2000s, private equity firms dominated the market for leveraged loans and were able to dictate the terms on which such loans were offered. Pricing on these loans was based on the London Interbank Offered Rate (Libor), which is the rate at which banks loan money to each other in the London banking market. The price of a loan was based on the spread (number of basis points or hundredths of a percentage point) above Libor that a borrower would be required to pay on a loan. As the market became increasingly overheated in the mid-2000s, spreads tightened and private equity firms were able to borrow at very low rates (Libor plus 125 to 250 basis points) and also negotiate extremely favorable covenants that gave them a great deal of latitude not normally accorded borrowers. These covenants, which were described in Chapter 3, allowed these borrowers to incur additional debt, pay dividends, and engage in many other activities that were contrary to the interests of lenders. The low cost of this financing, which generally came to less than 5 percent, enabled many transactions to be completed that could not have been done had money cost more. Alternatively, low-cost financing allowed private equity firms to pay higher prices for companies than strategic buyers who were no longer able to finance at lower rates than private companies (in part due to the costs associated with the Sarbanes-Oxley Act of 2002).[22]

One of the reasons the private equity industry is facing a difficult future in the aftermath of the 2008 crisis is that few expect low-cost bank debt to become available in large volumes without a revival of CLOs (or some similar structure that can absorb low yielding bank debt). And any such CLO or similar structure can only return if paper can be sold at the very low spreads that AAA paper was issued before the crisis (Libor plus 50 basis points or lower). In view of changes made by rating agencies in the way they rate CLOs and the large losses experienced by CLO investors during the crisis, the prospects for new CLO issuance is bleak. CLOs were able to purchase such low yielding bank loans because their own cost of capital was extremely low; their AAA liabilities yielded less than Libor plus 25 basis points on the cusp of the crisis. Now that the rating agencies have changed their assumptions underlying these ratings, no such low-cost AAA paper can be issued. This, in turn, means that

CLOs, which accounted for as much as 60 percent of the demand for leveraged loans in the mid-2000s, will no longer be available to buy this paper. With no investors to purchase low yielding bank debt, private equity firms will no longer be able to complete the types of transactions that were their bread and butter in the 1990s and 2000s. It is for this reason that the decision of several of them to go public, discussed in the next section, was particularly ill-timed from the perspective of any investor considering purchasing their stock.

Private Equity Goes Public: A Study in the Oxymoronic

The very idea of a private equity firm going public would be laughable if it weren't so deeply ironic. Then again, why should irony and laughter be mutually exclusive, especially on Wall Street, where a sense of humor is essential to survival? As unattractive as investing in private equity funds has proven to be on a true risk-adjusted basis, buying the stock of a publicly traded private equity firm has proven to be downright foolhardy. Not only do these transactions completely contradict the very *raison d'etre* of private equity, but they open multiple cans of worms in terms of exposing irreconcilable conflicts of interest for the owners of these firms. These owners have obligations to the pension funds and endowments that provide their private capital and to their new public shareholders. The firms argue that public offerings allow them to raise capital more efficiently than the normal time-consuming process of raising money from disparate institutional investors, give them a permanent source of capital, create a currency (their public stock) with which to attract new talent, and help them with succession planning. Of course, for funds that had experienced no trouble raising tens of billions of dollars of capital over the past two decades or attracting top talent with lucrative pay packages, these arguments ring completely hollow.

KKR completed the first major public offering of a private equity investment fund in Europe in May 2006, listing KKR Private Equity Investors L.P. (KPE) on the Euronext exchange in Amsterdam. The manner in which this offering was handled is strongly suggestive of why these offerings should be avoided by investors at all costs. KPE increased the size of its offering from $1.5 billion to $5.0 billion due to strong demand, but the shares themselves received a lukewarm reception, traded down on the opening, and never traded above the $25 per share offering price. The firm rewarded itself with E70 million of advisory fees immediately upon being listed, not only shifting a significant chunk of money from the pockets of the public shareholders to the insiders but also signaling to investors that going public would not change the general partners' practice of charging exorbitant fees every chance they could. (What other type of public company would have the gall to reward its executives for going public with such an egregious fee?) Within two months the stock had dropped to less than $22 per share, killing the chances of any other private equity firm pulling off a similar offering. Since then, the stock has been nothing but a disaster for investors, dropping to the high single digits. (See Figure 5.3.)

KKR's goal of listing its stock in the United States took three more years to realize. On June 24, 2009, KKR announced plans to have KPE, which was then trading at about $5.00 per share, purchase 30 percent of KKR's parent company. This was KKR's second attempt to bring the parent public through some type of backdoor offering, the first attempt having failed during the financial crisis in 2008. KKR finally accomplished its goal of becoming a public company on October 1, 2009, with the completion of this merger between KKR and KPE. The

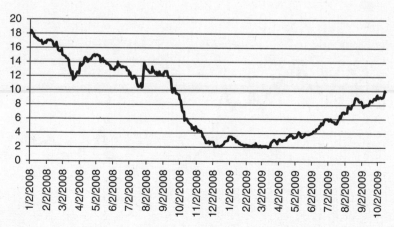

Figure 5.3 KKR Private Equity Investors, LP (KPE.EU) Stock Prices 1/1/08–12/9/09
SOURCE: Bloomberg.

new company was renamed KKR & Co. In the merger, KPE received interests representing 30 percent of the outstanding equity in KKR, and KKR's owners and employees retained the remaining 70 percent. In the period between the June 2009 announcement of the merger between KPE and KKR and the final merger, the price of the KPE units rose 65 percent to over $9.00 per share (the overall stock market was enjoying a strong rally at the time). The future performance of the stock will be a good barometer of the performance of the private equity industry.

KKR had earlier brought public another investment entity, KKR Financial Holdings LLC (KFN), in June 2005 at $24.00 per share. KFN was a real estate investment trust (REIT) that was turned into an entity primarily designed to invest in CLOs. The idea was that KFN could use these CLOs to purchase large chunks of the bank loans that were being issued in KKR-sponsored leveraged buyouts (as well as loans of other private equity deals) during the height of the LBO boom in the mid-2000s. KFN has arguably been KKR's biggest public embarrassment since the RJR Nabisco buyout (but at least the firm's investors didn't lose money on that mega-buyout). Since its IPO on June 23, 2005, through December 9, 2009, KFN stock has declined by approximately 80 percent due to a combination of poor loan selection, difficult market conditions, and the difficulties facing the private equity business. (See Figure 5.4.)

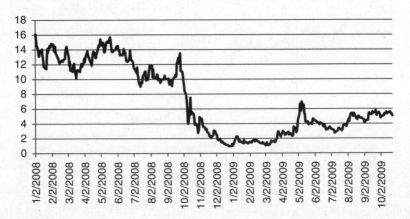

Figure 5.4 KKR Financial Holdings LLC (KFN) Stock Prices 1/1/08–12/9/09
SOURCE: Bloomberg.

It should be noted that KFN was only one of a number of examples in which private equity firms convinced their investors that they could translate their deal-making skills into money management skills. Other firms that attempted the same feat (another example of the copycat phenomenon that haunts Wall Street), causing their investors much pain in the process, include Apollo Management, L.P., Texas Pacific Group, The Blackstone Group's credit arm GMO Capital, LLC, and Bain & Co.'s credit affiliate Sankaty Advisors, LLC, all of which raised billions of dollars from investors in private formats to invest in bank debt in early 2008 and subsequently lost much of that money during the 2008 financial crisis.

The Blackstone Group LP was the first of the large private equity giants to announce a public offering in the United States. Blackstone filed its public offering plan with the Securities and Exchange Commission in March 2007. The prospectus it filed was lengthy, highly convoluted and disclosed little real information about the company's operations, a sure sign to wise investors that it was to be avoided. This offering came just a few weeks after Fortress Investment Group LLC completed its initial public offering in February of that year. Fortress's IPO was a huge (albeit short-lived) success, with its shares rising 68 percent on the first day of trading. Fortress was both a private equity and hedge fund manager, with about 60 percent of its assets devoted to leveraged buyouts. The offering made instant billionaires of its principals and, according to the *Wall Street Journal*, "had other hedge funds and private-equity managers scrambling to their calculators, gazing over their own potential worth if they were to follow the lead of Fortress and become public."[23] The bloom quickly came off the rose, however, and Fortress's stock has been among the worst performers in the market since it was issued at $18.50 per share in February 2007. As of December 9, 2009, it had lost more than 75 percent of its IPO value (not to mention almost 90 percent of its peak trading value of over $33 per share reached in April 2007), and even traded at under $1.00 per share on several days during the last week of 2008 before closing at $1.00 per share on December 31 of that year See Figure 5.5.

Despite some mild protests from some of Blackstone's limited part-ners, who were perhaps coming to realize that a public offering had little to offer them and would merely sacrifice their interests to those of the firm's principals, the firm made an unseemly rush to complete its

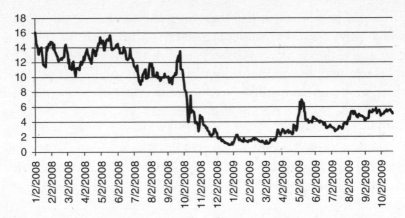

Figure 5.5   Fortress Investment Group LLC Stock Prices 1/1/08–12/9/09
SOURCE: Bloomberg.

offering in June 2007 just as members of Congress and the media were catching on and began calling for regulators to scrutinize the deal more closely. And stock market investors, thinking they were being let in on some kind of inside deal by being allowed to invest with Blackstone, piled into the IPO. The stock, which was issued at $18 per share, closed at slightly over $35 per share at the close of trading on the first day, June 22, 2007. Blackstone Chairman Stephen Schwarzman was worth $10 billion on paper and his archrival Henry Kravis was surely tearing out what was left of his hair at having been beaten to the public market trough in the United States. At the time—June 2007—I observed in *The HCM Market Letter* that the Blackstone offering would undoubtedly signal the top of the market and that Blackstone stock would prove to be a terrible investment.[24] *Barron's* also presciently called the Blackstone IPO the top of the private equity market. But the firm's competitors were not to be easily deterred when they saw that Blackstone's principals were able to monetize billions of dollars of their ownership interests in their firm.

Through December 2009, Blackstone's IPO had proven to be a bonanza for nobody other than Blackstone and its principals. Stephen Schwarzman deserved credit for rushing the offering through and timing what will likely prove in retrospect to have been the peak of the private equity business, as some of us predicted at the time. Figure 5.6 shows the performance of the stock since the IPO—as of December 9, 2009,

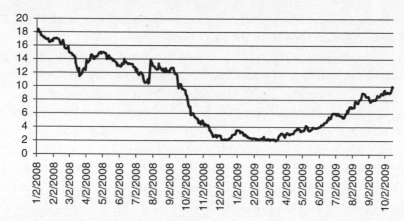

Figure 5.6 The Blackstone Group LP (BX) Stock Prices 1/1/08–12/9/09
SOURCE: Bloomberg.

it was trading at just above $13.00 per share, well below its IPO price of $18.00 per share and more than 60 percent below the closing price on its first day of trading (reminiscent of an Internet stock).

Next up at the plate was Leon Black. His firm, Apollo Management L.P., completed a convoluted backdoor merger into a public shell corporation in Europe called AP Alternative Investments L.P. in November 2007. This deal has also been nothing but a money-loser for public shareholders, with the stock declining by more than 60 percent since its offering in November 2007 and December 9, 2009. (See Figure 5.7.)

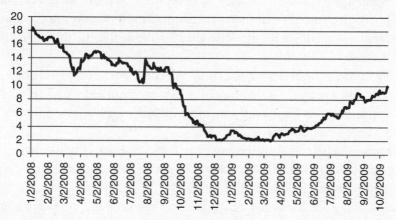

Figure 5.7 Apollo Management L.P. (AAA.EU) Stock Prices 1/1/08–12/9/09
SOURCE: Bloomberg.

This stock also had the dubious honor of spending much of late 2008 and early 2009 trading at under $2.00 per share.

After the Apollo offering, the window for these deals mercifully closed. KKR was able to complete its complicated offering in October 2009 and The Carlyle Group was reportedly trying to follow in these firms' footsteps. But investors will hopefully learn from the losses they have incurred on these early deals that they should run in the other direction when the private equiteers come calling for their money. This is a club on whose membership rolls they do not want to be included.

Investing in the public shares of private equity firms is a profoundly bad proposition for many reasons:

- Taking these companies public subjects them to the very pressures of public ownership that private equity is intended to avoid and exploit. These offerings (with the exception of KKR's U.S. listing) occurred in the middle of the biggest corporate debt bubble in history. Private equity firms were crawling all over each other to pay the highest prices for companies in auctions that resulted in increasingly leveraged transactions that served no purpose other than to generate fees for the general partners and their Wall Street servants.
- Private equity firms owe conflicting duties to their limited partners and public shareholders that simply cannot be reconciled. These firms touted the steps they took to supposedly limit these conflicts of interest. However, the very fact that these steps needed to be taken and were unusually elaborate was proof in itself that the conflicts were deeply embedded in the structure of these hybrid public/private entities.
- The prospectuses describing these offerings were completely opaque with respect to the valuation of portfolio companies and other key data points, making it all but impossible for public shareholders to evaluate the investment.
- Historical private equity returns are far less attractive than advertised, particularly when they are adjusted (as all investment returns must be) for leverage, liquidity, and fees.
- Financing for leveraged buyouts dried up after the 2008 crisis, and while Wall Street suffers from a perpetual dearth of long memories, it is unlikely that capital is again going to be extended to these firms

on anything like the favorable terms that were available in the 1990s and early 2000s. Accordingly, these firms are far less attractive as generators of profits than they were before, when their profitability on a risk-adjusted basis was overstated. Investors seeking equity exposure would be much better advised to invest directly in the public markets using leverage or to invest with a hedge fund manager with an established track record of investing well and treating his or her investors properly.

Taxing Labor as Capital

One of the truly unfortunate ways in which public policy encouraged private equity activity was the absurdly favorable tax treatment of the "carried interests" of private equity firms. Carried interests represent the share of the profits (generally 20 percent) that a general partner is paid when its fund sells a portfolio company and realizes a gain. Due to manipulation on the part of clever tax lawyers and accountants, as well as lobbying by the Private Equity Council, the industry's lobbying group, the private equity industry was able to garner capital gains treatment of its carried interest profits for many years. After the Bush administration lowered the tax rate on capital gains to 15 percent (which was generally a wise policy), private equity firms' principals were able to pay a much lower tax rate on the fruits of their daily labor than virtually any other individual in the United States was required to pay on his or hers. This unjustifiably favorable tax treatment was not only poor public policy that contributed to the widening gap between rich and poor in our society, but it generated disrespect for the tax system through its obvious unfairness. It was another example of the corruption of our moral sentiments.

A similar tax regime was introduced in the United Kingdom as well. In 1998, then Chancellor of Exchequer Gordon Brown introduced tax relief to encourage new business investment. Known as "taper relief," it lowered the capital gains tax on business assets, which were defined to include private equity carried interests. This regime was even more egregious than the U.S. one. The capital gains tax rate was lowered from 40 percent (which was clearly too high) to an almost irrelevant

10 percent, provided that the assets were held for 10 years (this period was subsequently lowered first to 4 years in 2000 and then to an almost laughable 2 years in 2002).[25]

There is a significant distinction between a carried interest, for which a private equity partner makes no investment of capital, and an investment by a private equity general partner in his fund or directly in a portfolio company. To the extent that any individual, including a private equity partner or executive, makes an investment of capital in a company and later makes a profit upon the sale of the company, he is entitled to capital gains treatment. But carried interests do not represent an investment of the private equity principal's capital—they represent an investment of his labor. And labor is taxed—and has always been taxed—at ordinary income rates. There is no intellectual justification for taxing one type of labor—a private equity partner's carried interest—as a capital asset when all other forms of labor are not taxed as capital assets. The fact that the private equity industry was able to convince the tax authorities, who ultimately answer to the U.S. Treasury and Congress, to allow this treatment was deplorable. Fortunately this treatment came to an end with legislation that was passed during the 2008 financial crisis, although for the moment capital gains were a thing of the past for private equity firms. Instead, many firms were wrestling with how to repay previously received carried interests that were wiped out by subsequent losses in their funds.

When Congress was threatening to begin taxing carried interests at ordinary income rates, a number of private equity chieftains hiked up to Capitol Hill to lobby against this change in an unseemly show of where their real interests lie. Among the arguments they trotted out was one that struck an especially insincere chord: They argued that taxing their profit participations at higher rates would make them stop taking risks. Considering that 60 percent or more of the income of a private equity firm is generated by fees that are unrelated to the outcome of their investments, and ignoring the fact that the individuals making these arguments already possessed personal wealth beyond the dreams of most Americans, this argument must rank among the most appallingly cynical and intellectually vacuous to have ever been made in the halls of Congress. Thankfully, Congress had the courage it exercises all too rarely to stand up to these fallacious arguments and end a practice that did nothing other than treat a small group of Americans better than the rest of us, a practice that damages all of us.

Calling Dr. Kervorkian?

The true toll that private equity has exacted from the U.S. economy will not be known for decades. A mind is a terrible thing to waste, and too many minds have been wasted on the types of financial engineering to which private equity is devoted. While many of the brightest and most promising students attending U.S. universities have been attracted to the exorbitant compensation offered by private equity firms and the investment banks that cater to them, American society and the entire world would have been far better served had these promising young men and women become scientists and teachers. Instead, as the U.S. economy struggles to recover from the 2008 financial crisis, the corporate landscape is littered with the carcasses of overleveraged companies that were seduced by the siren song of private equity profiteers. According to the research firm Preqin, one-year returns for the private equity industry fell 27.6 percent in 2008. But that hardly tells the full story of the damage these investors wrought, since private equity firms are not required to mark their assets to market in any meaningful way. As of late 2009, the industry remained exempt from registration with the Securities and Exchange Commission or any other governmental body and thus remained free to value their assets without government oversight. Moreover, even as they were losing hundreds of billions of dollars, private equity groups required investors to invest an additional $148 billion of cash under previous commitments in 2008 with virtually no prospects of investing it profitably while distributing back only $63 billion.[26] The outlook for 2009 was even bleaker; hundreds of billions of dollars were locked in partnerships that required further capital contributions from damaged limited partners even while the opportunities for making leveraged investments were slim or none. Rather than a source of funds for investors and a source of liquidity for financial markets, the private equity business had spent itself into exhaustion and inflicted significant systemic damage while doing so.

As the nation's largest institutional investors announced their losses for 2008, there was little hope in sight for a quick rebound in their private equity holdings. The California Public Employees' Retirement System (CalPERS), the nation's largest pension fund, announced a 23.4 percent loss for the fiscal year ended June 2008, a drop in value of $56 billion to $180.9 billion. It also reported that its returns from private equity were in the bottom 1 percent of its peer group with a 5.8 percent return for the past 10 years (compared to a median peer return of 9.6 percent for the period).[27] The California State Teachers' Retirement System (CalSTRS), the nation's second largest pension fund, lost 25 percent for the fiscal year ended June 2008 as well, losing $43 billion in assets to fall to $118.8 billion in size.[28] Among the largest contributors to these losses were private equity investments, although virtually every asset class (including public equities) plunged in value over the last half of 2008. Major universities like Harvard and Yale that had championed the so-called endowment model of investing that endorsed the private equity ideal (long-term investment inured from the short-term focus of public markets) were also severely damaged by private equity losses in their endowments in 2008.

Unlike public equities and fixed-income portfolios, however, private equity portfolios left these and other institutional investors stuck with illiquid holdings and commitments to fund similar investments in a climate in which private equity investments were virtually impossible to make due to the unavailability of leveraged buyout financing. Some private equity firms allowed their investors to back out of these financing commitments, while others begged their investors to honor their obligations. In the meantime, most of 2009 passed without new investments being made by private equity firms. Instead, these firms spent most of their time propping up their existing portfolio companies, negotiating with creditors, and trying to figure out how to justify their existence now that their business model had been definitively revealed to be a "heads-we-win, tails-we-still-win-but-our-investors lose" proposition.

To compound the affliction of their investors, some of these firms made the fatal error of confusing their deal-making skills for portfolio management skills in early 2008, just before the full force of the financial crisis hit. Apollo Management, LP, Texas Pacific Group, The Blackstone Group (through its acquisition of asset management firm GSO Capital Partners LP), Bain Capital, LLC's credit affiliate Sankaty Advisors, LLC (which actually was an experienced debt investor) and KKR (through KFN) all loaded up on leveraged loans in early 2008 using large amounts of borrowed money and significant amounts of their limited partners' capital. Apollo even managed to convince CalPERS to give it $1 billion to invest in leveraged loans in a separate account. These firms generally followed the same flawed formula, borrowing approximately 75 percent of the purchase price of the loans in which they invested. They thought they were getting a steal buying these loans at 25 percent discounts to par, licking their chops at the desperation of the banks that were unloading these albatrosses. Apparently they did not suspect that the banks' willingness to finance their investments in these loans was not a sign of their strong relationships with these institutions but rather an indication of how desperate the banks were to shrink their balance sheets as credit markets were collapsing around them. For once, the banks took the clever private equity firms for a ride. In the second half of 2008 the loan market came apart, with the average price of a leveraged loan dropping by approximately 35 to 40 percent, wiping out the private equity stake' holdings in these loans. By then, many of these firms' limited partners had reached the limits of their tolerance for the so-called privilege of belonging to the private equity clubs that would have them as members. Whether this newfound wisdom about an industry that should be viewed with a jaundiced eye will persist remains to be seen.[29]

Private Equity: The Long-Term Damage

While leveraged buyouts may have started with the legitimate purpose of increasing corporate efficiency, by the mid-1990s they had become little more than a speculative activity intended to generate fees for Wall Street and their private equity sponsors. Instead of feeding innovation and creativity, which even the ultimately overblown venture capital-funded Internet bubble accomplished to some extent (bringing us companies such as eBay, Amazon.com, and others), the private equity machine simply provided a market for changes in corporate control that substituted debt for equity on corporate balance sheets. Capital that could have been used for research and development, new buildings, jobs, or funding innovative new products was instead consumed by interest payments. The opportunity cost in terms of financial, physical, and intellectual capital is incalculable. Ultimately, private equity is where capital went to die, and it managed to bury too many bodies with the full complicity of virtually every member of the financial system.

But the indictment of private equity doesn't stop even there. The influence of these firms in terms of the fees they pay to financial institutions and the political influence they peddle on Capitol Hill have altered the incentives that drive the financial world and deeply corrupted the moral sentiments of our entire society. Private equity has been instrumental in forging a financial ethos that favors the interests of the individual over those of the group, debt over equity, and speculation over production. It has managed to perpetuate tax laws that have led to the overleveraging of the U.S. economy as well as unjustifiably favorable tax treatment of its own profits that has helped create an American oligarchy and contributed to the growing gap between rich and poor that threatens long-term social stability. As such, history should rightly look back on private equity as a deeply pernicious influence that contributed to the decline of U.S. financial and moral hegemony in the world.

The growing corporate sector indebtedness that was a defining feature of financialization was driven by the going private boom that began in the late 1970s and gained momentum in the 1980s. This phenomenon was justified by arguments that promoted return on equity (increasing shareholder value) at the expense of all other measures of value in a capitalist economy. The pursuit of shareholder value holds that the sole purpose of management is to maximize the short-term return to shareholders. Other considerations—the fair and equitable treatment of labor; sound environmental policies; enhancing the long-term health of the enterprise and surrounding community—were sacrificed at the altar of shareholders' demands for immediate gratification. This view dovetailed perfectly with the free market ideology that grew dominant during the 1980s when President Ronald Reagan and Prime Minister Margaret Thatcher reigned over the Western world and helped drive the Iron Curtain into submission (although the Communists inflicted much of the damage on themselves).

Into the breach stepped the private equity industry. Over the past three decades, private equity has gathered an inordinate amount of capital and power. The result has been a leveraging up, first of the U.S. economy and soon thereafter of Western European economies. Now Asia is on the radar screen of these financiers. What has been the result? The private equity industry's lobbyists will tell us, flying in the face of common sense and substantial evidence to the contrary, that they have made industry more efficient and productive. But there can be little question that crucial activities such as research and development have suffered tremendously at the hands of these owners. Moreover, rather than building businesses, the lion's share of private equity firms have made servicing debt the new Holy Grail of corporate management. This has led them to strip their portfolio companies of excess employees and assets in the name of efficiency instead of developing new products or adding new jobs or facilities or anything else of significance to the productive capacity of the economies in which their portfolio companies operate. What they have done is transferred an enormous amount of wealth from the pockets of public shareholders and their own limited partners into their own pockets. Due to the egregiously one-sided fee schemes that they have been able to foist on their investors, this has not even had the desired effect of transferring this wealth back into the pockets of institutional investors who have seen it disappear from their public equity portfolios. Instead, private equity managers have gotten rich at the expense of every other party with whom they have interacted in the economic system. The private equity industry has inflicted so much damage on the economy in terms of draining resources and wealth away from productive uses that it is doubtful that the United States will ever recover what it has lost. Rather than proving to be the innovators that would reawaken U.S. enterprise, private equity turned out to be the undertakers that buried a good part of it.

Reform of Private Equity Firms

Private equity would never have inflicted as much damage on the economy as it had if it had been subject to a modicum of sensible regulation. There are a couple of obvious measures that can be taken immediately to rein in the industry and contribute to the stability of the global financial system.

Registration as Investment Advisers

Private equity firms have been able to operate under the regulatory radar for too long in the United States and the United Kingdom. Until the financial crisis, there was little discussion in the United States of requiring these firms to register as investment advisers under the Investment Advisers Act of 1940, as amended (the "Investment Advisers Act"). As a result, despite following strategies that were identical to those offered by many hedge funds that are registered, these firms were operating in a regulatory black hole that allowed them to follow their own set of rules. In contrast, hedge funds that are registered under the Investment Advisers Act are subject to strict rules that govern how they value their investments. With respect to nonpublic securities, registered hedge funds must justify their valuation methodologies not only to their independent auditors but also to the Securities and Exchange Commission, which has the power to bring enforcement actions and to refer matters to the U.S. Justice Department for criminal action if abusive practices are found. Private equity firms face no such restrictions and have been free to value their holdings subject only to the demands of their limited partners. These partners have generally been unwilling to challenge the valuations since doing so would only depress the value of their own holdings. This is why so many private equity valuations must be looked at with a grain of salt (and a tumbler of Johnny Walker Red)—they are merely opinions that are untested in the marketplace. In 2008, private equity investors discovered not only just how illiquid these holdings were, but also that previous elevated valuations of these holdings were figments of their general partners' imaginations. This is one reason that private equity returns were never as high as they were purported to be even before adjusting them downward for liquidity and leverage.

There is no reason why private equity firms, which control hundreds of billions of dollars of capital, should be exempt from regulation. Moreover, there is no rationale for treating them differently than hedge funds and other investment management organizations that are required to register under the Investment Advisers Act if they have more than 14 clients. Just like hedge funds, private equity firms should be subject to regular inspections by the SEC staff and be required to adopt codes of ethics and specific procedures with respect to each part of their business designed to place the interests of their clients ahead of their own. While they purport to serve their clients' interests, their fee structures alone should definitively give the lie to that charade. The time for regulation to impose duties that this business has failed to adopt on its own is long overdue.

Fee Reform

Financial reform also needs to address the combination of opacity and egregiously asymmetric compensation schemes of the private equity business. For the most part, however, this is a matter that would be best addressed by investors. After all, nobody is putting a gun to investors' heads and forcing them to invest. Many of them would discover that they would be far better served by alternative, more liquid, less liquid investment strategies. The fact that investors have allowed themselves to be abused so egregiously by their private equity managers remains one of the more inexplicable phenomenon in today's investment world.

The first step to solving this problem is drawing back the curtain on the lack of value that all but a select few managers provide their clients. The evidence is available if investors want to seek it out. Better disclosure of returns and fees by private equity firms would go a long way to giving investors the tools to evaluate their managers in a meaningful way. This is one of the most compelling reasons why, as argued above, private equity managers should be registered as investment advisers and subject to the rules governing the reporting of returns and the disclosure of fees. This is a particularly curious discrepancy in view of the fact that private equity firms generally receive commitments to hold on to investors' capital for long periods of time (5 to 10 years) while hedge funds have much shorter commitment periods and are required to be in a position to return capital typically on an annual basis (with some exceptions for less liquid strategies that resemble private equity).

Private equity firms' fee structures are egregiously unfavorable to clients (and, in fairness, the same could be said of hedge funds' fees, so parts of this discussion should apply equally to that industry as well). This is the fault of both the firms and the clients and should be addressed through private negotiation and not legislation. There is no private equity strategy that merits a management fee of higher than 0.75 percent per year, or a performance fee of higher than 15 percent per year. Moreover, managers should be paid performance fees only after their investment returns exceed market performance or the rate of inflation. Accordingly, performance fees should only be payable above a hurdle rate. Investors should be paying for real performance, not fortuity. In no case should performance fees be paid for negative returns (for example, losing less money than a negative benchmark does not merit a performance fee although there have been instances where such fees have been paid). Performance fees should be used to reward absolute, not relative performance. Paying for negative performance is simply adding insult to an investor's injury and is the surest way to build distrust on the part of investors. All performance fees should be accrued for a period of not less than three years in order to discourage short-term risk-taking and speculation. Finally, all performance fees should be subject to both high water marks and clawbacks in the event that earlier years' profits are wiped out by poor performance in later years. Managing other people's money is a privilege, not a right, and should be treated as such.

If investors were able to ascertain more information about certain investment strategies that have attracted enormous amounts of capital in recent years but have also consistently been at the center of market dislocations, it is likely they would be far less enamored of them. As noted above, private equity returns, are far less attractive than advertised when they are properly risk-adjusted to take into account concentration risk and the risks of leverage, liquidity, and imposition of unjustifiably high fees. Other nonpublic market strategies like distressed debt have similar return profiles. What is most disturbing about these opaque strategies is the fact that they tend to follow the reverse-Black Swan model—they bump along for periods of time reporting decent returns based on unverifiable valuations of their holdings and then simply implode when the markets collapse as they did in 1998, 2001, 2002, and 2008. Investors get tagged with huge losses and are almost always unable to withdraw their remaining assets from the fund while their managers keep their previously earned fees. It has always been a point of curiosity why institutional investors have not been more disturbed by reading the names of their private equity or hedge fund managers on the list of the Forbes 400 reporting their Brobdingnagian wealth while they have been subject to earning mediocre returns with these men (they are almost all men) in charge of their capital.

CHAPTER 6

Welcome to Jurassic Park

In addition to being an enormously entertaining movie, *Jurassic Park* (1993) is a cautionary tale of technology gone wild. The film, and Michael Crichton's novel from which it was adapted, are modern twists on the ancient Prometheus myth and Mary Shelley's nineteenth-century horror story *Frankenstein*, in which an obsessed Dr. Victor Frankenstein dared to play God and created a monster that destroyed everything most dear to him. Misusing technology is an age-old tale that visited Wall Street in 2008 with dire results.

In one scene in *Jurassic Park*, the scientists who are brought to the park to evaluate its progress and safety for its insurers and financiers get into a heated debate over lunch with the park's founder, Dr. John Hammond, about the merits of trying to fool with Mother Nature. They had just witnessed a velociraptor devour a cow in a matter of seconds in a display of savagery that, among other things, renders them uninterested in their meal. Dr. Ian Malcolm, a professor of chaos theory (brilliantly played by the actor Jeff Goldblum) begins shouting at

Dr. Hammond that he is tempting fate by blindly using technology without respecting its potentially destructive power:

> The problem with the scientific power you've used is it didn't require any discipline to attain it. You read what others had done and you took the next step. You didn't earn the knowledge yourselves, so you don't take the responsibility for it. You stood on the shoulders of geniuses to accomplish something as fast as you could, and before you knew what you had, you patented it. . . . Your scientists were so preoccupied with whether or not they could that they didn't stop to think if they should.[1]

The hubris involved in creating extinct creatures out of the DNA stored in amber buried deep in the earth is an apt metaphor for the derivatives technology that was unleashed on the financial world through the creation of credit default swaps, and the ruins of the imaginary Jurassic Park serve as a vivid image of a damaged financial system once credit defaults swaps and other exotic derivative instruments backfired on their inventors in 2008. The fact that the film came out at roughly the same time that a group of investment bankers from J.P. Morgan created these new types of financial instrument simply lends some irony to the history of one of the greatest self-inflicted wounds in financial history.[2]

Isla Nublar

Financial derivatives are very odd animals. As Edward LiPuma and Benjamin Lee point out in a brilliant theoretical discussion of derivatives in their book, *Financial Derivatives and the Globalization of Risk*, derivatives are a unique form of capital. Unlike currencies, derivatives do not gain their value or legitimacy from the backing of any government or any precious metal.[3] And unlike bonds or bank loans, derivatives do not draw their value directly from an underlying obligor (in other words, the company whose financial condition will determine whether they will be repaid). Instead, a derivative is a hybrid creature whose value is drawn from two entirely separate sources. In this discussion, we will be focusing on credit derivatives in their most common (and potentially noxious) form: credit default swaps (CDS).

Financial derivatives are the ultimate (so far—there will undoubtedly be further applications of computer technology to financial instruments) example of the literal deconstruction of financial instruments. The importance of the ability to deconstruct financial instruments through computer technology cannot be overemphasized; it transformed the nature of financial assets by rendering them capable of being turned into immaterial objects of untold complexity. The digitalization of information was a key step in the process of financialization because it broke down the boundaries between different disciplines and modes of communication. Computers created the ability to reduce language or symbols into the common language of 1s and 0s in a manner that disguises or blurs differences in meaning between different types of underlying objects or forms.

Derivatives could not exist without the type of computing power that has developed over the past three decades. But the more important point is that digitalization takes one thing—a financial instrument (a bond, stock, mortgage, loan, and so on)—and turns it into another thing: another financial instrument (a derivative). This transformation reveals the fact that these instruments are really just different combinations of the same constituent parts, much like humans and animals are different combinations of DNA or each component of the periodic table is a different combination of electrons and protons. This is something that has tremendous ramifications for the way in which financial market participants come to view the world. It has also been an enormously destabilizing force because it separates the tradable instrument from the underlying reference instrument, just as securitization in the credit markets sundered the promissory relationship between the borrower and the lender. As relationships between things that were previously connected become further separated or mediated, the opportunity for confusion of meanings and intervening disconnections of meaning increases.

Derivatives disassemble bonds, loans, and mortgages into their constituent parts and then reassemble them into new configurations that can be sold to different investors (or speculators) with different risk appetites. Derivatives are the financial version of splitting the atom or dissecting the human genome. Just like nuclear weapons draw their potency from the ability of scientists to split the atom into its constituent parts, derivatives derive their power from the ability of mathematicians to separate financial instruments into 1s and 0s, the constituent parts of money. The problem with deconstructing money into its constituent parts is that it abstracts the new instrument—the derivative—from the underlying or reference obligation in a manner that attenuates the relationship between lender and borrower and vests economic power over the ultimate borrower in the hands of a party that has little or no knowledge about or interest in the actual business of this borrower.

To describe it in the language of Karl Marx, a credit derivative like a credit default swap is the quintessential fetish instrument, because it is the result of a process whereby an underlying financial instrument (a bond, bank loan, or mortgage) is deconstructed into its constituent parts and then reassembled or reconfigured into a new form that has no resemblance to the economic forces that created it. In most cases, these investors are speculators who have no interest in or understanding of the underlying instrument or the social relations that brought it into being. This is a far more radical state of alienation than simply saying that we are no longer getting our mortgage from our neighborhood banker. The relationship between lender and borrower, the two parties to a promise, has become so attenuated as to become almost spectral. Derivatives are the ultimate manifestation of disembodied financial relationships that are controlled by forces that are difficult to identify or control.

Highly mediated forms of finance such as securitization and derivatives impose enormous barriers between underlying financial instruments or securities and the forms in which they were traded. When every financial object is capable of being transformed into something else, all financial instruments are revealed to be, in their essence, the same. This chameleon-like quality introduces a degree of instability into the system that did not exist before derivatives technology existed. This instability arises from the fact that the identity and character of individual financial objects such as stocks or bonds or mortgages can be transformed into different types of objects. Just as the ability of a traditional convertible bond to be transformed into stock drastically changes the way it is valued compared to a nonconvertible bond, the ability of a traditional corporate bond to be pooled with other bonds into a collateralized bond obligation (CBO) or expressed in terms of a credit default swap alters its value in multiple ways by changing its liquidity and other characteristics.

For investors, this raises profound questions regarding asset allocation and other traditional theories of portfolio management that some of us have long questioned. For instance, the very concept of asset classes can be called into question in view of the ability of derivatives to turn one type of security into another type of security. Such questions have enormous consequences that are just beginning to be explored by thoughtful money managers and regulators.

If we turn our attention specifically to credit default swaps, the first thing to understand is that such instruments are legal contracts in which two parties enter into an exchange of promises with respect to some underlying financial obligation, for example, a bond, bank loan, or mortgage. Neither of these parties needs to have any legal relationship (for example, a preexisting ownership relationship) with the company that issued the underlying obligation. In fact, the presence of a preexisting relationship is the factor that separates speculative derivatives positions from hedged derivatives positions. The latter involves parties who already have an ownership interest in the underlying obligation and are using the derivative to protect themselves from losses, while the former involves parties with no such ownership position who are merely betting on price movements in order to earn a new profit. Another component of the value of a derivatives contract is found in the parties who enter into the contract. Their financial condition and ability to fulfill their promises are keys to the outcome of the contract into which they have entered.

The contractual nature of derivative instruments is essential to their understanding.[4] As contracts, derivatives share certain important similarities with other credit instruments such as mortgages, bank loans, and bonds. Wherever they circulate in the economy, they must return to their point of origin for redemption (i.e., payment). Once the contract is satisfied, it disappears from circulation. As we saw in an earlier chapter discussing mortgage derivatives, the disembodied nature of these contracts can cause serious practical problems, for example, when it becomes impossible to identify who holds the mortgage on a home because the mortgage contract was sold into a mortgage pool and cannot be tracked. Unlike the underlying cash obligations on which derivatives are based, derivatives are ungrounded from the flesh-and-blood borrowers whose economic performance determines their ultimate value.

An essential component of a derivative contract's value is based on the parties' ability to enforce their rights within a system of laws. There are two aspects of enforceability. First, theoretical or legal enforceability is based on the specific language of the derivatives contract. The contract sets forth the respective obligations of the parties and the consequences of failing to meet them. Second, practical enforceability is wholly dependent on the ability of the parties undertaking financial obligations under the contract to fulfill them. In theoretical terms, a legally unenforceable promise made by a solvent party is worthless, while in practical terms a legally enforceable promise made by an insolvent counterparty is an empty promise. Both the theoretical and practical aspects of enforceability must be present for a derivatives contract to be fulfilled.

The second component of value in a credit default swap contract is the underlying security itself. Changes in the price of this security play a determinative role in the value of the derivatives that are based on them. The indirect nature of a derivative obligation—the fact that its value is determined by reference to something outside of itself—renders it unusually complex and inherently unstable because it is subject to variables beyond the control of the parties comprising it. Moreover, unless regulatory or other legal limits are placed on the ability to issue derivatives with respect to an underlying obligation, there is no theoretical limitation on the volume of derivative contracts that can be written with respect to a specific underlying obligation. This raises particularly important systemic questions with respect to credit derivatives and credit default swaps specifically, which are discussed in detail in the following section.

At times during the 2008 financial crisis, it seemed as though the fiscal and monetary authorities were not going to be able to stop the markets from collapsing. The reason for this feeling of helplessness was not simply the volume of selling that was raining down on the markets, but the fact that it was difficult to identify the source of selling and the reasons for selling. This was particularly true with respect to the sale of credit instruments such as mortgages, bonds, and bank loans, the prices of which were driven to levels that made no rational sense unless one truly believed that the end of the world was at hand.

What was not apparent to market observers (in particular the media) was that selling pressure was being generated in the parallel universe of the credit derivatives markets, which were completely opaque and unregulated and whose prices were largely hidden from the media and the public. Price discovery—the term traders use to describe the point at which buyers and sellers come to a meeting of the minds—became a matter of shooting darts in the dark because there were no benchmarks against which to measure value. This was because the traditional benchmarks—the prices of cash credit instruments—were being driven by the shadow prices of their derivatives, whose markets were concealed from view and driven by mathematical formulas that had little or no relation to the real world in which these obligations were making their way and affecting real flesh-and-blood human beings. When the distance between lender and borrower, promisee and promisor, becomes so attenuated as to become like that between a body and its ghost, it is not unreasonable to fear that regulators and governments will not be able to put the genie back in the bottle again.

More frightening is the fact that the spectral world of derivatives is not subject to the physical limits of the underlying obligations to which they refer. The parallel universe of credit derivatives has come to dwarf the cash obligations with respect to which they are written. In the most widespread type of credit derivative and the one that will occupy most of our attention here—credit default swaps—the market grew to more than $60 trillion in size on the eve of the 2008 financial crisis, far greater than the volume of cash obligations it was insuring. The sheer size of this market came to exercise an enormous and often perverse influence on the world of cash credit obligations. Like Frankenstein, the creature who turned on and ultimately destroyed all that mattered most to his master, credit default swaps have created many unintended consequences for borrowers and lenders.

The New DNA of Finance

At its core, a credit default swap is an insurance contract in which one party (the seller of protection, that is, insurance) promises to pay the other party (the buyer) in the event that an underlying financial obligation (normally a bank loan, bond, mortgage, or pool thereof) defaults. The seller/insurer pays the buyer/insured an amount of money that will compensate for the loss. Most economists and educated market practitioners would agree that using a credit default swap to hedge an existing holding of a credit instrument is a rational and socially and economically valuable and useful activity.

A couple of simple examples will demonstrate the idea behind credit default swaps.

The first example involves bonds from IBM, a financially sound company:

> Institution A owns $10 million of IBM bonds. It is concerned that changes in interest rates may cause the price of these bonds to drop and wants to buy insurance against such an event. It goes to Institution B to purchase that insurance. The cost of such insurance is 150 basis points per year for $10 million of insurance for a five-year period, or $150,000 per year. This amount is paid annually pursuant to a standard contract known as an International Swap Dealers Association (ISDA) contract.

In addition, the buyer of protection is required to post some amount of collateral with the seller to insure his ability to make future premium payments. The collateral amount is determined by a combination of factors that includes both the credit quality of the buyer/insured as well as that of the underlying instrument. One of the reasons that the credit default swap market was able to explode in size was that collateral requirements were generally relatively small in the time leading to the 2008 crisis.

Collateral is a much bigger issue with respect to our next example, a financially distressed company like General Motors Corp., in the months before it filed for bankruptcy in early 2009. In the case of a failing company, default insurance is much more expensive to purchase because the likelihood of default is very high (the insurer is highly likely to be making good on his promise to make the insured whole for his loss). The buyer of protection will be required to post more collateral, and the cost of insurance will include a large upfront payment as well as large annual payments. Most of the premium, however, is captured in the large upfront payment.

> Institution A owns $10 million of General Motors bonds. It is concerned that General Motors may default on these bonds and wants to

buy insurance against such an event. It goes to Institution B to purchase that insurance. Because the odds of General Motors defaulting
are very high, Institution B demands both an upfront payment and an
annual premium for this insurance. The upfront payment is 45 points,
or $4,500,000, and the annual premium is $500,000, for a five-year
period. This insurance agreement is documented in a standard contract
known as an ISDA contract.

One might inquire why an investor would pay such an exorbitant
amount for default insurance. The answer is that he wouldn't. Trades
of this type occur among speculators, not investors looking to hedge
existing positions. Holders of General Motors bonds or loans who were
worried about credit losses arranged to hedge their positions much earlier, when credit insurance was still cheap. At the point where large
upfront payments are involved, speculators have taken over and are placing bets on the timing of default and the likely recovery value on the
swap contracts.

These examples illustrate the differences between the pricing on
credit default swaps for distressed borrowers and those for healthy borrowers. In fact, one might ask whether there is a need for credit default
swaps on healthy borrowers, and this is where the distinction between
hedging and speculation comes into play. Many investors must mark-
to-market their investments on a current basis, and other investors are
not required to do so. Increasingly, the investment world has moved to
a mark-to-market model in which institutional investors require their
investment managers to value their assets on a current basis. In recent years, this trend has been accentuated by the explosive growth of
hedge funds and changes in accounting rules aimed at increasing systemic
transparency.

Marking-to-market is a complex issue and a two-edged sword. In
the case of short-term oriented investors such as hedge funds, marking-
to-market is an appropriate requirement. If an investor has a short-term
time horizon, he should be required to value his assets on a current
basis. But in the case of banks, which are in the business of making
long-term loans on assets that are in many cases illiquid, or long-term
investors such as pension funds that are trying to match long-term liabilities with long-term bond holdings, marking-to-market may not be appropriate. Nonetheless, there is growing sentiment that mark-to-market

accounting should be used more broadly in the financial world. As a result, an increasing number of investors feel the need to hedge their investment holdings, particular longer dated ones; and one of the primary tools for doing so in the fixed-income world is credit derivatives, and specifically credit default swaps. The primary risk involved in investing in a high-quality investment grade bond is interest rate risk rather than credit risk. Accordingly, the holder of an IBM bond is primarily concerned about price changes in the bond resulting from changes in interest rates, not radical changes in IBM's financial condition. A credit default swap is a useful way to hedge this risk. The value of the credit default swap will change as the value of the underlying IBM bond changes in response to changes in interest rates (or, if there are significant changes in IBM's credit quality, to those changes as well). As a result, the investor will be able to counterbalance losses or gains in the underlying IBM bond with corresponding gains or losses in the credit default swap contract on those bonds. This hedging function is eminently reasonable and serves an important and useful purpose in financial markets.

The problem with these instruments arises from the fact that they are untethered from the underlying bonds and there is no practical or theoretical limitation on the amount of credit default swaps that can be written with respect to any given underlying bond, loan, mortgage, or pooled instrument. In practice, this means that if there are $2 billion of outstanding General Motors bonds, the amount of credit default swaps that can be written on those bonds is not limited to $2 billion. It can be $20 billion, or $200 billion, or $2 trillion. The net exposure (in other words, the actual amount of money at risk when offsetting trades are removed from the system) may be much less than the outstanding face amount of credit default swaps, but there is no systemic or regulatory limitation on the amount of these instruments that can be written by market participants. This is how the credit default swap market grew virtually undetected to over $60 trillion in size by early 2008 and came to threaten the very viability of the global financial system.

There are far more complex variations of credit default swaps. These are easier to understand if one keeps in mind that they are intended to be insurance against losses on underlying obligations. One such example is a credit default swap written on a tranche of a collateralized debt obligation (CDO) that holds pools of residential mortgages. These were discussed earlier in this book (see Chapter 3). In this example, a credit default swap is written with respect to specific tranches of a collateralized mortgage obligation (CMO) in order to provide insurance for an owner of that tranche's bonds against a default of those bonds. For example, if a holder of one of the 17 tranches in the CMO shown in Figure 3.3 in Chapter 3 wanted protection against a default on his bonds, which would result if enough of the underlying mortgages held by the CMO defaulted, he would ask a financial institution to sell him protection in the form of a credit default swap. Depending on whether the tranche in question was considered healthy or distressed, he might pay an upfront premium plus an annual premium (for a distressed tranche) or just an annual premium (for a healthy tranche). This would provide him protection if the CMO ran into trouble and defaulted.

Finally, there is an even more complicated variation, known as a credit default swap written on a synthetic CDO. A synthetic CDO holds a pool of other credit default swaps on underlying bonds, loans, or mortgages (rather than owning the underlying bonds, loans, or mortgages themselves). In other words, a synthetic CDO does not own a pool of individual bonds or loans or mortgages but instead is a counterparty to credit default swap contracts on underlying bonds, loans, or mortgages. Like other CDOs, this type of CDO is financed through the sale of different tranches of rated debt. Holders of these different tranches can buy insurance against potential losses on these tranches by buying protection through credit default swaps. Alternatively, speculators (those who don't own the underlying tranches) can place bets on whether the underlying tranches will increase or decrease in value. Needless to say, such instruments are highly complex and difficult to unwind when the feces hits the fan.

Warning Signs

By early 2006, the credit derivatives market was already spinning out of control. In any other industry, there would have been more than enough embarrassment to go around when it was discovered that a huge percentage of credit default swap trades had not been properly accounted for by Wall Street's back offices. As of September 30, 2005, the number of trade confirmations that were outstanding for more than 30 days stood at 97,000. Assuming an average trade size of $5 million, this meant that trades with a nominal value of \$485 billion, in the words of the *Wall Street Journal*, "lacked detailed confirmations—a problem that has left banks and brokerage firms uncertain who owes what to whom."[5] In a speech to the Global Association of Risk Professionals in early 2006, then New York Federal Reserve President Timothy Geithner stepped into the fray and read Wall Street the riot act about cleaning up its mess.

> The post-trade processing and settlement infrastructure is still quite weak relative to the significance of these markets. . . . The total stock of unconfirmed trades is large and until recently was growing considerably faster than the total volume of new trades. The time between trade and confirmation is still quite long for a large share of transactions. The share of trades done on the available automated platforms is still substantially short of what is possible . . . firms were typically assigning trades without the knowledge or consent of the original counterparties. Nostro breaks, which are errors in payments discovered by counterparties at the time of the quarterly flows, rose to a significant share of total trades. Efforts to standardize documentation and provide automated confirmation services has lagged behind product development and growth in volume . . . the assignment problems create uncertainty about the actual size of exposures to individual counterparties that could exacerbate market liquidity problems in the event of stress.

Wall Street, however, is not subject to embarrassment. The profit motives trumps everything else. So the large derivative trading firms promised to clean up the mess, and all was forgiven by the stern-faced Mr. Geithner and his regulatory brethren. The fact that Wall Street was unable to account for such a large portion of credit default swaps should have been a stark warning that trouble lay ahead. Little did anyone appreciate the depth of the problem or the risk it posed to the financial system. The monster was about to eat Manhattan.

Dinosaurs Turn on Their Makers

Credit default swaps create a structure in which lenders are so alienated from the flesh-and-blood labor of the businesses that are responsible for repaying them that the traditional relationship between borrower and lender is not only sundered but in certain circumstances is rendered adversarial. One of the dirty little secrets about credit default swaps is that they create in the buyer of protection (the insured) a strong economic incentive to see the borrower default; in many cases, a default is what produces the highest payout and highest rate of return for the buyer of insurance. In this way, credit default swaps create perverse incentives for the parties that enter into them. Credit default swaps can create strong economic incentives for investors to root for businesses to fail, because failure is what constitutes a credit event that triggers payment under standard credit default swap contracts known as ISDA agreements. Moreover, because the volume of credit default swaps can dwarf the amount of a company's outstanding debt, the derivatives market rather than direct lenders can determine the fate of a debtor. This means that the parties calling the shots are not those who have an interest in the underlying businesses and employees affected by whether a company can ultimately restructure its debts. Instead, power is vested in the hands of credit default swap holders who do not own the underlying debt instruments but who have instead been merely placing bets, usually with very little money down, on the future of flesh-and-blood businesses. From a public policy standpoint, this should raise serious concerns about the proper role of debt markets and derivatives markets in the economy.

The somewhat perverse phenomenon of creditors rooting for the demise of their borrowers in the credit default swap market has been termed the "empty creditor" phenomenon by Professor Henry T.C. Hu of the University of Texas Law School.[6] Professor Hu describes an empty creditor as "someone (or some institution) who may have the contractual control but, by simultaneously holding credit default swaps, little or no economic exposure if the debt goes bad." In fact, "if a creditor holds enough credit default swaps, he may simultaneously have control rights and incentives to cause the debtor firm's value to fall." This concept gives a whole new meaning to Karl Marx's concept of alienation. Marx was speaking about the alienation of labor, but today the alienation of labor is further exacerbated by the alienation of capital. We now see a type of alienation between borrower and lender that has an insidious effect on companies that employ labor by making it more difficult for them to reorganize their debts.

The advent of credit default swaps has created a situation in which lenders can hedge their exposure to borrowers to the extent that they effectively become indifferent as to whether their debts are repaid by the debtor. They will be just as happy to be repaid by their counterparty. In fact, such payment will come more quickly and is actually preferable to waiting for the debtor to pay. Accordingly, lenders aren't indifferent to the fate of their borrowers; they are incentivized to see their lenders fail. So-called "basis packages," in which investors own both a bond and a credit default swap related to that bond, are often structured to deliver a higher return if the borrower files for bankruptcy, thereby forcing a payout on the credit default swap contract at the time of the bankruptcy filing (as opposed to the end of the bankruptcy reorganization process, which can take months or years). Rather than leading lenders to participate in a consensual out-of-court restructuring that generally imposes much lower costs on the borrower, this structure pushes borrowers into highly expensive bankruptcy proceedings that create little economic value for anybody but bankruptcy attorneys. In the hands of speculators who have no interest in the ultimate survival of the business (if they even know what the business is and what it does), businesses are reduced to empty carcasses whose bones are more likely to be sold in liquidation than emerge as viable going concerns with new, deleveraged balance sheets.

In the period leading up to the 2008 crisis, this economically unhealthy phenomenon was exacerbated by the fact that many debts were incurred in private equity transactions where much of the value was skimmed off into the hands of the private equity sponsor through management and transaction fees rather than into the hands of the limited partners who represent endowments and foundations and other tax-exempt organizations. The combination of these factors led to a voiding of the value of leveraged companies into the hands of financial speculators. The government, through the offices of the bankruptcy process or, in the event of a systemically important company, through a bailout, was left to clean up the mess.

George Soros has written persuasively on the asymmetric incentives that credit default swaps have introduced into the financial system. Soros views these flaws as sufficiently profound as to have called for these instruments to be banned unless the purchaser of credit insurance owns the underlying instrument. In an essay in the *Wall Street Journal*, he wrote the following:

> Going short on bonds by buying a CDS contract carries limited risk but almost unlimited profit potential. By contrast, selling CDS offers limited profits but practically unlimited risks. This asymmetry encourages speculating on the short side, which in turn exerts a downward pressure on the underlying bonds. The negative effect is reinforced by the fact that CDS are tradable and therefore tend to be priced as warrants, which can be sold at anytime, not as options, which would require an actual default to be cashed in. People buy them not because they expect an eventual default, but because they expect the CDS to appreciate in response to adverse development. AIG thought it was selling insurance on bonds, and as such, they considered CDS outrageously overpriced. In fact, it was selling bear-market warrants and it severely underestimated the risk.[7]

Soros outlines what happens when you fool with Mother Nature. First, credit default swaps offer limited risk and unlimited reward when used to make negative bets on credit. Second, investments in credit default swaps require far too little collateral, which allows a small amount of capital to affect the market. This disconnection with the real economy is what raises concerns about the role that derivatives play in today's markets. The problem with this, as LiPuma and Lee point out, is that speculative derivatives positions (i.e., those not being used to hedge an underlying position) do not appear to involve productive labor, the organization of activities that have any real connection with material resources, the output of goods or services, or the satisfaction or promotion of further productive output.[8] As a result, these instruments can be used to speculate on credit without the speculators being sufficiently at risk to cause them to think twice about the potential systemic risks they may be posing.

Bear Stearns: First Casualty

The collapse of Bear Stearns in 2008 illustrated some of the systemic risks that unregulated trading in credit default swaps created. Speculators were able to take aim at the firm's stock and credit default swaps and engage in a variety of short-selling strategies in an effort to profit from price changes (a drop in the stock price, or an increase in the CDS spread) without any regard for the real-world consequences of their behavior. The rating agencies then stepped in and threatened to lower the company's credit rating based on these manipulative price movements, rendering the company all but incapable of financing itself. The inner workings of the CDS market were able to produce changes in Bear Stearns' borrowing costs that had little to do with the firms' financial condition but had tremendous consequences for the survivability of the firm.

In real-world terms, this is what happened to Bear Stearns in March 2008. At the time (and at all times), broker dealers had extensive counterparty exposure to each other. Each firm places limitations on how much overall exposure it is willing to have to another firm. If one trading desk has a certain amount of exposure to another firm, it will limit how much exposure other desks can have to that same firm. As a result, each firm has a limited ability to write CDS on another firm's credit. At the time, these limitations were even tighter because of the building crisis. Since firms had to limit their exposure to Bear Stearns, every time a firm was asked to increase its exposure to the firm by writing another credit default swap, it raised the price. Even relatively small price increases caused disproportionately large price hikes. This led Bear Stearns' credit default swap spreads to spiral out of control with little or no regard to the firm's underlying financial condition. In effect, the internal workings of the credit default swap market caused Bear Stearns' collapse to become a self-fulfilling prophesy by rendering Bear Stearns' cost of funding so expensive as to render the firm unfinanceable. Without the ability to finance itself, a broker dealer like Bear Stearns had to close its doors (or sell itself to someone like JPMorgan Chase & Co. for a nominal amount).

In the case of Bear Stearns, sharp increases in the spreads on its credit default swaps in the period leading to its takeover by JPMorgan Chase signaled to the media and markets that the firm was experiencing financial trouble. During the week of March 10, 2008, Bear Stearns' one-year credit default swaps spreads suddenly spiked up to nearly 1,000 basis points, a level that rendered the investment bank incapable of financing itself or running its business profitably. A financial institution uses money as its raw material, and when the price of its raw material is driven up by a factor of 10 virtually overnight, it is effectively priced out of business. This is exactly what happened to Bear Stearns.

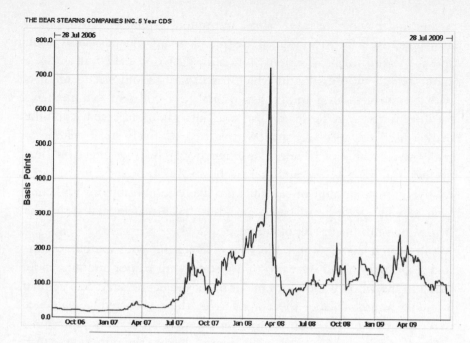

Figure 6.1   Bear Stearns' Death by CDS
Source: Goldman Sachs, July 2009.

Figure 6.1 shows the dramatic spike to unsustainable levels that Bear Stearns' credit default swap spreads were driven before the company was sold to JPMorgan Chase & Co.

An investment bank and trading firm requires low-cost overnight funding in order to profitably hold trading inventory, and these levels were telling the marketplace that Bear Stearns could no longer borrow at reasonable rates if at all. This was a far more important indication of financial distress than the firm's stock price, which was also plunging at the time.[9]

Credit default swaps spreads, because they are quoted in real time, are believed to be the most accurate and timely indicia of a borrower's credit quality. Unfortunately, there are several flaws with the concept of depending on the credit default swap market to determine the fate of important financial firms. Bear Stearns maintained active trading relationships with virtually every other financial institution in the world. Its failure would have caused severe disruption throughout the financial system (much as Lehman Brothers' bankruptcy six months later actually did cause). The credit default market was completely unregulated.

A few trades and a relatively small amount of capital were capable of moving spreads by an inordinate degree. A major financial institution and the entire financial system were allowed to be held hostage by a credit default swap market in which participants could place large bets with relatively modest amounts of capital (the collateral requirements for these trades were far lower than stock margin requirements) and the market itself was relatively shallow (that is, a relatively small volume of trades was capable of having a disproportionately large effect on Bear Stearns' spreads). As a result, a relatively small number of traders, and a relatively small amount of capital, were likely responsible for widening Bear Stearns' credit default swap spreads to levels that suggested that the firm was at imminent risk of failure.

In March 2008, swap traders were operating with extremely limited information, and were mostly working with rumor and innuendo. What in the world is more opaque or more subject to rapid change than a trading house's balance sheet? Moreover, there was credible evidence that some of the firm's competitors were participating in, or at least encouraging, what amounted to a "bear raid" (excuse the pun) on the firm through the credit default swap market. In Wall Street parlance, a bear raid involves a group of speculators acting together to raise doubts about the viability of a company and profiting from that firm's failure by selling short its stock (or in this case its bonds and other credit instruments). Since credit default swaps at the time were effectively unregulated, there was nothing Bear Stearns could do to stop the speculation and its sale to JPMorgan Chase (at the behest of the U.S. government) for $2 per share (later adjusted to $10 per share.) At its peak in January 2007, the stock had sold for as much as $171.50 per share (which was undoubtedly far more than it was worth). Bear Stearns was hardly a poster child for risk management, but being victimized by credit default swap speculators was not an appropriate ending for the firm.

American International Group (AIG)—Second Casualty

Credit default swaps appeared as the weapon of financial self-destruction six months later at insurance giant American International Group (AIG).

AIG was once the pride of the global insurance industry. The company morphed into a multifaceted financial institution that was part hedge fund, part investment bank, part asset management company, and part insurance company. Unfortunately, the firm came to be dominated by a group centered in London and Connecticut known as AIG Financial Products. This group of financial engineers came to believe that AIG's AAA balance sheet would allow it to write infinite amounts of insurance on investment-grade-rated risks without ever asking the question of what would happen if those credit ratings were questioned. By the middle of 2007, the company had insured a reported $465 billion of high-grade securities. But this exposed the company to two types of risks with respect to credit ratings. The first was that the ratings on all of the AAA securities that it was insuring would stay AAA. The second was that its own investment rating would remain AAA. Unfortunately, AIG came to learn that these were the same question, and the answer wasn't a pretty one.

In September 2008, AIG found itself facing approximately $27 billion of collateral calls on $62.1 billion of credit default swap contracts on synthetic collateralized mortgage obligations. A synthetic collateralized mortgage obligation is a collection of different credit default swaps on different tranches of underlying pools of mortgages. These assets are typical of those that lay at the heart of the financial crisis: They were highly complex, illiquid mathematical constructs that few people understood (least of all, apparently, the geniuses at AIG that were purporting to insure them) and few institutions wanted to own, which is why so much effort was made to lay off their risk. They traveled in the guise of securities, yet they are not securities in the traditional sense of the word. In fact, as the world came to learn much to its dismay, that term is the quintessential oxymoron—whatever these constructs are, they are the farthest thing in the world from secure. They have little to do with the fundamental credit quality or earnings quality of a company or an economic entity or actor. They merely reference some other entity that references some other entity and so on.

Yet in this case, the reason for AIG's crisis lay not in these monstrosities but in itself: AIG was about to lose its highly coveted AAA rating. On Friday, September 12, 2008, Standard & Poor's placed AIG on negative credit watch, suggesting that loss of its coveted AAA rating was imminent. The insurance giant didn't have to wait long to learn what "imminent" meant in the midst of a financial crisis. Just three days later, on Monday, September 15—the same day that Lehman Brothers filed for bankruptcy—Standard & Poor's and the two other major credit rating agencies, Moody's and Fitch Ratings Service, downgraded the long-term credit rating of AIG. The game was up. For many companies this might be bad news, but it would not trigger corporate destruction. However, AIG's credit default swap agreements included a clause that required the insurance giant to post additional collateral if it lost its AAA rating. Such a provision is not particularly unreasonable or even unusual; if a party's credit quality deteriorates, it is reasonable for those doing business with it to ask for additional assurance that they will be repaid. In the case of AIG, however, this clause triggered a requirement to post $27.1 billion of additional collateral with respect to the synthetic collateralized mortgage obligations in question. And AIG simply did not have that kind of cash lying around in its vaults. Obviously, nobody at AIG ever envisioned a ratings downgrade.

The U.S. government was faced with little choice but to step in and provide AIG with the cash to make these collateral payments. AIG was much larger and more interconnected than Lehman Brothers, whose bankruptcy was shaking the financial system to its core. AIG's failure would have been an extinction-level event for the global financial system because it would have triggered cross defaults on all of AIG's other contracts (derivative and otherwise) around the world. It would also have set off a maelstrom of defaults among the many financial counterparties that were depending on AIG for payment in order to meet their own obligations. It remains an interesting question whether the U.S. government solved the problem in the right way. The credit rating agencies could have been told to back off and maintain AIG's AAA rating (although that would have been unlikely to fool the market, and AIG's own credit default swap spreads probably would have widened significantly and driven the company into insolvency). Alternatively, the U.S. government could have simply stated that it would stand behind all of AIG's financial obligations, effectively lending AIG the U.S. government's AAA rating. While there was no express legal authority for such a move, the Federal Reserve had little trouble invoking its emergency powers at other times during the crisis in the name of systemic stability.[10] The advantage of this approach is that it would have avoided the necessity of the U.S. Treasury coming up with what ultimately became approximately $175 billion in support for AIG. The market was willing to accept U.S. government guarantees on other failed institutions such as Fannie Mae and Freddie Mac, so it likely would have been satisfied with one on AIG. But whether or not the bailout could have been done more effectively, the authorities clearly did the correct thing by stepping in and preventing AIG from failing. The real tragedy (and farce) is that AIG found itself in that position in the first place through the irresponsible issuance of hundreds of billions of credit default swap obligations.

The fact that the failure of Lehman Brothers and the near-failure of AIG occurred at virtually the same time was a sign that the financial markets had ceased to function. Capital had died. The damage soon spread to two other firms that were considered by most observers to be well-managed and well-capitalized: Goldman Sachs and Morgan Stanley. During that same week in September 2008, credit default swap traders had their way with these companies as well. To place the following numbers in context, remember that Lehman Brothers filed for bankruptcy on Monday, September 15, (and was obviously rumored to be in trouble in the days leading up to that date). The five-year credit default swap spreads for Goldman Sachs moved from 200 basis points on Friday, September 12, to 350 basis points on Monday, September 15, and then to 620 basis points two days later on Wednesday, September 17 (by then the government had announced an $85 billion rescue package for AIG). Morgan Stanley saw even more ominous widening in its spreads, from 250 basis points on Friday, September 12, to 500 basis points on Monday, September 15, to 997 basis points on Wednesday, September 17. Wall Street was devouring its own. At these spreads, no firm would be able to finance itself profitably for very long. Goldman Sachs and Morgan Stanley raised billions of dollars of new equity capital from outside investors in order to bolster their balance sheets and were granted bank holding company status by the U.S. government in order to obtain further protections.

The Bond Insurers—Third Casualty

Another group of companies that were ruined by their exposure to credit default swaps with serious systemic ramifications were the bond insurers led by Ambac Financial Group and MBIA, Inc. Both of these companies started out in the business of insuring municipal bonds, which requires very little intellect or imagination. Municipal bond insurance is a business that really should not exist in the first place because municipal bonds rarely default, but that is a story for another day. As the margins in that business shrunk, Ambac and MBIA looked for greener pastures and found them in the world of structured products. They could not have moved from a more mundane and simplistic product (municipal bonds) to a more arcane and complex one (collateralized debt obligations). As a result, they were poorly equipped intellectually and institutionally to deal with their new business. Nonetheless, like AIG, they were clever enough to discover (in another example of why we should not confuse intelligence with the ability to make money in the short-term) that they could use their own AAA ratings to begin insuring the AAA tranches of CDOs. As in the case of AIG, this strategy was wholly dependent on the rating agencies continuing to maintain their AAA ratings on both these bond insurers as well as on the underlying securities in the CDOs. And as with AIG, the rating agencies pulled both rugs out from under Ambac and MBIA. On January 17, 2008, Moody's placed Ambac's AAA credit rating on watch for possible downgrade. This was well after it was apparent to everyone other than Moody's that the mortgages in the CDOs insured by Ambac were defaulting in record numbers. Moody's cited Ambac's announcement that it expected to record a $5.4 billion pretax ($3.5 billion after-tax) mark-to-market loss on its portfolio of credit default swaps written on CDOs for the fourth quarter of 2007, including a $1.1 billion loss on certain asset-backed CDOs. Moody's stated with a straight face that "this loss significantly reduces the company's capital cushion and heightens concern about potential further volatility within Ambac's mortgage and mortgage-related CDO portfolios." When you read news releases like this, you really don't know whether to laugh, cry, or throw the telephone out the window.

Moody's announcement followed by a few days the issuance by Ambac's competitor, MBIA, of 14 percent AA-rated notes in a desperate attempt to salvage its AAA credit rating. At the time, the 14-percent coupon was 956 basis points higher than U.S. treasury notes of the same maturity, the rate that a CCC-rated company would have to pay. Clearly there was a serious disconnect between what Moody's was saying about the company's credit rating and how the market was viewing MBIA's financial prospects. Apparently 14 percent was the new AA interest rate for bond insurers that had chosen to enter the credit derivatives market to insure mortgage securities! MBIA was in serious straits, with exposure of bonds backed by mortgages and CDOs of $30.6 billion, including $8.14 billion of CDO-squareds (CDOs that own pieces of other CDOs). The death-knell for the bond insurers' new business model had been sounded.

The downfall of the bond insurers was a potentially catastrophic event for the Wall Street firms that were underwriting hundreds of billions of dollars of CDOs. These firms were not only relying on Ambac and MBIA to insure the AAA-tranches of these deals, making them easier to sell to gullible buyers, but were also counting on this insurance to protect them from losses on the huge amounts of this paper that they could not sell and ended up purchasing themselves to get these underwritings done. Over the coming months, these firms would work with New York Insurance Commissioner Eric Dinallo and others to reduce their exposure to CDOs, and the bond insurers ultimately survived in wind-down mode. But another piece of the financial model that led the markets to the edge of the cliff was carried out in a body bag.

Taming the Beasts (Regulating Credit Derivatives)

Fortunately, events have proved that the financial system will not go the way of Jurassic Park, at least not yet. But the obvious question once the smoke cleared was how to regulate the credit default swap market and the rest of the derivatives market to avoid a repeat of 2008. There were also similar questions being raised in the commodities pits about commodities derivatives contracts, which were being blamed for the spike in oil prices to over $140 per barrel in 2008 and the subsequent plunge to under $40 per barrel in the midst of the global financial crisis. The fact that the credit derivatives market had grown to over $60 trillion in size and then pushed the global financial system to the brink of collapse must rank as one of the greatest regulatory failures of the modern era. The fact that regulators had been cowed (or conned—pick your poison) by Wall Street into allowing credit default swaps to become the monster that ate Manhattan was inexcusable.

Credit derivatives remain a potential time bomb inside the financial system that could blow up any time. As long as naked swaps are allowed to be written, no firm is safe from a bear raid. A comprehensive approach to regulating these beasts is sorely needed. There are a number of practical solutions to the threat posed by unregulated credit derivatives. As noted previously, some respected investors like George Soros have recommended outlawing credit default swaps unless the purchaser owns the underlying instrument being insured. Certainly a strong argument could be made that naked credit default swaps—those in which the derivative buyer or seller does not own an interest in the underlying instrument—should be barred. Opponents of such a ban argue that these instruments improve market liquidity for the underlying instruments, but practitioners will tell you that these arguments are dubious. High yield corporate bond and loan markets are not particularly liquid and have become increasingly illiquid over the years. In fact, an argument can be made that so much capital has migrated away from cash markets and into the derivatives market that the result has been less capital available for trading the underlying instruments, significantly decreasing liquidity in those markets.

The real arguments supporting naked credit default swaps are economic; these are opaque, difficult to price instruments from which Wall Street earns enormous profits. Wall Street is not a public utility—it is a profit-seeking engine whose sole purpose is to generate money. The more complex and opaque the instrument, the easier it is for Wall Street to fool investors (even supposedly smart money investors like hedge funds and large institutions) and mark up these instruments to earn outsized profits from selling and trading them.

Proposals to regulate credit derivatives have generally focused on the following three areas:

1. Requiring these instruments to be listed on an exchange.
2. Monitoring counterparty risk.
3. Increasing collateral requirements.

Listing these instruments on an exchange would presumably enhance transparency, while increasing collateral requirements would arguably limit speculation by forcing participants to have more skin in the game.

While combining these measures with rules limiting financial institution leverage might reduce systemic risk to some extent, they would still leave unanswered the overriding policy question of whether society wants so much intellectual and financial capital devoted to speculation in naked credit default swaps. Banning such naked swaps might force some capital into more economically productive lending activities if the proper incentives (such as investment tax credits or accelerated depreciation deductions) were offered. While such a proposal would be part of a far more comprehensive economic program, it points to the fact that if regulation were to limit opportunities for mere speculation, it might increase the chances that money could find its way into more productive activities.

Listing Credit Derivatives on an Exchange

Listing and trading credit default swaps on an exchange without requiring full counterparty disclosure will accomplish little. In fact, the plan to trade complex financial instruments on an exchange, which does not include a provision requiring counterparty disclosure, is typical of the kind of facile thinking that tends to distract policymakers from genuine solutions while allowing the powers on Wall Street to keep minting money at the expense of everyone else. The argument that this approach will enhance transparency is a red herring since it relies on the ability of regulators and other non-specialists to decipher highly complex financial instruments. But giving market participants greater access to information on credit default swaps is a far cry from them being able to understand them and the risks they pose. This proposal is analogous to arguing that making quantum physics textbooks widely available will allow the average person to construct a nuclear power plant. The inspection staffs at the Securities and Exchange Commission and FINRA have already demonstrated their inability to conduct competent inspections of firms engaged in far less complex investment strategies than derivatives. How can we expect regulators to understand trading strategies involving complex financial instruments simply because they will be conducted out in the open rather than in private? This is a highly dubious proposition. Greek is still Greek to somebody who only speaks English. Despite the best intentions of new administrations and Congress, it is a virtual certainty that government work will never attract the type of talent necessary to untangle abuses that clever traders can construct in the credit derivatives area. Requiring these trades to be effected on an exchange simply passes the buck from legislators to regulators. And regulators will never be up to the task.

Furthermore, moving these instruments onto an exchange does nothing to eliminate the moral hazard regime whereby risks are socialized and gains are privatized. In fact, such a solution is likely to exacerbate the likelihood that such a regime will expand to new parts of the financial sector. Thus far, the "too big to fail" doctrine has been applied to institutions whose failures were deemed to pose a systemic risk. Moving credit default swaps onto an exchange would likely give the government an excuse to protect the exchange itself were the market to collapse due to a credit market meltdown. This would inevitably provide protection for many institutions (i.e., members of the new derivatives exchange) that are not systemically vital, further extending the government safety net and moral hazard to places where it does not belong.

Proponents of a listing requirement argue that an exchange-based system will allow regulators and others to better track trading volumes and exposures and thereby better measure overall systemic risk. It is questionable how useful such information will be, however. At the cusp of the crisis, the credit default swap market was reportedly $60 trillion in size, although that figure included many offsetting positions and the net exposure of financial institutions to these instruments was lower (again, nobody really knew or knows the real figures). Today, the figure is certainly smaller, as parties have worked doggedly to reduce their exposures after seeing what happened to AIG, the bond insurers, numerous hedge funds, and others who couldn't drink enough CDS Kool-Aid. But as noted above, the market is still vast and complex and filled with instruments that few if any regulators and non-specialists understand. It might be helpful for regulators to have some idea of the total number of outstanding credit default swaps as a first step to figuring out how to regulate them. More likely, however, it will prove completely meaningless since they still won't understand what they are regulating.

Moreover, most of the legislative proposals in Congress limit the types of contracts that must be listed to conventional or standard credit default swaps, and would not require nonstandard contracts or contracts used to hedge commercial business risks to be listed. Proponents for such exclusions argue, among other things, that such information is proprietary. Certainly steps can be taken to protect truly confidential information whose disclosure would be harmful to certain businesses. But the exceptions being proposed are sufficiently large to swallow the rule, particularly in the hands of clever Wall Street lawyers and derivatives experts. It is going to be extremely difficult to draft sufficiently specific legislation to render any listing requirement meaningful (if it is even meaningful or useful in the first place). If a listing requirement is deemed a good idea, then it should be a blanket listing requirement for all credit derivatives contracts with provisions to protect proprietary information from public disclosure. That still wouldn't accomplish very much substantively but it would at least let the members of Congress have something to boast about when they return home on recess to lie to their constituents.

Counterparty Surveillance

While simply listing derivatives on an exchange misses the mark, the goals of transparency and systemic stability would be much better served by requiring public disclosure by the parties trading these instruments. As some observers, including this author, warned in the period leading up to the financial crisis, one of the most serious flaws in the credit derivatives regime was the inadequacy of counterparty risk monitoring. Not only did regulators and important market participants have no idea of who owed what to whom, but they had no real understanding whether the parties involved in credit default swap transactions were capable of meeting their obligations.

One of the most egregious examples of what can happen when parties fail to perform proper (or any) due diligence on their counterparties involved the Swiss banking giant UBS. UBS purchased $1.31 billion of credit insurance on the oxymoronically termed "super-senior tranche" of a subprime collateralized mortgage obligation from a small Connecticut-based hedge fund, Paramax Capital, which had only $200 million of capital under management. Wisely unwilling to put all of its eggs in one basket, Paramax formed a special purpose entity to provide the credit insurance and capitalized it with only $4.6 million of its capital. The special purpose entity was subject to future capital calls if the value of the underlying CMO declined, which it inevitably did (this occurred in 2007), and ultimately Paramax defaulted after posting more than $30 million in collateral. Needless to say, when the hedge fund couldn't make good on its obligation, UBS sued it, and naturally Paramax sued UBS back. The odds of UBS recovering anything further on its *faux pas* are miniscule. If this transaction is typical of UBS's business practices, it is little wonder that UBS announced on December 10, 2007 that it was taking a $10 billion write-down in the fourth quarter of 2007, most of it related to the type of super-senior instrument that it had somehow expected the diminutive Paramax to insure.[11]

Counterparty risk is separate and apart from the risk associated with the underlying debt instrument that is insured under a credit default swap agreement. It is a measure of whether the party selling the credit insurance will be capable of making good on its obligation. In order to properly evaluate counterparty risk, a party entering into a credit default swap contract needs to be able to analyze the financial condition of the other party to the transaction. This requires full disclosure of all of that party's financial obligations, something that is an extremely tall order in today's opaque financial world in which typical counterparties are involved in numerous balance-sheet and off-balance-sheet transactions of various degrees of complexity.

The odds of a typical counterparty being in a position to adequately measure this type of risk are extremely low today. The current state of financial disclosure is inadequate to provide the type of information that is necessary to give counterparties the type of comfort they need to enter into these types of transactions. Reliance on financial institutions' publicly released financial statements or their credit ratings, however, would leave the system with insufficient information to evaluate counterparty risk on an institution-specific or system-wide basis. For a truly effective system to work, standards of disclosure would have to be significantly intensified and provisions to protect confidential and proprietary information would need to be strictly enforced. Requiring parties to disclose such information could create a huge disincentive for many of them to engage in such transactions and could be an effective way of limiting speculative trading in naked credit default swaps. Increasingly opaque financial markets cannot leave the monitoring of counterparty risk in private hands; government must step in to enforce high standards of disclosure. We have already seen the results of leaving this responsibility in private hands. Adequate disclosure would include not only counterparties' complete financial condition (including all balance-sheet and off-balance-sheet obligations), but also a complete listing of their derivative positions.

This proposal will undoubtedly be greeted with howls of protest by hedge funds and other investors who purport to claim that their trading positions and strategies constitute trade secrets that need to be protected like matters of national security. These protests should be dismissed for at least two reasons. First, regardless of what hedge fund operators like to claim, there is little that is proprietary about their positions or strategies. The only proprietary aspect of their operations is what occurs inside the heads of the funds' managers, the thought processes that cannot be duplicated merely by viewing their positions. Moreover, in markets that operate on the basis of milliseconds, a disclosure regime designed to rein in systemic risk could easily build in a sufficient time delay to render this concern moot. Second, the vast majority of these hedge funds' trades are speculative in nature; they are not increasing the productive capacity of the economy. Accordingly, the merits of disclosure in terms of enhancing systemic stability should surely outweigh any potential limitations on these funds' profitability. Regulation should favor stability and productive investment over instability and speculation. If such a disclosure regime were added to proposals to require all hedge funds to register as investment advisers and be subject to the rules of the Investment Advisers Act, the system would be moved much further down the road to both transparency and stability.

Increasing Collateral Requirements

Higher collateral requirements come closer to the mark but still fall short of creating the type of economic incentives that would effectively discourage speculation. It was far too easy for speculators to manipulate the short-term interest rates of firms like Bear Stearns and Lehman Brothers (or even Goldman Sachs and Morgan Stanley) through the credit default swap market in the midst of the financial crisis. Large investment banks or hedge funds could simply add these trades on to their existing credit lines and mount bear raids on other firms in a completely unregulated environment.

The real question comes back to the type of instrument represented by a credit default swap. These are insurance contracts that, in the case of naked swaps, do not require the party purchasing the insurance to own an insured interest. As a result, their economic interest in the outcome of the trade remains limited, and increasing collateral requirements does little to change the fact that their exposure will remain limited. Limited liability provides a great deal of incentive for investors to speculate and is just another component of the moral hazard problem that haunts the U.S. financial system today. Increasing collateral requirements in the absence of requiring an insurable interest will do little to stem the type of speculation that contributed to the 2008 financial crisis. At best, such a regime will force some weak hands out of the market.

At the end of the day, it is difficult to escape the conclusion that anything less than an outright ban on naked credit default swaps will accomplish the goal of directing more financial and intellectual capital into productive rather than speculative uses while improving systemic transparency and stability. The advent of credit default swaps has done little to improve liquidity in underlying cash markets; in fact, it has produced the opposite effect as trading capital has migrated out of those markets and into the derivatives markets.[12] Moreover, the types of perverse incentives these instruments create to see companies fail rather than succeed suggest that the system could do with fewer of them. Requiring purchasers of credit insurance to have an insurable interest in the underlying debt instrument would be the surest way of addressing the most significant regulatory challenges facing us today.

One of the arguments in favor of naked swaps is the same argument in favor of naked short-selling of stocks: Proponents argue that such a strategy imposes an important discipline on companies and provides an incentive for them to maintain strong credit quality. But as George Soros has pointed out, credit default swaps work in a completely different manner than stocks.[13] When an investor is short a stock, an increase in the stock price raises his exposure and renders it increasingly expensive to maintain the position. Moreover, the margin rules require the short-seller to post additional collateral to hold the position (although short positions effected through options and other derivatives can minimize margin requirements). These pressures discourage short-selling.

Credit default swaps do not discourage short-selling because they offer limited risk and unlimited reward. An investor who wants to short a credit can purchase a credit default swap for a fixed amount of money and limit his exposure to that amount of money. As that credit deteriorates, the value of his swap increases and he does not have to post additional collateral (and may, depending on his agreement with his lender, be able to withdraw collateral). This encourages the short-selling of credit. Taking the other side of this trade is much less attractive (that is, selling the credit insurance) because the seller of insurance must continue to post additional collateral as the underlying credit deteriorates. The asymmetry between selling insurance (going long) and buying insurance (going short) is so extreme that it encourages short-selling and introduces a significant short bias into the marketplace. This is far different from imposing an honest discipline on companies to improve their balance sheets and maintain strong credit quality. Instead, credit default swaps introduce a strong incentive to speculate on the short side, which is hardly conducive to directing capital to productive economic uses. The structure of credit default swaps therefore renders them far more destabilizing to markets than other types of hedging instruments and bolsters the case for limiting their usage to situations in which the buyer owns the underlying debt.

★★★

There is another wonderful scene in *Jurassic Park* when the scientists are touring the laboratory where the dinosaurs are bred. One of the scientists tries to explain to Dr. Malcolm that the park has bred only male velociraptors, a particularly dangerous breed of dinosaurs that come to wreak their own special havoc throughout the film (and its many sequels). Dr. Malcolm responds that it isn't possible to limit the breeding to males, and the scientist condescendingly explains that it's really a rather simple matter of excluding female chromosomes from the genetic mix. Dr. Malcolm disagrees and simply says, "Nature will find a way." The same is true of Wall Street when it comes to regulation. Wall Street will find a way to manipulate its way around restrictions placed on its ability to create new products and generate profits regardless of the systemic risks these products may pose. The constant cat-and-mouse game between regulators and traders is an age-old competition that will continue as long as there are markets. That is why it is incumbent upon every individual and institution that is affected by what occurs in the financial markets to not only understand derivatives but to appreciate why they can't be allowed to run wild like dinosaurs in a china shop.

CHAPTER 7

The Road to Hell

I n 1998, my partner Joe Harch was asked to visit with a prominent money manager in New York City. At the time, our money management firm was trying to raise additional money to invest in less-than-investment-grade corporate debt. To put it politely, Joe was given the brush off. That was no big deal—it happened all the time (and still does!). But what that money manager said struck us as very odd. "Why should I give you guys money?" he asked. "You can't make me one point a month like my friend Bernie." When Joe called me and told me about the meeting, I responded, "Joe, it's not a point-a-month world."

A few years later, in 2005, Joe and I were sitting in front of another group that said it was interested in raising money for us. The talks proceeded to the point where we were invited to meet with the company's founder and top lieutenants. These gentlemen explained that they were looking for another product to add to the offering of their largest existing manager, who was producing consistent monthly returns in the 80 to 100 basis point range. They stressed repeatedly that they could not employ a strategy that experienced losses of as much as 2 percent a month. We told them that it would be impossible to guarantee that there would not be monthly losses. Needless to say, the talks went nowhere.

The money manager we met in 1998 was Ezra Merkin, whose funds lost a reported $2.4 billion with Bernard Madoff. The money management firm we met in 2005 was Fairfield Greenwich Group, whose clients reportedly lost more than $7 billion in the Madoff fraud. The firm's founder Walter Noel attended that meeting but let his minions do most of the talking.

Satan in the Garden

Bernard Madoff Investment Securities offered investors what they are taught to seek out in all of their investments: steady returns and minimal risk. This is the mantra of fiduciary thought. Unfortunately, when the curtain was pulled back on this particular wizard, what was discovered was a virtual checklist of worst investment practices that knowledgeable investors such as Merkin and Fairfield Greenwich were paid obscene amounts of money to avoid. These practices included: lack of transparency; financial statements prepared by a hole-in-the-wall accounting firm; and an investment strategy that could not possibly be carried out in any markets on the planet earth (the so-called "split strike conversion strategy"). Yet fiduciaries such as Merkin and Fairfield Greenwich, as well as a laundry list of other respected investment institutions such as Tremont Group Holdings (owned by MassMutual), Banco Santander of Spain, the Swiss fund-of-funds firm EIM, and many other prominent investors were lured by the promise of month after month of consistently positive (but not *too* positive, which was an essential part of the scam) returns. The knowledge that such returns are virtually unattainable and that their purveyor refused to reveal how he produced them was apparently insufficient to dampen investors' hunger for them, suggesting just how rare and valuable such a return profile would be if it were truly achievable in the real world.

Madoff's scheme had a deeply pernicious effect on the investment business long before it was revealed to be a complete fabrication. In addition to casting a cloud of suspicion on other money management firms, particularly those that are not part of large institutional organizations, Madoff's scheme had the effect of distorting investor perceptions about the kind of returns they could reasonably expect. This aspect of the Madoff affair has been insufficiently acknowledged and is an essential part of the story about why capital has been and continues to be so badly abused by the professional investment class. The essence of Madoff's scheme was the proffer of consistent returns with low risk. To some people, this may seem like a reasonable proposition, but experienced and knowledgeable market participants should know better. This should particularly have been the case with respect to a track record that purported to show consecutive years of positive monthly returns with few if any negative months with no correlation to what was occurring in the financial markets. As I remarked to my partner in 1998, it is not a one-percent-a-month world; it is a world of fat tails and, in the term that Nassim Nicholas Taleb made famous a few years later, Black Swans. Yet Madoff's return pattern captured the imagination of the professional investment class and led it down the road to ruin. It also led to many imitators as institutional investors came to demand that other managers offer the same impossible model. This is how the road to investment hell became littered with fiduciary intentions.

Reverse Black Swans

It is hardly a coincidence that the explosion of so-called alternative investments in the form of hedge fund assets coincided with the growth of investment strategies that offered consistent low-risk returns. By the end of 2006, Hedge Fund Research, Inc., estimated that the global hedge fund industry held $1.43 trillion in assets. These assets were spread among 11,000 different funds of which approximately one-third were funds-of-funds, according to the European Central Bank. This was a huge jump from 1990, when hedge funds held less than $400 billion in assets, and even from 2005, when the $1 trillion mark was passed. This paralleled the growth of private equity assets and related strategies that invested increasing amounts of their capital in nonpublic securities that only could be valued by their managers rather than by reference to any objective market standard that could be independently verified. The two concepts—alternative investments and consistent positive returns—were joined at the hip in a symbiotic relationship that turned into a dance to the death. With some exceptions, the hedge fund model by and large became one in which managers offered investors the prospect of consistent, uncorrelated positive returns in exchange for exorbitant fees.

As we saw with private equity returns, when we pull back the kimono on hedge fund returns from a risk-adjusted basis (that is, adjusted for liquidity, leverage, concentration risks and fees), many hedge fund strategies turn out to be far less attractive than advertised. This is particularly true with respect to strategies that invest predominately in nonpublic securities, most of which lost enormous amounts of money in 2008. There were profound structural flaws in the investment strategies of hedge funds that were responsible for many of them ending up on the wrong side—and same side—of the market in 2008. These flaws included the following:

- They owned a lot of illiquid assets.
- They used too much leverage.
- Their positions were correlated.
- They took a lot of fat tail risk.
- They financed themselves with unstable capital on both the equity and debt sides of their balance sheets.
- They carried assets at book value (misrepresenting actual values).
- They tended to extrapolate the past into the future and ignore statistically or historically improbable events.

As a result, hedge funds—especially those that reported years of strong performance during the bull market in less liquid asset classes that involved the trading of corporate bonds, loans and credit derivatives—tend to be susceptible to blowing up at regular intervals. They did not disappoint in 2008.

What these funds have done is effectively adopt a reverse Black Swan investment model in which they offer the illusion of steady high returns with low risk. In his book, *The Black Swan: the Impact of the Highly Improbable*, best-selling author Nassim Nicholas Taleb explored the Black Swan investment strategy, which is characterized by trades that yield small losses over time but can generate extraordinary returns if the market or individual stocks make extreme moves. Many hedge funds marketing low volatility strategies flipped this strategy on its head and tried to create a series of small but steady returns against the small possibility of a large loss due to incidences of market volatility that were statistically unprecedented. Some funds did this using highly liquid securities and high degrees of leverage, such as credit arbitrage funds, and others invested in non-marketable debt and equity securities in the credit space, like the many highly leveraged credit-oriented hedge funds that blew up in 2008. These funds collected a lot of illiquid investments and ended up retaining the least valuable ones through a process of adverse selection. Many of these funds either blocked redemptions or offered to return assets in-kind to investors (which from an investor's standpoint is the equivalent of winning the booby prize). Realistically, there is nothing else they can do with them; they certainly couldn't sell these illiquid assets to anybody.

In order to deliver steady streams of positive returns, however, hedge fund managers were compelled to follow strategies that were allegedly uncorrelated with the financial markets. What does uncorrelated mean? We all know what it is supposed to mean—hedge fund returns are supposed to produce positive returns in all types of market environments based on the ability of these funds to engage in so-called alternative strategies that permit them to both buy and sell securities in response to changing market conditions. What uncorrelated really came to mean was opaque in two respects: Madoff-type returns, which were simply fraudulent, and private-market-type returns, which were based on non-public market valuations that could not be confirmed by liquidity events except on a sporadic basis. The latter type of investments included private equity, direct lending to small and mid-size companies, structured products, and similar investment strategies. Some of the largest hedge funds in the world managed by firms such as Cerberus Capital Management, LLC, Canyon Partners, GoldenTree Asset Management, L.P., and High-land Capital Management, LP, engaged in these strategies and grew to enormous sizes before running aground in 2008. Their downfall called into question their reported returns in earlier years to the extent those returns included unrealized gains that were later reversed by losses. But in order to compete to manage the money of institutions that bought the line of thinking that endorsed these strategies hook, line, and sinker, firms that wanted to grow had little choice but to adopt these so-called low-volatility strategies.

This shell-game worked out just fine as long as the markets were rising, or at least when they weren't experiencing extreme volatility. As long as global liquidity was robust and markets were rising, these strategies looked successful on the surface. Investors could continue to borrow to bid up the prices of financial assets, and managers could continue to convince investors that their investments were worth more each year. But when credit markets seized up, these strategies were swamped by three simultaneous tsunamis. First, the value of their leveraged assets started to decline precipitously. Second, their lenders became nervous and demanded more collateral to support their positions. And third, these firms could no longer convince investors to keep feeding them funds and in many cases were faced with requests to return capital. When the markets sold off, many investors wanted their money back. The problem was that these investments were completely illiquid and investor capital could only be returned in kind or not at all. Returning cash to investors was out of the question because capital had died. This was how Madoff's Ponzi scheme came apart: It relied on a continual stream of new money to pay interest on investor capital and to handle the return of capital to investors who requested their money back. But when such requests grew increasingly large (reportedly to $5 or $6 billion by late 2008), there simply wasn't enough new money coming in to handle them and the scheme fell apart. Many legitimate hedge funds (that unlike Madoff's actually engaged in real investing and trading strategies) suffered the same fate and were forced to suspend redemptions, return capital in kind, or close shop. This was not only another example (like the banking industry) of a flawed financial strategy that confused long-term solvency with short-term liquidity because they were effectively borrowing short to lend long, but also was emblematic of the fact that institutional investors had been seeking a Holy Grail of consistently high positive returns with low risk that had little chance of being available in the real world. One has to wonder how differently things might have turned out had Madoff's fraud been discovered much earlier and the investment community come to an earlier understanding that no such free lunches exist in the markets.

The real question that should be asked is how so many investors could be led to believe that such strategies were prudent. After all, the prudent man rule is the basis on which most fiduciaries base their conduct. How could an entire generation of investors be duped into believing things that are so blatantly false? Like many of the other corrupting influences that have been discussed in this book, investors were given a mighty helping hand by the political and intellectual authorities. In particular, the U.S. legal system developed a doctrine of fiduciary duty that narrowed the focus of those charged with investing other peoples' money to the single goal of economic gain. Other societal interests such as the rights of labor, the environment, and the distinction between productive and speculative investment, were pushed to the side.

Moreover, an entire industry of consultants and academics developed the intellectual scaffolding to dress up this mandate in pseudoscientific language. Concepts like "Sharpe ratio" and "R-squared" and the infamous Greek chorus of "alpha" and "beta" were used to justify the types of investment strategies that could deliver steady returns with low volatility and low correlation with the stock market. These arcana dressed the consultants in the garb of a secret ministry that held the keys to the kingdom of gold. The only problem is that when one pulls back the curtain, one finds that that there is no wizard and that the magic formula is malarkey. There is a perfectly good reason many of the strategies that are recommended by the consultant community and other investment advisers don't correlate with financial markets: They are not marked-to-market or even capable of being marked-to-market in any meaningful manner. Accordingly, the entire industry is operating under an illusion from which it would be extremely painful to break free.

Birth of the Prudent Man

There are two aspects to modern fiduciary doctrine that are deeply troubling. First, how did the prudent man rule become warped into a blind pursuit of financial profit at the expense of other, arguably equally important values? And second, how did substantive thinking about investing devolve into thinking that the Madoff model of consistent monthly returns is realistic?

The prudent man rule is usually dated back to the 1830 Massachusetts court case *Harvard College v. Amory*, 26 Mass (9 Pick.) 446

(1830). That court held that "all that can be required of a trustee to invest, is, that he shall conduct himself faithfully and exercise a sound discretion. He is to observe how men of prudence, discretion, and intelligence manage their own affairs, not in regard to speculation, but in regard to the permanent disposition of their funds, considering the probable income, as well as the probable safety of the capital to be invested." Most important, the case held that "trustees are not to be made chargeable but for gross neglect and willful mismanagement," standards of conduct that still apply today.

Like many legal standards, this one is extremely broad and leaves many of the details to be filled in by legislators, practitioners, and judges as specific situations arise. There have been a number of landmark advances in the thinking governing this rule in recent years. In 1942, the Model Prudent Man Statute was adopted that codified this rule and influenced the passage of many state statutes. In 1972, the Uniform Management of Institutional Funds Act was issued as a model law designed to guide institutional investors to adopt total return strategies for their investment portfolios. This was followed in 1974 by the Employee Retirement Income Security Act (ERISA), a comprehensive federal pension law that codified the prudent man standard of care. ERISA 29 USC § 1104(a) states that

[A] fiduciary shall discharge his duties with respect to a [retirement] plan solely in the interest of the participants and beneficiaries and—

    A. for the exclusive purpose of:
       i. providing benefits to participants and their beneficiaries; and
      ii. defraying reasonable expenses of administering the plan;
    B. with the care, skill, prudence, and diligence under the circumstances then prevailing that a prudent man acting in a like capacity and familiar with such matters would use in the conduct of an enterprise of a like character and with like aims;
    C. by diversifying the investments of the plan so as to minimize the risk of large losses, unless under the circumstances it is clearly prudent not to do so; . . .

But ERISA did more than simply codify the prudent man rule—it added a duty of diversification. This requirement was an endorsement of modern portfolio theory as developed by Harry Markowitz in one of the most famous papers in modern finance, "Portfolio Selection."

Markowitz's article appeared in the March 1952 issue of the *Journal of Finance* and was written when the author was only 25 years old. Markowitz followed this article up with a more detailed discussion in a book entitled *Portfolio Selection: Diversification of Investment,* which was published seven years later in 1959. In the key passage in the article, Markowitz argued that, "[i]t is necessary to avoid investing in securities with high covariances among themselves. We should diversify across industries because firms in different industries, especially industries with different economic characteristics, have lower covariances than firms within an industry."[1]

This means that securities in the same industry, for example, will not provide sufficient diversification because they will tend to react to the same types of business and economic risk factors in the same way. A portfolio composed of an undue concentration of companies in a single industry would be too vulnerable to the risks facing that industry. "A portfolio with sixty different railway securities," Markowitz wrote, "would not be as well diversified as the same size portfolio with some railroad, some public utility, mining, various sorts of manufacturing, etc. The reason is that it is generally more likely for firms within the same industry to do poorly at the same time than for firms in dissimilar industries."[2] Markowitz's paper was considered revolutionary at the time because it introduced the concept of risk-adjusted returns. Previously, the concept of diversification had not been considered essential to portfolio management. Instead, investors were primarily focused on maximizing their returns without regard to the risks involved. Markowitz introduced the important concept that returns are related to the amount of risk associated with an investment. As noted previously with respect to the discussion of private equity returns, this is an essential insight that is too often overlooked even today.

In constructing portfolios that were sufficiently diversified to pro-tect against risk, Markowitz added the mathematical concept of mean variance optimization, which in layman's terms means "efficiency." In mathematical terms, efficiency means maximizing output for a given input, or minimizing input for a given output. In portfolio terms, this means maximizing the anticipated return for the amount of risk taken, or minimizing risk for the amount of return achieved. In Peter Bernstein's words, an efficient portfolio "offers the highest expected return for any given degree of risk, or that has the lowest degree of risk for any given expected return."[3] This concept still guides much of the money management industry today. Unfortunately, it has done little to help the industry avoid repeating the same mistakes over and over again.

The other theory that has exercised enormous (and undue) influence on fiduciaries is the wholly discredited efficient market theory, which was set forth in a 1965 article by economist Eugene F. Fama. An efficient market is defined as one in which:

> There are large numbers of rational, profit-maximizers actively competing, with each trying to predict future market values of individual securities, and where important current information is almost freely available to all participants. In an efficient market, competition among the many intelligent participants leads to a situation where, at any given moment in time, actual prices of individual securities already reflect the effects of information based both on events that have already occurred and on events which, as of now, the market expects to take place in the future. In other words, in an efficient market at any point in time the actual price of a security will be a good estimate of its intrinsic value.[4]

Although this is clearly a definition that only someone completely lacking in market experience could actually accept as a reflection of reality, it has exercised an undue influence on fiduciary thought.

In fact, the efficient market theory was endorsed in the *Restatement Third of Trusts* (1992), where the Reporter's General Note on Restatement Section 227 reads:

> Economic evidence shows that, from a typical investment perspective, the major capital markets of this country are highly efficient, in the sense that available information is rapidly digested and reflected in the market prices of securities. As a result, fiduciaries and other investors are confronted with potent evidence that the application of expertise, investigation, and diligence in efforts to "beat the market" in these publicly traded securities ordinarily promises little or no payoff, or even a negative payoff after taking account of research and transaction costs. Empirical research supporting the theory of efficient markets

reveals that in such markets skilled professionals have rarely been able to identify underpriced securities (that is, to outguess the market with respect to future return) with any regularity.[5]

The introduction to the *Restatement* and the prefatory note to the Uniform Prudent Investor Act that was passed two years later stressed the influence of modern portfolio theory, of which Markowitz was one of the founding fathers. In fact, this landmark restatement of the law of trusts was primarily intended to incorporate modern portfolio theory into the rules governing fiduciaries. Among the principles laid out in the *Restatement* was that both passive and active investment strategies would be deemed prudent, but that active strategies would be required to meet a higher standard in justifying that they were adding value (which came to be known as "alpha," one of the Greek gods of current investment wisdom). The *Restatement* outlined five principles of prudence for fiduciaries to follow: diversification; a reasonable relationship between risk and reward; minimizing unnecessary and unreasonable fees; balancing preservation of capital and production of current income; and giving trustees the duty and authority to delegate investment decisions to others. With the exception of the bald assertion of the necessity of diversification, this is a reasonable list.

It is little wonder that typical fiduciaries at large institutions tend to stumble into one investment trap after another; they invest as though they actually believe that the markets are efficient and that diversification really pays off. They might as well believe that the earth is flat or the moon is made of green cheese, two propositions for which there is just as much empirical proof as there is for the efficient market theory and Harry Markowitz's "Portfolio Selection." This is the type of thinking that leads institutions into the private equity trap, the distressed debt trap, and other illiquid strategies that they are told do not correlate with public equity and debt markets when, in fact, they correlate strongly with such markets with the added handicap of enjoying limited liquidity, employing greater leverage, incurring higher fees, and producing lower risk-adjusted returns. These theories completely overlook market realities. The efficient market theory ignores not only the wisdom of thinkers like Smith, Marx, Keynes, and Minsky that markets are highly inefficient because they are driven primarily by human emotion, but the reams of data that illustrate beyond a shadow of a doubt that market prices are imprecise measures of underlying valuation metrics that are themselves unstable indicia of value. The Portfolio Selection thesis overlooks the fact that the concept of correlation has changed dramatically since the time that Markowitz wrote his paper. Investors treat the concept of correlation like it is a law of nature rather than a human construct, and therefore engage in a profound intellectual error. In fact, it is ironic that when Markowitz wrote the paper in 1955, it was difficult to test his thesis because of limited computer power and that today advanced computer power that permits every conceivable type of financial instrument to be deconstructed into 1s and 0s renders the very concept of diversification obsolete.

The Fallacy of Diversification

In Chapter 2, we discussed the role that the prudent or reasonable man played in the work of Adam Smith as he tried to design a just society based on commercial exchange. We saw the flaws in that approach as it cedes power to groupthink and the madness of crowds. Add that to what came to be an almost religious belief in diversification and efficient markets and one can begin to understand how the evolution of fiduciary law created the conditions for most shepherds of capital to consistently produce sub-optimal returns.

Diversification came to be taken for granted as the gravamen of prudent investment management. But the world changed, and diversification in the early twenty-first century no longer means what it did half a century ago before derivatives and Ponzi finance came to dominate the financial landscape. So while the concept of diversification had a great deal to recommend it in the investment world of the 1950s, it has turned out to be a trap for investors in the twenty-first century. Today, asset classes that are not ostensibly covariant (to invoke Markowitz's terminology), such as equities and debt, have been rendered covariant by new financial technology. The ability to deconstruct all types of securities and financial instruments into their constituent parts (1s and 0s) has erased the differences between asset classes, breaking the boundaries between different types of holdings in ways that render the concept of diversification completely outmoded. Investors have discovered, much to their distress, that while they thought their portfolios were invested in different types of risks, they were, in fact, largely exposed to the same types of risk. The most significant type of risk was the enormous amount of leverage that was embedded in all types of asset classes, including both equity and debt. Another way of saying this, in the terminology of Hyman Minsky, is that they were at greater risk than they realized that the Ponzi finance structure of the U.S. and global economy would come apart. The economy became populated by so many economic actors—individual homeowners, corporations—that were so highly leveraged that virtually their entire capital structures (equity and debt) effectively consisted of borrowed money. As a result, both the equity and debt components of their capital structures were equally vulnerable not only to changes in the individual debtor's financial situation but also to deterioration in the financial markets. What once was not correlated suddenly turned out to be highly correlated because all asset classes were vulnerable to the risk of a credit crisis.

Perhaps the grossest abuse of the concept of diversification occurred in the hands of the U.S. credit rating agencies, Moody's and Standard & Poor's, in their ratings of structured products. The intellectual poverty of the agencies' approach to modeling correlation is writ large in the fact that the agencies subsequently found themselves compelled to reject their earlier ratings and admit that the models on which the entire trillion dollar edifice of structured finance was constructed was completely incorrect. Aided and abetted by large Wall Street underwriters of CDOs, these oligopolists concocted so-called black box models that they claimed measured the correlations among individual mortgages, bonds, or loans. In the case of mortgages, as noted earlier in Chapter 3, they simply ignored the fact that the borrower data (FICO scores) they were using had never been tested in an economic downturn. In the case of corporate bonds and loans, they applied grossly understated corporate default and recovery assumptions (ones that predated the 2001–2002 period in which corporate defaults exceeded 10 percent for two consecutive years) and then categorically restated their assumptions in 2009 after the worst of the crisis had passed without little rationale and without distinguishing among different transactions. Their actions effectively forced those collateralized loan obligations that had not stumbled on their own into slow motion liquidations and rendered them incapable of purchasing additional bank loans. The fact that hundreds of billions of dollars of transactions were completed based on the default assumptions that they unilaterally decided to alter (at a time, by the way, when the default outlook was improving due to companies enjoying better access to capital that enabled them to refinance their debt) was apparently of no account to these self-appointed doyens of credit that had demonstrated beyond a shadow of a doubt that they know nothing about credit. With banks having exited this market, this unilateral and ill-considered post hoc action further shrunk the sources of capital available to fund less-than-investment-grade companies in the United States and Europe.

The only positive sign that the credit agencies were going to be held accountable for their fecklessness was the fact that New York Federal Court Judge Shira Scheindlin rejected their argument that their intellectually vacuous credit opinions were protected by the First Amendment. Judge Scheindlin held that First Amendment protection does not apply "where a credit rating agency has disseminated their ratings to a select group of investors rather than to the public at large." We would simply add that when rating agencies are paid for their opinions, the First Amendment veneer of free speech should not be available to protect them.

The high-yield bond area has been a Petri dish for misapplied financial theories and assumptions as well. As noted earlier, high yield bonds are properly understood as hybrid securities that possess the characteristics of both debt and equity. Yet most investors in this asset class focus on the spread at which a bond trades. The spread is the number of basis points (1/100s of a percent) above a benchmark yield at which a bond trades. In the case of high yield bonds, Treasury bonds are considered the benchmark on the basis that they are riskless securities (an assumption that itself is questionable in view of the United States' increasingly precarious fiscal posture). Spread represents the risk premium that investors demand for owning a security that is riskier than a Treasury bond.

There are two problems with this approach. First, conceding the argument that Treasury securities are riskless in the sense that their repayment by the U.S. government is assured, the rate at which they trade has been kept artificially low since the early 1990s by procyclical Federal

Reserve policy. These low rates are signs that all is not well in the economy, a condition that adds further risk to high yield bond investments that are generally highly sensitive to economic conditions. In periods when interest rates have been extremely low, these low rates have generally been indicative of economic weakness, not strength. Accordingly, high yield bond investors have been grossly underpaid for the risk they are assuming.

Second, spread is a fixed-income measurement and high yield bonds are not simple fixed-income instruments; they contain a significant component of equity risk (that far too many investors have swallowed firsthand, to their dismay). The market is applying a tool designed to measure fixed-income risk to what is in large part an equity security. This is particularly true with respect to lower rated bonds (bonds rated Ba1/BB or lower by Standard & Poor's and Moody's). Lower rated bonds are extremely risky and are really not fixed-income instruments; they are best described as "equities in disguise" or "equities with a coupon." In fact, these bonds always end up trading at equity-like returns (which translates—meaninglessly—into very wide spreads) when the market recognizes their subordinated, equity-like character.

Combining the wrong benchmark with the wrong tool to measure risk almost assures investors of a bad outcome. The primary reason spread is used to value high yield bonds is because it appeals to the quantitative side of the investment universe. Unfortunately, it is an extremely poor tool that continues to be used by investors to their detriment.

Another bogus assumption in the high yield bond area that led to billions of dollars of investor losses in the 2001–2002 credit collapse were those underlying a now mercifully extinct product, the collateralized bond obligation (CBO). CBOs were a form of CDO whose collateral was comprised primarily of high yield bonds. CBOs were underwritten by the largest and most respected financial institutions in the world using the basic assumptions that only 2 percent of the bonds in a diversified portfolio would default each year and that the recovery rate on these bonds would be 40 percent. These assumptions had little basis in reality, as the bond market collapses of 1990–1991, 1998, 2001–2002 and 2007–2008 demonstrated. Yet for some reason, the major credit rating agencies, Standard & Poor's and Moody's, continued to issue investment grade ratings on the upper tranches of CBOs based on the strength of these erroneous assumptions. Even worse, highly respected investment firms continued to hawk these products based on these same assumptions, and large institutional investors continued to purchase securities by believing them.

★★★

Interestingly enough, Harry Markowitz would be very open to suggestions that investment mantras like diversification should be subject to question in view of changing conditions. In 1995, Markowitz wrote a fascinating paper for the *Financial Analysts Journal* entitled "Market Efficiency: A Theoretical Distinction and So What?" in which he subjected William Sharpe's Capital Asset Pricing Model (CAPM) to some revisionary thinking. The CAPM is among the most influential theories in the recent history of investment management despite the fact that it depends on wholly unrealistic assumptions about the way in which markets and investors operate in the real world.[6] Among the assumptions of the CAPM that do not jive with the real world of investment are first, the assumption that taxes, transaction costs, and other friction costs can be ignored, and second, that investors share the same predictions for expected returns, volatilities, and correlations of securities. Both of these assumptions are obviously false. Moreover, the predictive record of this model is notoriously poor. As Eugene F. Fama and Kenneth R. French wrote in 2004: "the empirical record of the model is poor—poor enough to invalidate the way it is used in applications. . . . The CAPM, like Markowitz's . . . portfolio model on which it is built, is nevertheless a theoretical tour de force. We continue to teach the CAPM as an introduction to the fundamentals of portfolio theory and asset pricing . . . But we also warn students that, despite its seductive simplicity, the CAPM's empirical problems probably invalidate its use in applications."[7] Despite these flaws—it is based on bogus assumptions and has poor predictive power—the CAPM has exercised an enormous influence on the thinking of investment professionals. There are valuable lessons to be learned from this model. But it is also a lesson that the investment management business—and on a broader basis, human knowledge—is built on error. The trick is learning from those errors and building on them to come to a deeper understanding of the truth. Peter Bernstein argued powerfully in his final book, *Capital Ideas Evolving*, that "investors have learned from

CAPM that they must recognize the fundamental distinction between investing in an asset class and selecting individual securities on which they hope to earn an extra return. The choice of asset classes—for example, stocks, bonds, emerging market equities, real estate, or subdivisions of those markets—is in essence the choice of beta risks, or the volatility of entire markets rather than their individual components."[8] This may be true, but this does not help solve the conundrum facing investors when all asset classes correlate because they have been reduced to 1s and 0s. Theory has yet to catch up to practice and fiduciaries need to understand the new reality if they are to properly fulfill their obligation to first do no harm before worrying about how to generate attractive risk-adjusted returns for their flocks.

Market dislocations like those that occurred in 1998 and 2008 demonstrated that allegedly noncovariant asset classes like debt and equity can (and likely will) collapse at precisely the same time, and that stocks in different industries are far more interconnected than Markowitz's theory contended. True diversification turns out to require a far more radical approach than that required by Markowitz's model and legislated by ERISA and other codifiers of fiduciary standards in the mid-to-late twentieth century, as market events have demonstrated. Fiduciary law, like much of the thinking governing financial markets as they edged closer to crisis in the mid-2000s, has been left in the dust.

CHAPTER 8

Finance after Armageddon

For many men and women who spent most of their professional lives on Wall Street, the year 2008 must have felt like Armageddon. Not only did they lose their jobs, but many of them lost the wealth and financial security they had spent decades accumulating. Regulators and others in the seats of government surely felt as though they were facing the end-of-days when confronted with the death of capital. The global financial system was virtually paralyzed in September and October of 2009, and unimaginable measures had to be taken to resuscitate it.

Accordingly, it does not seem farfetched to treat the question of where we go from here as a question of fixing finance after the survival of a near-extinction-level event. Anybody who believes that the system can continue without drastic reform after the events of 2008 is probably beyond convincing, or stands to profit too much personally from maintaining the status quo. Each succeeding financial crisis of the last three decades has been more severe than the last because the underlying imbalances that caused it were left unaddressed. As a result, these imbalances have grown larger, distorted the economy in more profound ways, and become less susceptible to correction without causing severe instability. After each of the previous crises, serious financial reform was sloughed off and the reins on risk-taking were further loosened in the name of free markets. For example, conduct that increased systemic instability, such as the creation of off-balance-sheet entities to conceal debt, continued to receive favorable treatment under bank capital rules even after the abuse of these entities by Enron Corp. caused a crisis of confidence in 2001 that inflicted untold damage on the markets. Increasing tolerance for behavior that escalated systemic risk created a system characterized by extreme moral hazard in which gains are privatized in the hands of a small elite while losses are socialized among the effectively disenfranchised and overburdened American taxpayer. Ronald Reagan's trickle-down economics became socialism for the rich and capitalism for the poor (if it was ever anything else).

For those who still believe that capital can be a force for good in the world if wisely managed and regulated, it is time for serious discussion about what can be changed within the limitations of a highly flawed political system or, as argued earlier in this book, a financial-political complex that exercises power over all aspects of our society. The time is long overdue for a serious call to arms to reform a system that has the capability of doing so much good but has inflicted so much harm by being repeatedly diverted into wasting its resources on leverage and speculation.

Despite the profound crisis that capitalism experienced in 2008, serious discussion of reform was quickly sidelined by powerful lobbying interests. After markets hit their nadir in March 2009, a veneer of stability returned to the financial world. But below the surface, serious instabilities continued to boil. The enormous mountains of debt that were incurred to triage the global economy continued to weigh down sovereign balance sheets and limit governments' ability to deal with future challenges before they lurch into new crises. The weakened condition of the global system renders reform more urgent than ever.

For this reason, regulatory reform must be addressed within the context of what economic instability really means, and what it can lead to. This will require a much greater focus on the long-term consequences of failing to act rather than concerning ourselves exclusively with addressing short-term emergencies. The failure of a single institution is, in the

long run, a relatively minor event. The system and its constituent parts
will find a way to survive. But the long-term consequences of rescuing
every poorly managed firm are extremely negative because of the moral
hazard they create in a system that has grown accustomed to seeing risk
socialized and profit privatized.

In order to be able to think long-term, one must learn to think
in terms of the arc of history. Modern markets and media have short-
ened our attention spans to the point where historical consciousness
has been all but obliterated, and it requires a special effort to focus on
anything beyond the immediate moment. Despite the urgent necessity
to remember the past and learn from it, people today have forgotten to
think historically. As the social and literary critic Frederic Jameson has
written, people need "to think the present historically in an age that
has forgotten to think historically in the first place."[1] This is particularly
imperative at junctures when it feels like the center cannot hold, periods
in which prior assumptions fail us and new answers are needed.

And what better place to start thinking about the consequences of
Armageddon than to return to the gates of the place where barbarism
last reigned when humanity failed us? In 1969, Theodor Adorno called
for an uncompromising standard for education that should be applied
more widely to all areas of human endeavor:

> The premier demand upon all education is that Auschwitz not happen
> again. Its priority before any other requirement is such that I believe
> I need not and should not justify it. I cannot understand why it has
> been given so little concern until now. To justify it would be monstrous
> in the face of the monstrosity that took place. Yet the fact that one
> is so barely conscious of this demand and the questions that it raises
> shows that the monstrosity has not penetrated people's minds deeply,
> itself a symptom of the continuing potential for its recurrence as far as
> peoples' conscious and unconscious is concerned. Every debate about
> the ideals of education is trivial and inconsequential compared to this
> single ideal: never again Auschwitz. It was the barbarism all education
> strives against.[2]

Some readers may view it as alarmist to compare the obligation
to prevent genocide from reoccurring to the obligation to maintain
stable financial markets. In fact, other than being long overdue, such a

connection is absolutely necessary. It is blindness to such comparisons that leads to barbarism, and the conditions that led to the monstrosities that occurred in Germany 70 years ago are no less present in our world today. Just ask the people of the former Yugoslavia or the modern Middle East. If we fail to imagine the worst, we will be unprepared to deal with the worst when it descends upon us. If nothing else, the 2008 financial crisis surely taught us that.

Adorno also wrote in the same essay quoted above: "[a]mong the insights of Freud that truly extend even into culture and sociology, one of the most profound seems to be that civilization itself produces anti-civilization and increasingly enforces it." Thirty years after Adorno's warning, insufficient attention is being paid to the fact that without functioning financial markets that are capable of raising capital for productive uses and creating opportunity for the disenfranchised, the world is far more likely to spin into anarchy. The economic grievances that led to Nazism's vicious rise to power in the 1930s are echoed in similar inequalities around the world today. Having exported economic disaster to all corners of the world, the dominant Western powers need to reorder their priorities as they heal their economies in order to create a more equitable and stable global order.

As the tools of finance become more sophisticated, the obligation to regulate them prudentially increases exponentially. With great power comes great responsibility. In *Modernity and the Holocaust* (1991), the sociologist Zygmunt Bauman argued that two of modernity's signal achievements made the holocaust possible: technology and bureaucracy.[3] In fact, he argues, the genocide of the Jews (and murder of millions of others) was carried out in a manner that was completely consistent with the norms of how business was conducted at the time. In other words, Auschwitz was an example of modernity cannibalizing itself. Why shouldn't the same be said about modern finance and the succession of increasingly destabilizing financial crises that have consumed the financial markets over the past two decades? Beginning with portfolio insurance, which contributed to the stock market crash of 1987, and continuing through credit default swaps, which swept away some of the world's largest financial institutions in 2008, financial technology itself became the tool that almost destroyed the very system it was designed to protect from risk. What could be a better example of Adorno's "civilization creating anticivilization"? And if it is indeed the case that our most advanced tools are also the ones that are most capable of destroying us, mustn't we better educate ourselves to prevent that from happening? As the perpetrators of the crisis try to sneak away from the scene of their crimes unseen, it is incumbent upon the rest of us to ensure that the intellectual and moral lapses that caused so much damage are exposed for what they are. Only after this flawed thinking is exposed can it be disposed of.

Yet Congress is fiddling while Rome is burning, cheered on by special interests that serve to benefit from the status quo. Proposals for reform are being derailed and diluted by Wall Street interests that would like the rest of us to forget that 2008 even happened. According to the Center for Responsive Economics, the finance, insurance, and real estate industries spent $223 million on lobbying in the first half of 2009, a period in which these very institutions were still in serious financial distress and could have used that money to bolster their weakened balance sheets.[4] Nobody should be fooled. The enemies of reform are not just enemies of reform; they are enemies of a more just and fair society in which the rewards of capital are shared not slopped up by a small elite like pigs feeding at a trough. Reform must start from within and it must begin now.

It is almost impossible to overstate the urgency of global financial reform if we are to avoid the social and political consequences of economic instability. Maintaining stable and equitable financial markets is a moral and practical imperative. The status quo, and any system that resembles it, is certain to lead the world into further cycles of boom and bust that will exceed the abilities of both markets and governments to repair. As our readings of Smith, Marx, Keynes, and Minsky suggest, and as our historical experience demonstrates, boom-and-bust cycles are deeply embedded in the nature of capitalism. While some may argue that the authorities effectively prevented a wholesale collapse of global finance in 2008, the fact that they needed to resort to unprecedented actions to do so should serve as *prima facie* evidence that previous policies were seriously deficient. The fact that financial markets suffered from imbalances of such extremity that they caused near-collapse illustrates that the system requires radical reform. In 2008, the markets were not remotely capable of fixing themselves (despite all of the accolades paid to free markets), and governments managed to return the system to stability only by throwing the traditional rule book (and rule of law) out the window.

Moreover—and this point is of the utmost importance—*the unprecedented measures governments were forced to take in 2008 are certain to impose long-term destabilizing effects on the global economy.* These actions were not permanent solutions to the economic imbalances that led to the crisis; they were temporary bandages applied to triage the patient. And this wasn't the first time the underlying imbalances that caused a crisis were left unresolved. In fact, the pattern of the last three decades is one of a series of crises caused by flawed monetary and fiscal policy that were addressed by short-term fixes that left the underlying imbalances unresolved. The result is a continuing buildup of imbalances that, like layers of sediment, have distorted the global economy beyond any chance of reaching equilibrium. The last layer of sediment comprised trillions of dollars of additional debt loaded onto government balance sheets that will have to be repaid or otherwise monetized.

If the past is prologue to the type of draconian measures that will be taken by governments to restore order and stability when the next crisis arrives, everything possible must be done today to address the underlying causes of the 2008 crisis. In economic terms, the actions by governments around the world in 2008 to prevent an outright economic catastrophe are likely to lead to some combination of the following negative repercussions for the United States: a weaker dollar; higher inflation; and an accelerated shift in relative economic strength away from the United States toward Asia. Moreover, there are likely to be a variety of other consequences that cannot be predicted with certainty but will undoubtedly be negative for the United States' global economic standing.

The misbegotten policies that led the United States into the crisis have placed the world's greatest economic power into a situation where its balance sheet is greatly encumbered with debt. It appears that this debt can only be repaid by extraordinarily high rates of economic growth, debasement of the currency, inflation, or a combination of all three. If history—meaning the history of government policy and the conduct of fiscal and monetary policy by Congress and the Federal Reserve—is any guide, most of the heavy lifting to repay this debt will not come from strong economic growth. Instead, the debt will continue to grow and end up being monetized through currency devaluation and inflation. These are not the ingredients from which economic hegemony can be sustained.

There is a further reason why the financial system desperately needs to be reformed to minimize the chances of future crises. Emergencies give government license to flout the rule of law. The death of capital can become the death of liberty and human rights, which is another reason why the moral obliquity of financiers who contribute to the serial financial meltdowns is so reprehensible. Their conduct is not only wrong in and of itself, but tempts the government to abuse its power. Each time there is a financial crisis, the SEC and Justice Department throw out the rule of law at the behest of politicians ducking their own complicity and prosecute newly fashioned "crimes," criminalizing conduct that was previously accepted as legal in order to quell public outcry. As each financial crisis grows in severity, this type of post hoc criminalization of finance is becoming a greater threat to our liberty. While privileged individuals who bleed the system for their own benefit deserve no special pleading, it remains incumbent on the government in a crisis to respect the rule of law. Unfortunately, all too often it does the opposite. Government by show trial should be associated with a gulag not a republic.

The steps taken to address the 2008 crisis were in many ways a natural extension of the government's conduct after the 9-11 attacks. The passage of the Patriot Act had already seriously weakened civil liberties by giving law enforcement the power to do virtually anything it deemed necessary in order to protect the country from potential terrorist attacks. This came to include such questionable practices as warrantless wiretapping of U.S. citizens, the practice of "extraordinary renditions," the suspension of habeas corpus, and the torture of suspected terrorists (and these are only the practices we know about). The financial crisis of 2008 threatened such extreme economic and social anomie that the government took it upon itself to again ignore the rule of law by abrogating the bankruptcy laws in the General Motors and Chrysler bankruptcies. The U.S. government demonstrated its proclivity to exercise raw power in the name of crisis management. The most effective way to limit its opportunity to rob us of our liberties in the future is to limit the potential for future crises to occur in the first place.

By the time the imbalances being created today come home to roost, it will be too late to introduce the reforms necessary to strengthen institutions and capital flows to withstand the coming instability and the increasingly draconian measures governments will feel licensed to take to deal with them. Accordingly, dramatic financial reform must be instituted as soon as possible to prepare the system for the instability that is certain to come when everyone least expects it (for that is what instability is, a disruption that occurs when the system is least prepared to handle it). A well fortified and stable system will be the best protection against government again overstepping the bounds of law to manage the next crisis.

The consequences of failing to act are not theoretical. On a global basis, they include a widening gap between rich and poor, high levels of hunger and poverty in disenfranchised areas of the world, ecological devastation, and political instability. On a local level in the United States, the effects include the ruination of neighborhoods and communities, sustained high levels of unemployment, high amounts of unused capacity in manufacturing, retail, and commercial real estate, a health care system that leaves tens of millions of people uninsured, and a seriously deteriorating fiscal situation. Despite all the advances that mankind has made, there is much more work to do to fulfill even our most modest obligations to billions of people around the world. We will not have even the smallest chance of doing so without a stable financial system. Only a strong and wisely regulated global financial system whose benefits are shared equitably will be able to effectively meet the challenges posed by these threats. We do not have such a system today, and we certainly did not have one leading into the financial crisis. Instead, the system encouraged speculation at the expense of production, debt at the expense of equity, short-term gain at the expense of long-term investment. True financial reform must be designed to reverse these priorities in order to prevent capital from dying again.

Obama Goes to Wall Street

In September 2009, on the first anniversary of the day Lehman Brothers filed for bankruptcy, President Barack Obama flew Marine One up from Washington, D.C., to make a lunchtime speech at Federal Hall on Wall Street to discuss financial reform. By this time, much of Wall Street (or what remained of it after 2008) had returned to the practices that had contributed to the financial crisis: exorbitant, asymmetric compensation schemes; trafficking in highly complex and highly leveraged credit derivatives; and the issuance of record levels of debt, including debt associated with leveraged buyouts and other speculative forms of investment. By mid-September 2009, it was obvious to many observers that the battle for meaningful financial reform had already been lost.

The president's speech repeated proposals contained in a white paper authored by Treasury Secretary Timothy Geithner and the director of the National Economic Council Lawrence Summers that was released on June 14, 2009, entitled "Financial Regulatory Reform: A New Foundation." President Obama brought all of his considerable oratory skills to bear on his audience that day, a group that included many of the most influential legislators in the financial arena as well as key representatives from the largest financial institutions and hedge funds. His message was blunt: "We will not go back to the days of reckless behavior and unchecked excess that was at the heart of this crisis, where too many were motivated only by the appetite for quick kills and bloated bonuses," he warned his audience. "Those on Wall Street cannot resume taking risks without regard for consequences and expect that next time, American taxpayers will be there to break their fall." To say that Obama's plea fell flat, however, would be an understatement. His words were largely greeted with silence, according to *New York Times* reporter Andrew Ross Sorkin,[5] who was in the audience. Most of the financial executives in attendance were trying to position the traumas of 2008 as ancient history and were actively lobbying the government to allow them to go back to their old ways. The model of socializing risk and privatizing gain had worked exceedingly well for the financial elite sitting in Federal Hall that day while impoverishing significant portions of the general population and weakening the economic fabric of the United States. This audience was not interested in changing the status quo.

The sad truth was that the reform train had left the station a long time ago. While just one year earlier the entire financial system had been staring into the abyss, trillions of dollars of intervention from the U.S., European, and Chinese governments had created the appearance that all was well with the world economy. Credit markets were functioning again; the stock market had risen approximately 50 percent from its March 2009 lows of 666 on the S&P 500 and 6,547 on the Dow

Jones Industrial Average, and many Wall Street firms had repaid the government money they had taken (or been forced to take) in late 2008 and were now focusing on how to overpay their employees once again. While Wall Street firms were not as leveraged as they were before the crisis, they were again taking outsized risks with their balance sheets. And while there were competing legislative proposals before Congress regarding how to overhaul financial regulation, the old set of laws was still in place with diminishing prospects for meaningful change.

A year after the death of capital, comprehensive regulatory reform of the type needed to truly stabilize the financial system was all but dead. There were some small signs of progress, such as potentially aggressive actions taken by the Federal Reserve and Treasury Department on compensation reform and by the SEC on dark pools. But on more systemically serious matters such as derivatives legislation and monetary policy management, there was little sign that serious change would be effected. This is profoundly disappointing because future financial instability, which is highly probable, renders radical regulatory reform an urgent necessity.

Principles of Reform

Regulatory reform must be comprehensive in nature in order to maximize financial stability. Earlier in this book, I proposed specific reforms with respect to two areas that have contributed to the overall instability of the economic system—private equity (see Chapter 5) and derivatives (see Chapter 6). On a broader basis, six key areas must be addressed in order to provide a proper foundation for a more stable financial system that no longer rewards speculation at the expense of productive investment or socializes risk and privatizes profit:

1. Taxing speculation.
2. Creating a unified regulator.
3. Addressing the "too big to fail" doctrine.
4. Improving the capital adequacy of financial institutions.
5. Reforming monetary policy management.
6. Improving systemic transparency.

Each of these areas is highly complex and requires a comprehensive approach. The complexity of the modern financial system is the major challenge of financial reform, but one that can be overcome by thoughtful and patient legislation. *Partial solutions will leave too much room for abuse and the return of instability. A reform program must integrate all of the principles enunciated above in order to be effective.*

The current regulatory system is based on the assumption that markets are efficient and investors are rational. Accordingly, regulation has been designed to minimize governmental interference with the efficient and rational operation of markets. (Not to put too fine a point on it, but that is a polite way of saying, "garbage in, garbage out.") Those who have warned that markets are obviously inefficient and investors far from rational beings have been largely marginalized in terms of influencing policy. That is unfortunate, because markets have consistently demonstrated their inefficiency, and investors have repeatedly exhibited their irrationality. Regulatory reform must start from the premise that markets are inefficient[6] and investors are irrational. Our society should not have to continue to pay such a high price for clinging to beliefs that events have consistently shown to be false. Working with any other set of assumptions will lead reform down the wrong path.

The election of Barack Obama offered some promise that things would change, but his choice of Timothy Geithner as treasury secretary and Lawrence Summers as his top economic advisor delivered the two most important economic posts in the administration to individuals who were highly credentialed but also deeply entrenched in the financial-political complex that had long endorsed the deregulatory agenda. Far more disappointing was the choice of lifelong regulator Mary Schapiro as head of the SEC, an agency that cried out for new blood after abjectly failing in its mission to protect investors. If change is going to occur, these key players are going to have to shed their previous skins and emerge with some new ideas and the political courage to push them forward. Truly comprehensive and meaningful reform will ultimately depend on the raw power of ideas and the political courage to put them into effect rather than just paying lip service to them.

If financial reform is going to be effective, it must address the two most profound flaws that currently plague Western capitalism. The first flaw is the phenomenon that has been discussed throughout this book—the predominance of speculative over productive investment. This issue has been addressed with far more forthrightness in the United Kingdom than in the United States, where Britain's chief financial regulator, Adair Turner, has raised the ire of bankers and other members of the financial services establishment by publicly questioning the purpose of much of the activity in modern finance. In September 2009, Turner told a group of financiers at a dinner held at Mansion House, the grand residence of the Lord Mayor of London, that banks "need to be willing, like the regulator, to recognize that there are some profitable activities so unlikely to have a social benefit, direct or indirect, that they should voluntarily walk away from them."[7] While honest observers welcome such outspokenness, this message was greeted with a fair degree of disdain by the audience. But Turner, who in March 2009 authored "The Turner Review," a fairly scathing report on the financial crisis, is onto something. The global economy simply cannot sustain a regime in which increasing amounts of capital are devoted to churning money out of money rather than adding to the productive stock of the world. Banks in particular, but other financial institutions as well, especially those that operate under the aegis of some sort of government licensure that gives them certain rights that nonlicensed businesses do not enjoy, possess a public utility function that has been thrown to the wayside in recent years by the obsession with free markets. It is time to restore some balance to these institutions to ensure that society is not completely sacrificed at the altar of profit motive.[8]

The second flaw is the model that socializes risk and privatizes reward. This model is not only economically defective because it places an undue burden on governments and the taxpayers that fund them, but is morally retrograde in absolving individuals of responsibility for their actions, imposing the highest costs on those least responsible for harming society. This regime has also widened the gulf between rich and poor that leads to social instability.

The basic premise of any regulatory regime must be that it creates the proper incentives that favor productive investment over speculation and more fairly distributes economic gains and losses among the populace. Society must come to understand that the way investors generate profits is just as important as the amount of profits they generate. This is why human beings were vested with moral sentiments, so they could distinguish the quality of human conduct from the quantity of those results. And only by appreciating the quality of economic output as well as its quantity will society be able to increase productive investment and improve the quality of life for all of its citizens.

Impose a Tax on Speculation

Toward the end of 2009, proposals were being floated in Congress to impose a modest tax on certain types of securities transactions. One proposed piece of legislation, titled "Let Wall Street Pay for the Restoration of Main Street," would impose a 0.25 percent tax on the sale and purchase of stocks, options, derivatives and futures contracts. Wall Street is unalterably opposed to any such tax, but it is a good idea for a number of reasons:

- Tax policy should be used to create the proper types of economic incentives, and to discourage types of behavior that damage the economic system and society at large. One of the indisputable lessons of the 2008 financial crisis is that far too much capital is being devoted to speculation and far too little is being channeled to productive investments. Increasing the cost of speculation is a logical and economically efficient way of discouraging unproductive activities.

- The U.S. government is running unsustainable deficits and is desperately in need of revenues. In addition to ending egregious tax breaks for financial interests such as taxing private equity interests at favorable rates and permitting hedge fund billionaires to defer their taxes for periods of as long as 10 years, the government should be raising revenue from activities that are contributing the least to society and taking the most from society. The financial industry can easily afford to pay a tax on its speculative activities. Moreover, a significant amount of securities trading today is not for the purpose of providing growth capital for corporations but is merely done to churn financial profits. Accordingly, a tax on these activities would be a perfectly reasonable and economically harmless way to raise revenues.

Transactions such as credit default swaps and leveraged buyouts and recapitalizations have extremely wide profit margins built into them by their Wall Street promoters and can easily bear the type of tax proposed here. As someone who has worked in these markets for two decades, I can assure readers that Wall Street arguments to the contrary are both self-serving and false. One of the points of such a tax would be to make Wall Street firms and their clients think twice about engaging in speculative activities that contribute nothing positive to society, and force them to give something back economically if they are hell-bent on engaging in such activities.

Rather than a flat 0.25 percent tax on securities trading, I would propose a sliding scale tax rate applied to the face amount of the following types of transactions:

- Naked credit default swaps if they are not banned entirely (1.25 percent tax).
- Debt and preferred stock issued in leveraged buyouts, leveraged re-capitalizations, or debt financings used to pay dividends to leveraged buyout sponsors (0.60 percent).
- Quantitative trading strategies (0.35 percent).
- Equity derivatives (options, futures contracts) (0.25 percent).
- Large block trades (0.25 percent).
- All other stock, bond, and bank loan trades (0.15 percent).

Coupled with other measures aimed at reducing systemic risk (i.e., increasing capital adequacy at financial institutions, increasing collateral requirements, and imposing listing requirements for credit default swap trades, and so on), such a tax would impose a cost on activities that add little in the way of productive capacity to the economy and increase systemic instability. Obviously any such tax would have to include provisions to prevent forum shopping by investors and traders to prevent them from avoiding the tax by moving their activities abroad. Such a tax regime would also contribute to the progressivity of our tax system by asking those who benefit the most from our economy to pay a little more in the way of taxes. The tax should not be imposed on stock, bond, and bank loan investments in retirement accounts (IRAs, 401ks, etc.).[9]

End Balkanized Regulation

One aspect of the current regulatory regime that must be improved in order to fortify systemic stability is its balkanized structure. The

fractured structure of the current regulatory system must be replaced
with a unified system. Whatever the historical and political sources of
the existing multiple (and often conflicting) agencies that regulate the
financial industry (the Securities and Exchange Commission, the Federal Deposit Insurance Corporation, the Commodities Futures Trading
Corporation, FINRA (the former NASD), state banking and insurance
regulators, and the Federal Reserve), this structure has been rendered
archaic by changes in markets and financial technology. In a world where
all financial instruments can be deconstructed into 1s and 0s, effectively
erasing the barriers between insurance, financial, and real estate firms
and rendering any one of them capable of creating systemic risk, the
existing regulatory regime has been a surefire recipe for disaster. There
is no longer a rationale for regulating securities firms, commercial banks,
and commodities firms from separate federal agency silos while leaving
states to regulate mortgage brokers and insurance companies. Instead,
a single regulatory body should assume responsibility for overall regulation of the financial industry and then form separate subagencies to
regulate each separate type of firm. In a networked global economy, all
of these industries are closely linked (for instance, they all trade with each
other as counterparties) and must be regulated at the federal level by a
powerful regulatory body that is guided by the principles of regulation
discussed here—encouraging production over speculation, transparency
over opacity, and stability over instability.

Moreover, a single, independent regulatory body is needed to monitor and regulate systemic risk. The Federal Reserve has been touted by
some observers (and by its own chairman) as the most qualified candidate for the role of super-regulator. Such a choice would be unwise for
several reasons.

First and foremost, the central bank's track record in managing monetary policy has been nothing short of disastrous. Despite the fact that
monetary policy is almost impossible to get just right, the Federal Reserve's monetary policy methodology has been a case study in procyclicality, has been based on deeply flawed intellectual premises, and has
placed the U.S. economy on an unsustainable path of speculation and
indebtedness. A central bank that sat idly by while obvious bubbles built
up and burst hardly seems qualified to prevent the same thing from happening in the future.[10] This track record alone renders the institution

a poor choice to serve as the party responsible for monitoring the very systemic risk its own policies have consistently exacerbated.

Furthermore, the Federal Reserve's own practices set a poor example of the type of transparency that the system requires to improve stability. It is frankly anachronistic that the central bank refuses to issue real-time releases of the minutes of the Open Market Committee meetings, and instead discloses this information only after significant time delays that leave the markets guessing as to the thinking of the most powerful monetary regulator in the world. In a day and age in which information travels around the globe in the blink of an eye, and markets uncover information with astounding speed, the attempt to delay disclosure of the central bank's deliberations borders on absurdity (and antiquity). Moreover, the central bank needs to make a greater effort to make its operations understandable to laymen rather than to economists and market experts. Chairman Ben Bernanke has been far more constructive in this respect than his predecessor Alan Greenspan, who never met a sentence he couldn't mangle whenever he testified before Congress or otherwise spoke publicly. The decision-making of the Federal Reserve should not be a state secret—it should be a process subject to public scrutiny and debate. That does not mean that the Federal Reserve should lose its independence; one can only imagine the damage that would be done to the economy if monetary policy were subject to more direct influence by Congress, which demonstrates with every passing year its inability to manage complex long-term economic issues with any degree of foresight and responsibility. But the system needs an independent risk monitor that will lead by example, and the Federal Reserve is not that body. Instead, an independent nonpartisan oversight board should be appointed to fill such a role.

Too Big to Fail

The reality is that institutions still exist that are too big to fail without jeopardizing the stability of the financial system both within the United States and globally. Moreover, there is little political inclination to force these firms to shrink, and there are good business reasons why such firms exist provided they conduct their businesses responsibly. Accordingly, we must establish an equitable system for dealing with their potential failure.

The 2008 financial crisis taught the world a valuable lesson: Institutions that are too big to fail are equivalent to government protectorates. Or put another way, only the government is too big to fail, so any institution that is too big to fail must be taken over by the government. The problem with the regime that has been in place is that these institutions' profits were being privatized before they ran into trouble and then, when they hit the skids, their losses were socialized. This is unacceptable. Only the government should be considered too big to fail, and, frankly, if the United States continues on the fiscal and monetary path that it has set itself upon, that belief will be tested as well. But the concept of permitting private institutions to grow to a size that permits them to pose systemic risk in a system that privatizes their profits but socializes their losses must come to an end immediately. As a practical matter, there is little prospect that the government is going to break up JPMorgan Chase, Bank of America, Goldman Sachs, Morgan Stanley, or any other firm whose failure would pose systemic risk. Accordingly, we must accept the reality that there are institutions that are too big to fail but must also impose a regime that requires a bailout of such firms to result in government ownership so that the American taxpayers can share in both the gains and the losses of the enterprise, rather than limiting the gains to insiders and shifting the losses to outsiders.

There are currently several institutions whose failure could pose a serious systemic risk. In one category are institutions that are already owned by the U.S. government, like Fannie Mae, Freddie Mac, Citigroup, and AIG. Then there are other ostensibly healthy institutions like JPMorgan Chase; Wells Fargo; Goldman Sachs Group, Inc.; Bank of America; Morgan Stanley; and several major insurance companies that are not owned by the government whose demise, while currently unlikely, would cause severe systemic stress. Nonetheless, the collapse of this latter group of firms is not unthinkable, particularly without meaningful reform of credit default swaps that can be used to drive a firm's financing costs to unsustainable levels. The Obama administration and the Federal Reserve quite properly have made the issue of too big to fail an important focus of their policy. The combination of lowering balance sheet leverage, reducing the risk embedded in asymmetric compensation schemes, and improving transparency through the elimination of structured investment vehicles (SIVs) are important steps in minimizing the possibility that a single large firm could destabilize the financial system.

Nonetheless, systemically important firms have a special dual role in the economy and in society. They are not simply profit generators; their size and reach effectively render them public utilities whose continued health is vital to the continued viability of the economy. They have gained that status in part through government licensure, which should be considered a privilege rather than a one-way grant of a right to print private profits. The best approach to the too-big-to-fail doctrine is one that ensures that gains and losses are properly allocated among different societal constituencies. Merely limiting the size of an institution will not ensure that result.

Accordingly, there must first be a regime under which large institutions are regulated to minimize the risk that they will suffer large losses that can place them—and therefore the system—at risk. Such a regime would address issues such as capital adequacy, vulnerability to financial products of mass destruction such as naked credit default swaps, and the imposition of countercyclical approaches to balance sheet management. Secondarily, the system must no longer be designed to address failures, which are inevitable in any capitalist economy, by socializing the losses and privatizing the gains. This would entail reforming compensation practices to better align executive rewards with risk, as well as providing the government with an ownership stake in businesses that have to be bailed out. The fact that the U.S. government profited from its investment in Goldman Sachs, Morgan Stanley, and other companies that received TARP funds was entirely appropriate. It was also entirely appropriate that the government took major ownership stakes in Citigroup and AIG when those giants came hat in hand to the government. If we want to have an ownership society, gains and losses have to be shared far more equitably than they have in the past.

Improving Capital Adequacy

One of the lessons of the 2008 crisis is that financial institutions rarely have sufficient capital cushions to sustain themselves through true market calamities or even severe economic downturns. Financial institution shareholders demand high returns on equity to boost the value of their stockholdings, particularly where employees own large amounts of stock.

Unfortunately, such demands conflict with sound balance sheet practices and lead to excessive leverage and other reckless management practices. One of the frustrating characteristics of capital is that it is most available when least needed, and least available when most desperately needed. Policy must be changed to ensure that financial institutions are encouraged or required to maintain stronger balance sheets in prosperous times, even if this reduces their return on equity and lowers their stock prices. In the end, this will reduce the volatility of their stock prices and reduce their odds of failure.

Limiting Banks' Balance Sheet Leverage

Important steps have already been taken to reduce the balance sheet leverage of commercial and investment banks from the dangerously high levels that contributed to the financial crisis. Bear Stearns and Lehman Brothers both sported leverage ratios of more than 30-to-1 when they failed in 2008, a direct result of the loosening of their net capital rules in August 2004. These levels did not include any off-balance-sheet leverage that these firms had tucked out of sight. Such high leverage was the financial equivalent of playing Russian roulette with five of the six chambers of the gun loaded. Once the off-balance-sheet leverage with legal or reputational recourse to the sponsoring institution was added, it was the equivalent of placing a bullet in the sixth chamber. Less than a 3 percent drop in the value of these firms' assets was sufficient to wipe out their equity. Such a thin cushion is insufficient for a traditional bank and is woefully inadequate for an investment bank whose business model is based on proprietary trading and trafficking in highly complex financial instruments whose liquidity (and value) can suddenly evaporate.

Today, most of the large commercial banks and investment banks have reduced their leverage ratios significantly below where they were when the crisis began. As of June 30, 2009, Tier 1 common equity ratios for U.S. banks had increased to 7.5 percent (13.3-to-1 leverage) from 5.3 percent (19.8-to-1 leverage) at the end of 2008.[11] This is a definite improvement but still insufficient. Many institutions are still holding significant amounts of illiquid assets of dubious value on their balance sheets, such as complex mortgage-related securities. Moreover, current leverage levels hardly render these institutions bastions of stability considering that their businesses are increasingly focused on highly risky speculative trading strategies rather than low-risk lending strategies. For example, by mid-2009, Goldman Sachs (admittedly one of the best managed firms on Wall Street) was earning approximately 80 percent of its revenues from trading and investments rather than traditional banking and investment banking activities. Accordingly, it would be more prudent to further lower the maximum allowable leverage to 10-to-1, lower than the 12-to-1 level that existed before the ill-conceived 2004 lifting of previous limitations.

Lower leverage will undoubtedly mean that these firms will be less profitable in strong markets because they will be limited in their ability to speculate in securities and other financial assets. The flip side of that observation is that these firms will be more profitable and less prone to large losses in falling markets and thereby still be able to fulfill their public utility roles when most needed. *Regulation should be geared toward ensuring the stability of financial institutions, not maximizing their profitability. The fact that reducing their balance sheet leverage will reduce their profitability should be completely irrelevant in determining the best manner in which to maintain their capital adequacy.* Moreover, if financial institutions were less profitable, they would likely be in a weaker position to lure America's most talented students with lucrative compensation offers to become investment bankers and derivatives and mortgage traders. That would be nothing but a boon for U.S. society, which would greatly benefit if these talented individuals were instead to become scientists, engineers, doctors, and teachers.

Capital requirements also need to be maintained on a countercyclical rather than procylical basis. For too long, financial institutions have been permitted or encouraged to reduce their capital when times were good, leaving them with insufficient capital cushions when economic conditions deteriorated. The old adage about saving money for a rainy day may be quaint, but it has survived for hundreds of years because it makes a great deal of sense. Regulators and stockholders frown upon banks and other financial institutions overreserving for losses because this results in understating earnings, but a more sophisticated approach to reserves (and measuring bank profitability) is needed. Annual financial results are nothing more than an accounting convention, and many of the financial arrangements into which banks and other institutions enter are far longer in tenor than one year. Accordingly, it would be far more appropriate to tie reserves on longer-dated contracts to their tenor on a fully disclosed basis to permit investors to make a more informed evaluation of an institution's reserve policy. Moreover, regulators are generally ill-equipped in this day and age to set predetermined reserve requirements for complex financial instruments, and if anything should be encouraging institutions to err on the side of overreserving rather than underreserving in order to ensure that there will be adequate capital cushions when markets inevitably seize up again. A far more flexible regime is needed than the current one-size-fits-all capital model that has been adopted. Finally, little attention should be paid to stock market investors on this issue. Reserves are intended to prevent exactly the type of irrational panics to which stock market investors are particularly prone, and they are the least qualified arbiters of capital adequacy in the marketplace.

FDIC insurance should also become subject to an anticyclical regime. In the past, prosperity has given rise to reductions in the amounts of insurance that banks have been required to pay into the insurance fund. This has proven to be a fateful mistake as the FDIC has been rendered seriously insolvent in 2009 by a rash of bank failures (approximately 140 through December 2009 and still counting). It would be far wiser for insurance rates to be maintained at high levels in strong markets, when banks can afford them, than to create a situation where these fees have to be drastically increased in the middle of a crisis to keep the fund from running out of money. Like many things, management of the FDIC has been subject to the human proclivity to believe that current conditions will persist, particularly when such conditions are healthy. Regulators need to exercise a little imagination and consider that benign conditions are likely to encourage risk-taking and lead to trouble for which a bigger insurance fund will be needed.

Compensation Reform

Any attempt to rein in financial institutions' balance sheet leverage must include compensation reform. Asymmetric compensation schemes that favored short-term profitability over sustainable long-term financial health greatly exacerbated the balance sheet weaknesses that contributed to the financial crisis. Paying out hundreds of millions of dollars of cash compensation to their executives left firms such as Bear Stearns and Lehman Brothers with diminished cushions to absorb losses on their mortgage and loan portfolios when the crisis occurred. Compensation reform is not needed to satisfy the torch and pitchfork brigades demanding retribution for the sins of the past, as satisfying as it would be to punish those who profited from damaging the system; it is needed to stabilize the capital bases of systemically important institutions.

The good news is that the Obama administration (as well as European governments) has taken important steps to rein in—at least for the moment—the most egregious pay practices in the financial industry. On October 22, 2009, the Obama administration's Special Master for Compensation Kenneth Feinberg, and the Federal Reserve, unveiled a two-front attack on Wall Street's pay practices. Feinberg, working out of the Treasury Department, set limits on the compensation practices of those companies that had received financial aid from the government during the crisis and had not yet paid it back: Citigroup; Bank of America, AIG; GMAC, General Motors Corp., Chrysler Corp., and Chrysler Financial Corporation. While these limits reportedly still left several dozen employees at these firms earning in excess of $1 million of long-term compensation, they can fairly be described as draconian (at least in Wall Street terms).[12] On the same day, the Federal Reserve announced that it would incorporate compensation reviews into its routine regulatory supervision of banks, which would affect all institutions regulated by the central bank, including those that received government support during the crisis and were able to pay it back. Federal Reserve Chairman Ben Bernanke said the purpose of the new rules was to tie pay to long-term performance and to ensure that pay schemes do not create "undue risk for the firm or the financial system."[13] While these steps will not cure the plague of overcompensation in the financial services industry, they are a constructive attempt to remove the asymmetry from previous pay schemes that led executives to make one-way bets with what turned out to be other peoples' (that is, the government's or the American taxpayer's) money.

The payment of huge amounts of cash compensation severely weakens the balance sheets of financial institutions. Accordingly, limits must be placed on the amount of cash compensation that is paid out every year by these firms. A much greater percentage of compensation should be paid in the form of stock that vests over an extended period of time. This will strengthen balance sheets in two ways—first by increasing the firms' cash balances, and second by increasing the amount of equity on their balance sheets. It will also hopefully help to align the incentives of

the biggest earners with those of the stockholders and other stakeholders who want the firm to survive by taking prudent risks. But even if
it doesn't align these interests, it will at least keep more cash where it
belongs: inside the firm.

While the senior executives of failed firms owned enormous stock
positions (worth hundreds of millions of dollars or more at their peak
valuations), these large ownership stakes still failed to instill the necessary
ownership mentality and fear of risk. This is likely because these executives were not only granted obscenely large stock option grants annually,
but were also paid tens of millions of dollars of cash compensation and
retirement benefits each year by the boards of directors and compensation committees that were stacked with their cronies. A recent study
by three Harvard Law School professors showed that executives at Bear
Stearns and Lehman Brothers cashed out $1.0 billion and $1.4 billion,
respectively, of performance-based compensation from cash bonuses
that were not clawed back and from stock sales during the 2000–2008
period.[14] Lehman Brothers' former chairman and chief executive officer
Richard Fuld reportedly cashed out more than $500 million of compen-
sation while Bear Stearns' former chairman and chief executive officer
James Cayne made off with more than $350 million. Though these men
lost hundreds of millions of dollars in stock value when their firms failed,
they remain among the wealthiest Americans in the wake of the crisis
and the collapse of their firms. This is the epitome of the heads-I-win,
tails-I-win-anyway compensation schemes that most executives on Wall
Street enjoyed in the years leading up to the 2008 crisis.

Moreover, simply as a matter of common sense and moral decency,
Wall Street compensation became grossly disproportionate to any contributions any individual could possibly be making to a public company
or to society. It is one thing when the owner of a private company earns
outsized compensation; that individual is assuming the entire risk of the
enterprise. In a public company, all of the expenses of operating the business are paid by others and do not fall on individual executives. Public
company executives are sheltered from business risks (for example, the
costs of defending litigation) by the financial wealth of the corporation,
and there should be some sort of limitation on the upside that accom-
panies that protection from the downside. Effectively, public company
executives have a one-way ticket to earn cash compensation with no
return ticket to put any of that cash at risk. This is the real objection

to the sky-high bonuses that were paid on Wall Street—they reflected a completely one-sided compensation arrangement in which executives suffer limited pain if their firms experience failure. These types of arrangements must be terminated because they breed a loss of confidence in the fairness of the system, which in turn erodes the moral bonds that encourage the types of constructive conduct that allows markets to function. If the directors of these firms are not prepared to make the necessary changes to these schemes, then the government must step in. The government properly has a role to play in limiting such schemes if losses are going to be socialized when financial firms fail. Firms simply cannot be permitted to perpetuate such asymmetric compensation schemes in an era where the ultimate risk of payment falls on the U.S. taxpayer.

In view of the fact that large amounts of money will continue to be paid to financial executives (even with the Federal Reserve and Treasury Department breathing down their necks), the lion's share of compensation should be paid in the form of stock whose ownership vests over an extended period of years. Stock compensation should be based on several years of performance and include provisions that adjust awards appropriately (known in Wall Street parlance as clawback provisions) in order to avoid the error of rewarding executives for short-term performance that later turns out to be illusory. For example, an investment banker should not be rewarded with a blank check for working on a transaction that later turns out to fail; his ultimate compensation should be related to the success or failure of the deal. This would be an important step to leading the investment banker to work on deals that are likely to succeed and avoid working on deals that are likely to fail (such as a highly leveraged private equity transaction). Regulators should permit firms to maintain reserve accounts and make other arrangements to facilitate these types of compensation structures and require detailed disclosure to keep investors fully informed.

Moreover, such compensation arrangements would ideally focus executives on the overall financial health of their firms and lead them to be more prudent when taking risks. They would also be designed to inculcate a culture focused on shared responsibility and respect for risk-taking, two attributes that are far too rare in the financial services industry. This might also encourage firms to develop cultures in which professionals are required to speak up when they spot reckless behavior or wrongdoing, which would further enhance systemic health. These are ideals, of course; we all know that individuals go to Wall Street primarily to make large sums of money, not to rescue puppies. Nonetheless, it is long past the time when society divorced doing well from doing good. Generous compensation and respect for the system and the institutions that pay compensation should not be mutually exclusive. In fact, the sooner people realize that these values are mutually reinforcing, the healthier and wealthier the financial system will be.

Compensation is particularly important because the powerful interests in our society have decided repeatedly to bail themselves out at the expense of the disenfranchised. Financial institutions—particularly banks that operate with federally-granted banking licenses—continue to speculate rather than engage in productive economic activities. Former Federal Reserve Chairman Paul Volcker has pointed to this flaw in the system and urged bank speculation to be reined in. "I do not think it reasonable that public money—taxpayer money—be indirectly available to support risk-prone capital market activities simply because they are housed within a commercial banking organization. Extensive participation in the impersonal, transaction-oriented capital market does not seem to me an intrinsic part of commercial banking. . . . I want to question any presumption that the federal safety net, and financial support, will be extended beyond the traditional commercial banking community."[15] Volcker is suggesting—correctly—that it is a profound policy error to continue to permit institutions to speculate in a system that socializes their losses.

One way of dealing with this problem would be to return to the regime of the Glass-Steagall Act of 1933 that previously separated investment and commercial banking. As noted earlier, this Depression-era law was repealed after heavy lobbying by the commercial banking industry in 1999. Reinstituting Glass-Steagall may not be the most effective way of addressing this issue in today's world, however. The argument in favor of a return to that law is that deposit-taking institutions should not be able to speculate (that is, trade for their own accounts) when the ultimate risk falls on the government that insures these deposits. That argument appears to have lost much of its validity in view of the fact that the government not only protected bank depositors in the 2008 crisis but also came to the rescue of credit default counterparties like

Goldman Sachs and non-U.S. institutions like Societe Generale when it rescued AIG with its other support programs. If there is not going to be a distinction between deposit-taking and nondeposit-taking institutions when it comes to government buyouts, reinstituting Glass-Steagall would accomplish nothing. The cost of rescuing all types of institutions fell squarely on the American taxpayer.

The distinction between deposit-taking and nondeposit-taking institutions is rendered largely irrelevant when the government stands ready to protect both types of institutions from failure. Instead, uniform regulation of the capital, compensation and other capital adequacy practices of all types of financial institutions would be far more effective because it would reflect the fact that so many of them operate under an implicit assurance that the government will exercise its lender of last resort function in a crisis. The real question is whether private institutions that serve any kind of public utility function in terms of providing access to capital for businesses should be permitted to become sufficiently large or interconnected to pose a systemic threat if they were to fail. As noted above, the answer to that question is that we are already past that point with respect to several such institutions and therefore we need to insure that future bailouts provide for public ownership of the rescued entity.

Reforming Monetary Policy

It is time to acknowledge that the procyclical policies of the Federal Reserve have placed the United States' economy on an unsustainable path and that a countercyclical policy approach must be adopted. The evidence for this is the pattern of booms and busts that has dominated the financial markets over the past 20 years. This pattern has proved to be highly disruptive to economic growth as well as damaging to the returns that investors have been able to earn on their capital. Furthermore, important trends in the financial markets have exacerbated the procyclical bent of monetary policy: globalization of markets, the digitalization of finance, and consolidation of the financial industry.[15] With the markets increasingly likely to lean in the same direction, it has become imperative that monetary authorities learn to lean in the opposite direction to temper imbalances. The age of allowing imbalances to build until they burst and then cleaning up the mess should come to an end with the crisis of 2008.

Alan Greenspan will probably spend the rest of his life defending his tenure as chairman of the Federal Reserve (of course, that statement might be more meaningful if he were 20 or 30 years younger, but I wish him nothing but good health and long life). Once considered the elder statesman of the Committee to Save the World, his tenure has been significantly discredited by the financial crisis that unfolded within a short period after he departed the most powerful position in global finance. The "Greenspan put," which morphed into the "Bernanke put" in the hands of his successor, current Federal Reserve Chairman Ben Bernanke, created an environment of moral hazard that has been repeatedly exploited by the private sector. By constantly resorting to what some economists have termed "preemptive easing" to prevent short-term pain.[17] Greenspan may have won individual battles but managed to lose the war. His policies set the United States on an unsustainable path.

The pattern of policy making since the mid-1980s was clearly pro-cyclical and created an environment that encouraged moral hazard, beginning with the reaction to the stock market crash of 1987. In order to reassure the markets in the aftermath of their 508-point drop on October 19, 1987, Chairman Greenspan assured them that the Federal Reserve stood ready to make available whatever liquidity was necessary to assure their smooth operation. This was a highly appropriate response to an unprecedented one-day drop in the stock market averages. Unfortunately, however, it became the canned response to far less critical threats. Monetary easing in response to real or perceived crises spawned bubble after bubble.

Easing in the late 1980s led to a property bubble that resulted in the savings and loan crisis in the United States in the early 1990s. Low rates in the early 1990s that were invoked to deal with fallout from the savings and loan crisis and resulting recession spurred a decline in the U.S. dollar in the mid-1990s (and linked Asian currencies in Thailand and Indonesia) and contributed to the Asian bubble that burst in 1997. Low rates also played a large role in the Long Term Capital Management debacle of 1998 (allowing the hedge fund to borrow virtually infinite amounts of cheap money to leverage itself into oblivion) as well as the Russian default of that year, which led to further emergency easing that contributed to the absurd and unsustainable boom in technology stocks beginning in 1999 and ending in tears in 2001. Greenspan also didn't miss a chance to react to the false alarm that all of the world's computers would supposedly shut down at midnight on December 31, 1999 (we all might be better off if they had shut down) by keeping rates lower than they should have been in the middle of what was the most obvious stock market bubble in recent memory (the NASDAQ peaked at a price/earnings ratio of 351 times during that farce). When the Internet bubble burst and dragged down the corporate credit markets that had been dominated by billion-dollar offerings for telecommunications and technology companies that in many cases didn't even qualify as early stage venture capital start-ups, the Federal Reserve maintained low rates in order to protect the markets from themselves once again. This led to the credit bubble of the mid-2000s that fed into mortgages and corporate credit with the able assistance of the shadow banking system of structured credit, SIVs, and derivatives. By the time this bubble burst, the systemic imbalances that had been permitted to build up under the aegis of the Federal Reserve were so profound that it was little wonder that capital had to be given its last rites in the fall of 2008.

The Federal Reserve and its misguided chairmen didn't accomplish this alone. The nation's inability to bear the least amount of economic pain contaminated every level of the financial and political system. Every time the "R" word was mentioned, the political classes went into a trance and began quoting Joseph Conrad's Mr. Kurtz—"The horror! The horror!" The United States had fallen far from the days of the Greatest Generation. The American body politic has grown insufferably intolerant of the least degree of hardship. The possibility of a mere recession has become such an anathema to the political classes of this country that it leads policy makers to pull out all the short-term stops to prevent a downturn while completely ignoring the long-term consequences of such a strategy.

This inordinate fear of the slightest economic downturn ignores the fact that recessions are completely normal and absolutely necessary in a capitalist economy. More important, it neglects the basic economic truth that pain deferred is pain increased. Little or no attention was paid each time the potential of an economic slowdown was raised to whether the remedies would sow the seeds of deeper problems later. The Federal Reserve chairman found more-than-willing coconspirators in the United States Congress, whose inability to rein in spending over the past three decades illustrates beyond a shadow of a doubt that today's

U.S. government bears little resemblance to the one envisioned by the Founders. No doubt there was corruption back when the country was formed, and there has been corruption ever since in various forms, but today's corruption has become so deeply embedded into the system that it threatens the very future of U.S. hegemony. Drastic measures are needed to reverse course.

The Federal Reserve has been justifiably subject to intense criticism by certain members of the political class not only for its actual performance, which has fed one bubble after another, but also for its lack of transparency. Congressman Ron Paul has been in the forefront of this movement. Certainly there should be no reason why the central bank should not be setting an example for standards of transparency. In fairness, under its current Chairman Ben Bernanke, the central bank has taken major steps to become more open in its operations. But the bigger issue is one of substance, not form. The Federal Reserve must make an intellectual shift toward a countercyclical policy approach and away from the procyclical policy regime that it followed first under Chairman Greenspan and then under his successor. Effectively, the Federal Reserve has functioned as a massive momentum machine, feeding liquidity into the market at points when it perceived that it was needed and letting it run too long. This has left the U.S. economy with a massive unresolved problem—after creating serial bubbles, it has left in its wake an over-indebted economy filled with too much capacity in too many industries and too few sources of internal growth. In September 2009, capacity utilization in the U.S. and European factory sectors (they are linked in today's global economy) was running at a depressed 65 percent with modest prospects for meaningful recovery. Other sectors of the U.S. economy, such as retailing, hospitality, commercial real estate, and financial services (the latter after shrinking significantly in 2008 and 2009), were also suffering from significant overcapacity. The repercussions of procyclical policy will reverberate through the economy for years to come.

Private sector actors are going to do whatever they can to maximize their profits. After all, as discussed in the previous chapter, it is their fiduciary duty to do so, even if their actions hurt the overall economy. If low-cost leverage is available and can increase profits, economic actors will use it. Accordingly, the maintenance of artificially low interest rates is an invitation for people to borrow and spend.[18] Part of the goal of monetary policy at various times in recent years has clearly been to encourage and discourage risk-taking and the use of leverage. Until the financial crisis forced Chairman Bernanke and his colleagues to become far more aggressive and creative in employing the tools of the central bank (some might argue in contravention of the law), the primary tool used to manage monetary policy was the Federal Reserve's ability to set the overnight lending rate between banks, known as the discount rate. The problem is that the overall policy bent has been highly asymmetric—the Federal Reserve has been much quicker to lower rates and ease liquidity at the least sign of economic stress than to raise rates and tighten the flow of money when conditions improved.[19]

But during the Greenspan years, and the first couple of years of Bernanke's term that preceded the crisis, the Federal Reserve also refused to aggressively address growing imbalances in the economy. One reason for this hands-off approach was the oft-stated rationale that monetary policy should only be tightened to battle inflationary threats. This approach was based both on a narrow interpretation of the central bank's mandate and on Alan Greenspan's belief that it is impossible to identify a bubble when it is occurring. Hopefully by now the latter view has been completely discredited.

Contrary to Greenspan's oft-repeated assertion that it is impossible to identify a bubble, there are clear indicia of when asset prices are rising at unsustainable levels. Moreover, it doesn't require a bubble to justify the imposition of countercyclical policies. Any significant departure from long-term valuation trends should capture the attention and concern of central bankers and trigger a response. But the types of deviations from the norm that occurred in the decade preceding the crisis of 2008 were far more than mere departures from long-term trends; they were obvious bubbles that required no special economic knowledge to identify. Stock prices traded at a multiple of 351 earnings on the NASDAQ Stock Exchange at their peak on March 10, 2000; the average price/earnings multiple at previous market peaks has been no higher than 20 before that.[20] The risk premium (known as spread) on Credit Suisse's High Yield Index reached 271 basis points over Treasuries on May 31, 2007, a record level that exceeded the historical average of 570 to 580 basis points by over 50 percent.[21] Asking central bankers to rein in liquidity when markets reach such extreme points of overvaluation is a far cry from asking them to micromanage the financial system. Central bankers have the tools at their disposal to counteract such trends, and they should use them more proactively than the Federal Reserve has done. There is a better answer than simply choosing between stepping aside and letting bubbles run their course and creating a command economy with too much government intervention and control.

It was apparent to many observers, including this author,[22] that technology and Internet stocks were experiencing a bubble at the turn of the millennium. The NASDAQ was trading at a valuation of more than 20 times higher than its previous peak. The housing market was experiencing a similar unsustainable rise in prices in the mid-2000s when housing prices were well outpacing the growth in personal income. The corporate debt market was trading at unsustainably tight levels on the eve of the financial crisis when spreads were more than 50 percent tighter than historical norms. The fact that the Federal Reserve either did not recognize these bubbles or simply ignored them is either a severe indictment of its monetary management or a clear sign that formal reform of its mandate is overdue. Today's economy and markets would be unrecognizable to the people responsible for founding the Federal Reserve in 1913, and the central bank's original mandate needs to be revisited. The world cannot afford more procyclical policies that ignore bubbles that are blowing up in central bankers' faces and inflicting damage for which future generations will be left to pay.

Respected authorities such as the Bank for International Settlements have begun to call for countercyclical monetary policy management in recent years. Such a policy is often confused—deliberately perhaps by opponents—as a form of targeting asset prices, but such criticism is misplaced. Asset prices are a symptom of an underlying disease, not the disease itself. Monetary policy is designed to treat diseases, not symptoms, and should be more proactive in addressing burgeoning imbalances in order to help avoid the immense damage that market crises impose on economies and societies. No system can be perfect and eliminate imbalances, but a better system than the one operating today would proactively tighten policy by raising interest rates and tightening liquidity conditions based on movements in certain economic indicators.

Economist William White suggests the following indicators as some of those that might give rise to proactive tightening: "unusually rapid credit and monetary growth rates, unusually low interest rates, unusually high asset prices, unusual spending patterns (say very low household saving or unusually high investment levels). . . ." He also suggests that "unusually high external trade positions" be considered.[23] I would add a series of more specific indicators, including corporate credit spreads, mortgage spreads, differentials between changes in house prices and changes in personal income levels, and the absolute level of existing interest rates. The key question monetary authorities should be asking is whether markets are underpricing risk. The proper pricing of risk (which is obviously an art and not a science) is one of the most effective ways to prevent systemic imbalances from growing out of control and creating threats that turn into crises. Consideration of these factors in the fashioning of monetary policy would be a major improvement over the current narrow focus on inflation, which is itself a far different phenomenon than it was in 1913 when the Federal Reserve's original mandate was implemented.

Enhancing Systemic Transparency

One of the keys to encouraging productive investment and discouraging speculation would be to improve systemic transparency. Obscurity is the enemy of stability. If investors are deprived of the information necessary to evaluate specific securities or markets, they are incapable of accurately determining the level of risk they are assuming or that financial institutions are assuming. If they are not provided with the information regarding the holdings of financial institutions because these holdings are being concealed in off-balance-sheet entities, investors can't possibly evaluate the financial condition of these institutions. Without the ability to make that determination, investors are deprived of the ability to accurately evaluate financial industry or systemic risk. This increases uncertainty, which in turn leads investors to lose trust more easily in their counterparties and the markets themselves. Increasing uncertainty and decreasing trust in market mechanisms leads to less rational behavior as investors act to protect their own interests regardless of the consequences for the system, leading to full-blown market sell-offs like those we saw in 2008. Opponents of transparency need to understand that they are not only harming the system but they are hurting their own interests by ultimately promoting systemic instability.

If there is one common denominator among speculative practices in the financial markets, it is that they tend to be opaque. Earlier chapters in this book have examined two of these practices in detail: private equity (and related strategies that invest in nonpublic market securities) and derivatives. Each of these strategies depends in part on the ability to obscure investment holdings (and their valuations) from the prying eyes of investors and regulators. This is done in a number of different ways. For private equity and other nonpublic market strategies, obscurity is obtained through investments in securities that are not traded on a public market and can only be valued through highly subjective procedures that are unverifiable with any degree of certainty by reference to independent pricing sources. For derivatives (and related quantitative strategies), prices are obscured by how the instruments or trades themselves are dressed up in mathematical complexity that most investors and regulators are incapable of understanding. As a result of these strategems, these investment programs are effectively operating in regulatory and due diligence vacuums with few checks and balances. At best, it is up to auditors to confirm the validity and the accuracy of prices and investment returns, and auditors only offer after-the-fact reviews of investments and trades and can do little to prevent fraud or other abuses while they are occurring. Moreover, auditors generally have limited knowledge of the substance of what they are reviewing, so any protection they afford is extremely limited. Accordingly, the link between nonproductive investment strategies and opacity is deeply embedded and intentional. That link must be identified, and then these strategies must be forced into the light.

Ban Structured Investment Vehicles

There were times during the 2008 crisis when it felt as though the authorities were not going to be able to stop the stampede of panic selling that was threatening to send the markets into a tailspin from which they would never recover. Perhaps the greatest fear motivating panic sellers was fear of the unknown, which was hardly surprising in view of the revelations about hundreds of billions of dollars of highly risky assets that the world's largest financial institutions were concealing in undisclosed SIVs. The assets held in these vehicles were not included in traditional measures of these firms' leverage, which left regulators and investors in the dark with respect to the risks that these institutions were facing. As these entities lost their access to short-term funding in late 2007, legal commitments as well as reputational concerns and governmental and regulatory pressures forced tens of billions of dollars of these assets back onto the balance sheets of their sponsoring institutions, further burdening already overleveraged balance sheets and in some cases threatening outright insolvency. These SIVs were a large part of the shadow banking system that was able to operate outside the purview of regulators and permitted financial institutions to employ even more leverage than the already high levels of leverage they used on their balance sheets. Figure 8.1 shows the growth of these vehicles in the years prior to when the walls came crashing down.

Off-balance-sheet entities have produced nothing but trouble over the past decade. The regulatory solution to this problem is very simple. All types of off-balance-sheet entities should be banned, plain and simple. They serve no purpose other than to conceal information from regulators and investors. As economist Roger W. Garrison writes, "a market system whose credit markets involve risks that are partially concealed from the lender and partially shifted to others will be biased in the direction

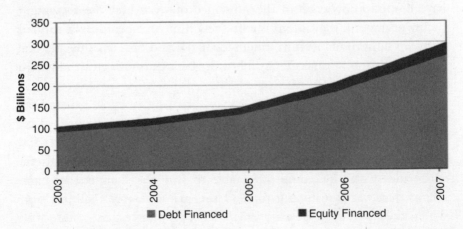

Figure 8.1   Growth of SIVs' Total Assets
SOURCE: Standard & Poor's.

of excessive risk-taking. And excessive risks are converted in time into excessive losses."[24] Banks in the United States and U.K. ended up having to take failed SIVs' assets back on their balance sheets and then go hat in hand to their governments for multibillion dollar bailouts. These losses landed on the doorsteps of taxpayers and their heirs, who are going to be paying the bills for the losses caused by these borrow-short lend-long schemes for decades to come. When it comes to reckless financial ideas (borrowing short-term funds to purchase complex, illiquid long-dated securities), SIVs were at the top of the list. There is no other solution than to remove them from the list permanently.

Virtually without exception, these vehicles were designed to reduce the amount of debt that financial institutions were allowed to incur directly on their balance sheets, which in turn preserved their credit ratings and lowered their borrowing costs. That was how Enron was able to maintain an investment-grade credit rating while the company teetered on the verge of insolvency; the debt that was so dangerous to its survival was effectively concealed from the eyes of investors in nondisclosed entities. Other companies, including some of the Big Three automakers and NYNEX Corp. before it became part of Verizon Communications, Inc., used these structures to their advantage to finance large building projects. NYNEX, for example, financed the multibillion dollar construction of its cable and telephone franchises in the United Kingdom through the use of complex off-balance-sheet structures developed by Citigroup in the 1990s. Outside investors (including the author's firm) were brought in and guaranteed a fixed return by NYNEX in exchange for serving as the so-called equity in the transactions. There was, of course, no real equity in these transactions because these investors were provided with a corporate guarantee on their investment by NYNEX's parent corporation, but tax attorneys were willing to provide opinions that granted the necessary equity qualification to the investment to keep the project off NYNEX's books. NYNEX was able to construct modern telecom and cable systems in the United Kingdom while preserving its credit rating, something it could have done at a slightly higher cost on its balance sheet. That project and many others had happy endings. Enron's story did not.

Enron's utilization of off-balance-sheet finance turned into a total debacle. What was once an innovative industrial and manufacturing company transformed its balance sheet into a house of cards by shuffling an increasing percentage of its assets into hidden entities with the active assistance of Citigroup, JPMorgan Chase, and Merrill Lynch. Enron took the idea of off-balance-sheet financing to its logical conclusion; by the time the company collapsed, most of its most valuable assets had been transferred off of its balance sheet and Enron Corporation had been rendered virtually an empty shell. Due to Enron's obfuscation of its true financial condition (ably assisted by its attorneys and accountants), the energy company was able to hang on to its investment-grade credit rating until shortly before its collapse.[25]

Enron's failure caused a sharp sell-off in the credit markets that inflicted serious losses on investors in the United States and around the world. Previously, few if any investment-grade companies had ever collapsed in such a dramatic fashion, plummeting from investment grade to insolvency in a short period of time. The very validity of an investment-grade rating was thrown into doubt, although the market regained its confidence soon enough to permit the issuance of hundreds of billions of dollars of mis-rated AAA-rated mortgage securities. Little did anybody realize that the losses caused by Enron's demise would be nothing compared to what would come to pass when hundreds of billions of dollars of AAA-ratings turned out to have been issued in error by Moody's and Standard & Poor's just a few years later.

The Enron story was sad enough on its own in terms of the losses of jobs and pensions suffered by its many well-intentioned employees. But there were actually more tragic (Karl Marx would call them farcical) aspects to what happened at Enron. The company's abuse of off-balance sheet vehicles and corporate disclosure laws was just a warm-up for the much larger abuses of off-balance sheet financing that were committed by the world's largest financial institutions.

One would think that the Enron collapse would have given rise to serious reforms to prevent further abuses of off-balance sheet vehicles. Yet nothing of the type occurred. After Enron collapsed, members of Congress pulled out their torches and pitchforks and took a brief break from the rubber chicken circuit to swear that off-balance sheet entities would never again be permitted to damage the U.S. financial system. While they were making these statements for the cameras, the largest financial institutions in the world were busy as beavers sponsoring and underwriting even larger off-balance-sheet entities whose subprime mortgages and other financial instruments were far riskier than the industrial assets held by Enron in its side-pockets. Moreover, these entities were hiding in plain sight because the debt obligations they issued had to be rated by Moody's and Standard & Poor's.

In a report dated March 13, 2002, entitled "Structured Investment Vehicle Criteria," Standard & Poor's wrote that it "rates the senior liabilities of all of the SIVs in the market 'AAA/A-1+,' [Standard & Poor's] highest long- and short-term rating categories. Standard and Poor's also provides counterparty ratings of 'AAA/A-1+' for all such vehicles." The methodology Standard & Poor's used was "to determine whether the senior debt of the vehicle will remain 'AAA/A-1+' rated until the last senior obligation has been honored in the event that the SIV needs to be wound down for whatever reason." In other words, the credit agency's "focus is on the tail end of the transaction." This focus on the end of the transaction is difficult to reconcile with the gross mismatch between the entity's assets and liabilities. When Standard & Poor's analyzed the risks that an SIV may face, it clearly acknowledged this mismatch, noting that "their weighted-average liability maturity is usually about four to six months, whereas the assets in the vehicle will have considerably longer average maturities." It is precisely at the end of the transaction that this mismatch will matter.

The report reads like a very reasonable document on its face until one realizes that these entities were almost entirely comprised of the "AAA/A-1+" securities that were being rated and had very little capital below them (a typical SIV held less than 5 percent equity capital as a cushion against losses). Moreover, the quality of the assets that were being purchased were wholly dependent on credit ratings being granted by no less than the same agencies that were rating the liabilities, the oligopolists Moody's and Standard & Poor's. The rating agencies' complicity in rating SIVs should have raised serious concerns about the competence and good faith of these agencies and served as a warning that the rating agencies were unsuited for the job to which the regulators had anointed them.

It is inexcusable that none of the leaders of the firms that financed or traded with these SIVs ever spoke out against them or took any action to reduce the systemic risk they posed. Anyone who presumed to be qualified to manage a bank or investment banking firm should have possessed the intelligence to understand that borrowing short to lend long is and has always been an idiotic proposition. Using enormous amounts of short-term leverage to purchase complex securities that in the most liquid markets only trade by appointment could only lead to one result. SIVs were not simply an accident waiting to happen—they were actually perfectly designed to impose systemic risk and any other outcome would have been a miracle. Each of these men (there are no women in such positions) bears a grim responsibility for allowing the SIV farce to have continued for so long and inflicted so much damage on the markets. It is also the height of hypocrisy for any member of the Senate Finance Committee or House Finance Committee to pretend that they were surprised that these time bombs existed. Yet no individual was ever held to account for the damage these entities wrought. There is no place for such Ponzi-structured entities in our financial system, and they should never see the light of day again.

Prohibit Dark Pools and High-Frequency Trading

Apparently hiding hundreds of billions of dollars of assets beyond the purview of regulators and investors did not sate Wall Street's hunger for making money in places where it can be concealed. Because even before all of the insolvent SIVs were liquidated, Wall Street was actively building covert trading networks that fed its insatiable desire for secrecy and opacity. Appropriately called "dark pools," a name that could have been torn from the pages of a novel by the paranoid science fiction writer Philip Dick, these private trading exchanges became major profit centers for large financial institutions and hedge funds in the mid-2000s. Dark pools are electronic trading networks that allow institutional investors to buy and sell stocks anonymously. These networks allow investors to conceal their identities as well as the number of shares they are buying or selling. Goldman Sachs operates one such network called SIGMA X; Credit Suisse Group AG operates one called Crossfinder; and there are others called Liquidnet, BATS, and Direct Edge. According to *The Economist*, there were 40 dark pools operating in the United States in mid-2009 that accounted for an estimated 9 percent of traded equities. Other sources estimated the volume to be higher, which highlighted the fact that nobody could know exactly what was going on in these hidden corners of the investment universe because their very *raison d'être* was to conceal information from the eyes of regulators and investors. Having just experienced an unprecedented financial crisis that was caused in part by a lack of transparency on the part of the world's largest financial institutions, dark pools qualified as one of the most dangerous ideas to come to life on Wall Street since SIVs and naked credit default swaps. These secret trading networks pose significant systemic risks because they suppress the very transparency that builds confidence in markets. The minute these networks came to light, they should have been closed down.

High-frequency trading is a phenomenon that often takes place on these dark pool exchanges. Actually, the correct term is high-frequency algorithmic trading, because it is a trading strategy based on using algorithmic formulas to analyze market data and then predict and exploit likely market movements. High frequency trading is closely linked to something called "flash orders," a particularly noxious Wall Street invention in which dark pool exchanges allow traders to briefly see and react to certain orders ahead of the rest of the market. Flash orders are nothing other than a thinly disguised version of front-running, a blatantly illegal activity. By giving certain traders a preview of order flow, it gives these traders an unfair advantage over other traders who are not privy to such information. The fact that some of the world's largest financial institutions were engaging in this practice right under the noses of regulators is a sad commentary on how deeply inequities have become embedded in the financial system.

Wall Street loves these private trading networks, where business is booming and profits are growing. For example, Citadel Investment Group LLC disclosed in litigation that its high-frequency trading business produced more than $1 billion in profits in 2008 (a year in which the firm's hedge funds lost billions of dollars). Needless to say, quantitative trading of the type that occurs on these dark pools is nothing more than mere speculation and adds nothing to the productive capacity of the economy. Moreover, these strategies have had a deleterious effect on markets in recent years by increasing volatility and causing securities prices to move without any connection to fundamental changes in the underlying company's financial condition. Proponents of these activities argue that dark pools enhance market liquidity, but liquidity without transparency breeds market volatility and uncertainty. Add higher volatility to the mix and you have a singularly bad idea. Why can't these trades be done with full disclosure and in the full light of day? How does hiding these trades in the shadows enhance liquidity or market stability?

No less than Paul Wilmott, a highly respected figure in the quantitative investing world (and founder of the quantitative finance journal *Wilmott*), warned of the dangers of high-frequency trading in an opinion piece in the *New York Times:* "Thus the problem with the sudden explosion of high-frequency trading is that it may increasingly destabilize the market. Hedge funds won't necessarily care whether the increased volatility causes stocks to rise or fall, as long as they can get in and out quickly with a profit. But the rest of the economy will care."[25] Moreover, the economy will care because the financial markets do not simply provide an outlet for financial speculation; like banks, they also provide a public utility function whereby they serve as a source of growth capital for companies. Dark pools are private playgrounds that hedge funds and investment houses use to trade in secret; allowing them to operate is singularly bad public policy. As we saw in 2008, when the markets fail and can no longer perform their public utility function because of damage caused by excessive speculation, the economy suffers severe damage. One of the best ways to ensure the healthy operation of markets is to require them to operate transparently, and high-frequency trading on dark pool exchanges is designed to do precisely the opposite.

Dark pools stand in sharp contrast to other recent regulatory efforts to bring greater transparency to trading markets. Several years ago, corporate bond trading was forced into the open through the introduction of the TRACE system, which requires all broker-dealers to report all public bond trades within 15 minutes of execution. In view of the consensus in favor of transparency, and the obvious dangers of opacity, it makes absolutely no sense to permit large parts of the equity markets to retreat into the shadows while at the same time forcing corporate bond trading into the light. Such a regime can only contribute to market confusion and instability.

Fortunately, proponents of reform are likely to be able to claim a victory in this area. It appears that dark pools and flash orders will not enjoy nearly as long a run as SIVs and other abusive practices. In the summer of 2009, the Securities and Exchange Commission (at the urging of Senator Charles Schumer of New York) began taking steps to ban flash trading, which was an important step to leveling the playing field for all participants in the stock markets. In October 2009, the Securities and Exchange Commission voted to propose lowering to 0.25 percent from 5 percent the daily volume in a company's shares that can be executed on such secret exchanges before quotes must be made public. The agency decided against permitting a much higher 1 or 2 percent limit because it felt that such a limit would allow too much room for dark pools to operate freely and conceal meaningful trading information from the public markets. This rulemaking should sound the death knell for this singularly dangerous idea that, if not derailed, would undoubtedly lead to illegal activity, market volatility, and systemic risk.

★★★

It is unlikely that the financial reforms that are ultimately legislated will be sufficient to prevent another market crisis in the relatively near future. The finance industry still has far too much influence in Washington, D.C., to permit any kind of reform that significantly reduces instability. This is both a tragedy and a farce. It is a tragedy because future crises are not avoidable but could be rendered far less damaging if meaningful reforms are adopted. It is a farce because the world suffers every day from its previous regulatory failures. To put it bluntly, we know better and we still refuse to do what is necessary to enhance financial stability. Accordingly, we will have nobody but ourselves to blame the next time we are staring into the abyss.

CONCLUSION

"This Is Later"

O n April 16, 2007, the American novelist Cormac McCarthy was awarded the Pulitzer Prize for his novel *The Road*. *The Road* is an unbearably painful tale of a father and son, seemingly among the last surviving men on earth, traveling an American landscape that has been rendered a postapocalyptic charnel house by a faintly hinted-at nuclear conflagration. The love between father and son are the last shards of human feeling left in a world destroyed by hatred and war. Technologically advanced man has left behind a gray and ruined landscape.

> In those first years the roads were peopled with refugees shrouded up in their clothing. Wearing masks and goggles, sitting in their rags by the side of the road like ruined aviators. Their barrows heaped with shoddy. Towing wagons or carts. Their eyes bright in their skulls. Creedless shells of men tottering down the causeways like migrants in a feverland. The frailty of everything revealed at last. Old and troubling issues resolved into nothingness and night. The last instance of a thing takes the class with it. Turns out the light and is gone. Look around you. Ever is a long time. But the boy knew what he knew. That ever is no time at all.[1]

Two and a half years later, in December 2009, the film version of
the novel was released. In bringing this bleak and complex novel to
film, the producers reportedly had a difficult time identifying shooting
locations. In the end, however, they didn't have to travel far from the
American heartland. Most of the film was shot near Pittsburgh, Pennsylvania. As one of the film's producers explained to *Rolling Stone* magazine,
Pennsylvania was chosen because "it offered such a pleasing array of postapocalyptic scenery: deserted coalfields, run-down parts of Pittsburgh,
windswept dunes."[2] Had the film been made after the 2008 financial
crisis, which saw the closing of dozens of manufacturing plants around
the country to accompany thousands of empty foreclosed homes, the
filmmakers undoubtedly would have had many more locations from
which to choose.

In the end, it is not the media or politicians who are going to lead
us out of the mire of ill-begotten policies. With very few exceptions,
these two groups were co-opted a long time ago into serving the status
quo. Instead, we need to look at artists whose loyalty is to their personal
vision of the world. It may seem odd to some readers to conclude a
book on finance with a discussion of Cormac McCarthy, but careful
readers of the preceding pages should not find the appearance of one
of our greatest living novelists jarring at all. *The Death of Capital* has
maintained from the beginning that finance serves a larger purpose in
the world than a merely economic one. Capital is the lifeblood of society, making it possible for people to eat and be sheltered and learn
and heal. Only after people fill these needs can they begin to appreciate
the beauty and love that life offers instead of focusing on its struggle and pain. If there is passion in this book, it is because I believe
that the forces responsible for the death of capital, if successful, will
extinguish the best hope for mankind to move forward and meet the
challenges of his future. I, for one, will not allow that to happen without
speaking out.

Look around at our culture and society. We must be nearing the end
of things, the end of something. McCarthy could have been writing
the coda for our last days when, in *The Road*, he wrote in the voice of
the father: "No list of things to be done. The day providential to itself.
The hour. There is no later. This is later. All things of grace and beauty

such that one holds them to one's heart have a common provenance in pain. Their birth in grief and ashes. So he whispered to the boy. I have you."[3] The father does not survive in McCarthy's tale, and the son is left to carry on without him. While bereft, the son is fortified by the memory of his father's love and the words that they shared as they struggled on the road together, trying to simply survive the wreckage that other men wrought for them and the rest of mankind.

It is not too late to make the necessary changes to stabilize our financial system against instability and avarice. But time is running out, both for those of us well into our lives as well as for our children. In the novelist's words: "There is no later. This is later." At the heart of every technical discussion about finance lies a simple truth: Without a functioning and stable economy, civilization will ultimately fall into barbarism and chaos. That is the undeniable and redundant lesson of history.

The Jewish-German philosopher Walter Benjamin, who committed suicide at the Spanish border in 1940 rather than surrender to the Nazis, set a very high standard for critical thought when he wrote that, "only that historian will have the gift of fanning the spark of hope in the past who is firmly convinced that even the dead will not be safe from the enemy if he wins. And this enemy has not ceased to be victorious."[4] In 2008, we met the enemy—and the enemy was us.

It may not say anything very positive about the human species to argue that it requires economic well-being in order to keep from destroying itself, but that is the undeniable reality that history has taught us. The most compelling reason to reform our financial system—for pragmatists as well as moralists—is to ensure that society continues to move forward in a manner that improves human life on this planet for all people, not just a small elite that continues to fool itself into believing that it will be able to defend itself against the leagues of sufferers when they rush the ramparts.

The Death of Capital has had harsh words for many of the established ideas and institutions that control the world's capital. These words are deeply felt but they have been offered in the spirit of the great Romantic poet William Blake's adage, "Opposition is true friendship." We are running out of time. We continue to cling to faulty financial theories, invest in unproductive strategies that enrich managers but impoverish investors, and refuse to address the instabilities bred by procyclical monetary policy and complex financial products that fail to enhance the quality of human life on the planet. Karl Marx never wrote what comes in history's third act, after tragedy and farce. We still have a chance to write that it ends in triumph if we start taking bold action now.

NOTES

Introduction: The 2008 Crisis—Tragedy or Farce?

1. Karl Marx, *The Eighteenth Brumaire of Louis Napoleon* (International Publishers: New York, 1972), 15. Actually, what he wrote was the following: "Hegel remarks somewhere that all facts and personages of great importance in world history occur, as it were, twice. He forgot to add: the first time as tragedy, the second as farce."

2. There is a fourth characteristic that receives less attention in this book than it deserves, the fact that the world's economies and financial markets connected through vast networks in which information is exchanged at the speed of light 24 hours a day. As a result, what happens in one market often has consequences in other markets that are seemingly unrelated and inexplicable in fundamental economic terms. The proverbial anecdote about a fly flapping its wings in Africa causing a hurricane in Miami is a reality in modern markets. Because economies and markets function through networks, they generate both negative and positive feedback loops that tend to significantly increase volatility and risk. This completely redefines key investment concepts such as correlation and diversification as they have been traditionally understood. Today, short-term price movements in securities are primarily the result of so-called "technical" factors, which means that the mechanisms of interlinked markets move prices in ways that can only be understood in terms of the structural logic of these markets and not in terms of what is happening to the underlying companies whose securities prices are being affected.

259

3. The growth of finance is amply supported by statistical evidence. Between 1994 and 2000, the profits earned by the financial sector doubled and accounted for 75 percent of the increase in total corporate profits after payment of interest accrued. By 2000, financial profits accounted for 40 percent of total corporate profits. Even during the recession of the early 2000s, these profits came to constitute as much as 50 percent of total corporate profits, according to Morgan Stanley. See Steve Galbraith et. al, "Bank of America" and "Fading Fog" in Morgan Stanley *U.S. and the Americas Investment Research*, June 21, 2001, and September 21, 2003, respectively.

4. Lawrence E. Mitchell, *The Speculation Economy: How Finance Triumphed Over Industry* (San Francisco: Berrett-Koehler Publishers, Inc., 2007), 3. Mitchell's thesis is that "[t]he giant modern corporation was a phenomenon distinct from the forms and processes of industrialization. . . . The giant modern corporation was created for a new purpose, to sell stock, stock that would make its promoters and financiers rich." (9)

5. Ibid., 3.

6. Charles Kindleberger, *Manias, Panics and Crashes: A History of Financial Crises* Revised Edition (New York: Basic Books, 1989), 19.

7. The fact that capacity utilization in the United States and Europe was running at approximately 65 percent during 2009 suggested that lending to build new facilities would not have been productive.

8. Others argue, with some support, that the bailout had little to do with preserving these institutions' ability to serve the public but was instead another example of a small financial elite bailing itself out without paying heed to the long-term consequences of what it was doing.

9. Unfortunately, these mathematical trading models have turned out to do little more than dress up a variety of momentum-driven leveraged investment strategies. They tell us little about how real-world markets behave. Benoit Mandelbrot, the mathematician who founded fractal theory, calculated that if the DJIA followed a normal bell curve distribution, it should have moved by more than 3.4 percent on 58 days between 1913 and 2003; instead it moved by that amount on 1,001 days. It should have moved by 4.5 percent on six days but moved that amount on 366 days. And it should have moved by more than 7 percent only once in 300,000 years but in the twentieth century did so 48 times. Source: *The Economist*, "A Special Report on the Future of Finance," January 24, 2009, 14.

10. Robin Blackburn, "The Subprime Crisis," *New Left Review* 50 (March/April 2008): 67.

11. Fortunately, this differential was narrowed when the tax on corporate dividends was lowered by President George W. Bush.

12. See Thomas I. Palley, "Financialization: What It Is and Why It Matters," The Levy Economics Institute of Bard College, Working Paper No. 525, December 2007, 4.

13. A third manifestation of this changed world, which would play itself out most publicly and painfully in the slow-motion meltdown of the U.S. automobile industry in the first years of the twenty-first century, was the increasing flexibility of global labor markets. By 2008, labor markets had grown much more flexible than they were two decades earlier, and organized labor had lost much of its power. Labor was subject to temporary contracts, immigration pressures, and off-shoring in ways that had emasculated its economic strength. Western manufacturing, particularly in industries like autos and textiles, had been decimated as the outsourcing of plants to lower-cost jurisdictions, just-in-time production, and other changes rendered high-cost U.S. and European countries uncompetitive. U.S. labor unions effectively negotiated themselves out of business with their demands for lax work rules and expensive health and pension benefits that helped their members in the short-term but contributed to the bankruptcies of their employers in the long-term. It would not be far off the mark to argue that the approach taken by labor leaders in the United States to try to extract as much as possible for their unions was analogous to the approach adopted by fiduciaries in terms of focusing on maximizing economic gains at the expense of other noneconomic interests, with similarly damaging results to the overall economic interests of their constituents. See Chapter 7.

14. Source: Federal Reserve's Flow of Funds data.

15. The other major economic power that suffers from a comparable debt-to-GDP ratio is Japan, which has been hanging in economic suspended animation for two decades. The Organization for Economic Cooperation and Development (OECD) projects that Japan's debt-to-GDP ratio will reach 197 percent in 2010. While the U.S. and Japanese economies are profoundly different, they are also increasingly linked in today's globalized world. The lesson of Japan should not, therefore, be dismissed. And the trend that country represents is not one the United States wants to follow.

16. Moreover, the currency links between developed countries and developing countries forced both groups to pursue similar expansionary monetary policies in the aftermath of the 2008 financial crisis despite the fact that developed countries were highly indebted, deficit-ridden economies while many developing countries were creditor nations running major surpluses. In 2009, this appeared to be creating a series of new bubbles around the world, for instance, in Chinese stock and commodities markets.

17. Consider, for example, the theories that were developed to support the Internet bubble by writers such as George Gilder, Kevin Kelly, Ray Kurzweil,

and research analysts such as Mary Meeker and Henry Blodget. See Michael
E. Lewitt, "New Math or New Economy? Some Ruminations on the 1999
Stock Market Bubble," *Trusts & Estates* (February 2002).

18. Scott Lanman and Steve Matthews, "Greenspan Concedes to 'Flaw' in His
Market Ideology," Bloomberg.com (October 23, 2008), www.bloomberg.
com/apps/news?pid=20601087&sid=ah5qh9Up4rIg. See also David Leon-
hardt, "Greenspan's Mea Culpa," Economix (blog), *New York Times* (October 23, 2008), http://economix.blogs.nytimes.com/2008/10/23/greenspans-
mea-culpa/.

19. Hyman P. Minsky, *Stabilizing an Unstable Economy* (New Haven: Yale University Press, 1986), 250–251.

20. Niall Ferguson, *The War of the Worlds: History's Age of Hatred* (London: Allen
Lane, 2006), xli.

21. Ferguson, *The War of the Worlds*, p. lix. Italics in original.

22. Ibid, lxi–lxii.

23. "The State of Public Finances: Outlook and Medium-Term Policies after
the 2008 Crisis," International Monetary Fund (March 6, 2009), www.
imf.org/external/np/pp/eng/2009/030609.pdf. I am indebted to Thomas
Gallagher of the ISI Group for bringing this chart and its implications to my
attention.

24. "Federal Government Faces Balloon in Debt Payments," *New York Times*,
November 23, 2009, page A1.

Chapter 1: The Death of Capital

1. The Baltic Dry Index is issued daily by the London-based Baltic Exchange. It
"provides an assessment of the price of moving the major raw materials by sea.
Taking in 26 shipping routes measured on a time charter and voyage basis, the
index covers Handymax, Panamax, and Capesize dry bulk carriers carrying
a range of commodities including coal, iron ore, and grain." The Baltic Dry
Index is considered to be an accurate barometer of economic activity because
dry bulk consists of raw material inputs into the production of intermediate
or finished goods such as concrete, electricity, steel, and food. It is also one
of the data points to which hedge funds and other influential investors pay a
great deal of attention.

2. Wealth itself is defined by the *Oxford English Dictionary* as "the condition
of being happy and prosperous; well-being" and also "an instance or kind of
prosperity; a felicity, blessing," as well as "spiritual well-being" and "prosperity
consisting in abundance of possessions; 'worldly goods,' valuable possessions,
esp. in great abundance, riches, affluence."

3. Capital is not money per se, but money is one form of capital as it is viewed by economic actors exchanging economic values in the economy. Money is itself a highly complex form of capital, but it is only one form of capital.

4. See, for example, "College Try: Chicago's Stock Sale—How the University's Unloading of $600 Million in Shares Divided Its Managers," *Wall Street Journal*, August 21, 2009, C1. "The endowment model contained a colossal intellectual error in thinking—that long-term investors don't need short-term liquidity," says Robert Jaegar of BNY Mellon Asset Management.

5. There is a significant difference between a capitalist economy and a democratic society, as China exemplifies. Democracy arguably remains the best system for engendering political stability in the context of a variety of different economic systems.

6. Peter Bernstein, *Capital Ideas: The Improbable Origins of Modern Wall Street* (New York: The Free Press, 1992), 2.

7. Peter Bernstein, *Against the Gods: The Remarkable Story of Risk* (New York: John Wiley & Sons, 1996), 334.

8. See, for example, William A. Fleckenstein with Frederick Sheehan, *Greenspan's Bubbles: The Age of Ignorance at the Federal Reserve* (New York: McGraw Hill, 2008); Peter Hartcher, *Bubble Man: Alan Greenspan and the Missing 7 Trillion Dollars* (New York: W.W. Norton & Company, 2006); Frederick Sheehan, *Panderer to Power: The Untold Story of How Alan Greenspan Enriched Wall Street and Left a Legacy of Recession* (New York: McGraw Hill, 2009). Moreover, despite his now infamous 1996 warning that stock prices had reached levels of "irrational exuberance," often it seemed like Greenspan was looking to the stock market for economic guidance.

9. Peter Bernstein, *Capital Ideas Evolving* (Hoboken, NJ: John Wiley & Sons, 2007), xviii.

10. In its most dangerous form, debt came to be disguised as equity in the form of various types of bonds such as lower rated corporate bonds (junk bonds) and mortgage bonds (subprime and Alt-A mortgage bonds).

Chapter 2: Capital Ideas

1. Professor Robert Brenner of UCLA has done comprehensive work analyzing corporate profitability (or the lack thereof). See Robert Brenner, *The Boom and the Bubble: The U.S. in the World Economy* (New York: Verso, 2002) and Robert Brenner, *The Economics of Global Turbulence* (New York: Verso, 2006). Professor Brenner's work dispels the myths surrounding U.S. productivity growth and demonstrates that much of the economic expansion of the last two decades has been little more than a mirage.

2. Fernand Braudel, *The Wheels of Commerce: Civilization and Capitalism, 15th–18th Century, Volume II,* (New York, Harper & Row, 1982), 28–29. Footnotes omitted.

3. This discussion was heavily influenced by the interpretation of Adam Smith's work found in James Otteson's study, *Adam Smith's Marketplace of Life* (New York: Cambridge University Press, 2002).

4. Adam Smith, *The Wealth of Nations*, 15.

5. The famous phrase "invisible hand" appears only once in *The Wealth of Nations* in a discussion of imports: "By preferring the support of domestic to that of foreign industry, he intends only his own security; and by directing that industry in such a manner as its produce may be of the greatest value, he intends only his own gain, and he is in this, as in many other cases, led by an invisible hand to promote an end which was no part of his intention. Nor is it always the worse for the society that it was no part of it. By pursuing his own interest he frequently promotes that of the society more effectually than when he really intends to promote it." (484–485) The phrase also appears in *The Theory of Moral Sentiments* (242) in a section making the dubious argument that the wealthy end up consuming no more than what they need and sharing the rest with the poor: "They [the wealthy] are led by an invisible hand to make nearly the same distribution of the necessaries of life which would have been made had the earth been divided into equal portions among all its inhabitants; and thus, without intending it, without knowing it, advance the interest of the society, and afford means to the multiplication of the species."

6. *The Theory of Moral Sentiments*, 3–4.

7. This statement was included in the second, third, fourth and fifth editions of *The Theory of Moral Sentiments* and excluded from later editions, including some popular modern editions. It can be found on page 152 of the Cambridge Texts in the History of Philosophy edition of Adam Smith, *The Theory of Moral Sentiments*, Knud Haakonssen, editor (New York, Cambridge University Press, 2002).

8. For a thoughtful interpretation of Smith's "impartial spectator," see James R. Otteson, *Adam Smith's Marketplace of Life* (New York: Cambridge University Press, 2002), 42–64.

9. Dennis C. Rasmussen, *The Problems and Promise of Commercial Society: Adam Smith's Response to Rousseau* (University Park, PA: The Pennsylvania State University Press, 2008), 114.

10. Ibid,. 121.

11. Ibid, 122.

12. *TMS*, 206, 207.

13. *TMS*, 205.

14. Irving L. Janis, *Groupthink* (Boston: Houghton Mifflin Company, 1982), 10.

15. *TMS*, 22.

16. Otteson, *Adam Smith's Marketplace of Life*, 124. Footnotes omitted.

17. Stuart Kauffmann, *At Home in the Universe: The Search for the Laws of Self-Organization and Complexity* (New York: Oxford University Press), 8.

18. Ibid., 15.

19. Ibid.

20. See, for example, Christopher Hitchins, "He's Back: The Current Financial Crisis and the Enduring Relevance of Marx," *The Atlantic* (April 2009): 88–95; Leo Panitch, "Thoroughly Modern Marx," *Foreign Policy* (May/June 2009): 140–45.

21. Francis Wheen, *Marx's Das Kapital: A Biography* (New York: Grove Press, 2006), 4. See also Francis Wheen, *Karl Marx: A Life* (New York: W.W. Norton & Company, Inc., 1999), p. 304–311.

22. See David Harvey, *The Limits to Capital* (New York: Verso, 1999), 20.

23. Karl Marx, *Capital*, Vol. 1 (New York: International Publishers, 1967), 154, 155.

24. Ibid., 154–155.

25. Karl Marx, *Grundrisse.* (London: Penguin Books, 1973), 260–261.

26. Marx, *Capital,* Vol. 1, 153.

27. This formulation raises profound questions about the moral values a society places on different kinds of work. For example, why does American society value the work of investment bankers more highly than the work of teachers?

28. Marx, *Capital*, Vol.1, 72.

29. Ibid.

30. Harvey, *The Limits to Capital*, 17.

31. David Harvey, *The Condition of Postmodernity* (Cambridge, MA., Blackwell Publishers, Inc., 1990), 100.

32. Leszek Kolakowski, *Main Currents of Marxism* (New York: W.W. Norton & Company, Ltd., 2008), 227.

33. Ibid., 227.

34. Marx, *Capital*, Vol. 1, 76.

35. Mark C. Taylor, *Confidence Games Money and Markets in a World without Redemption (*Chicago: University of Chicago Press, 2004), 8.

36. Marx, *Capital*, Vol. 1, 102.

37. Ibid., 196.

38. Ibid., 102.

39. Hyman Minsky, *John Maynard Keynes* (New York: Columbia University Press, 1975), 59.

40. John Maynard Keynes, *The General Theory of Employment, Interest and Money* (New York: Harcourt Brace & Company, 1964), 158.

41. Ibid.

42. Ibid., 155.

43. Ibid., 156.

44. Ibid., 202.

45. Ibid. 161–62.

46. Ibid. 162–63.

47. Ibid., 37.

48. Ibid., 145.

49. Ibid., 154.

50. Ibid., 155.

51. Minsky, *John Maynard Keynes*, 1.

52. Ibid. 11–12.

53. PIMCO's Paul McCulley deserves credit for being the earliest to bring Minsky's work to a wider audience. During the 1998 Russian debt crisis, McCulley coined the term "Minsky moment" to describe the market meltdown. In December 2004, I wrote in an issue of *The HCM Market Letter* entitled "The Ponzi Museum" that I was "firmly of the view that the credit markets are experiencing a bubble no less overblown than the stock market bubble of 1998–2000." *The HCM Market Letter*, December 21, 2004.

54. Minsky, *Stabilizing an Unstable Economy*, (New Haven: Yale University Press, 1986), 206–208.

55. Hyman Minsky, "The Financial-Instability Hypothesis: Capitalist Processes and the Behavior of the Economy," in Charles P. Kindleberger and Jean-Pierre Laffargue, ed., *Financial Crises Theory, History & Policy* (New York: Cambridge University Press, 1982), 25.

56. Minsky in Kindleberger, ed., 37. And in a warning that unfortunately came too late for many investors, Minsky pointed out the risks inherent in many investment structures that involve indefinite entry and exit points: "Incidentally, what in retrospect appears to be a fraudulent operation often has its root in a 'speculative' or 'honest Ponzi' financial arrangement where the 'payoff' is not forthcoming as anticipated. 'Fraud' often is an ex-post result and is not always ex-ante in conception."

57. Ibid., 37.

Chapter 3: Empty Promises

1. Source: The Bank Credit Analyst.

2. Martin Wolf, *Fixing Global Finance* (Baltimore: The Johns Hopkins University Press, 2008), 10–11.

3. Ibid, 12.

4. Diversification is designed to prevent individual securities in a portfolio from acting in a correlated manner. As discussed in Chapter 7, this thesis breaks down in many modern markets due to hidden correlations.

5. Robert J. Shiller, *The Subprime Solution: How Today's Financial Crisis Happened, and What to Do about It* (Princeton, N.J.; Princeton University Press, 2008), 22.

6. Peter Bernstein, *Against the Gods: The Remarkable Story of Risk* (New York: John Wiley & Sons, 1996), 334.

7. See Gretchen Morgenson, "If Lenders Say 'The Dog Ate Your Mortgage'," *New York Times*, October 25, 2009. Morgenson describes a case that was decided in federal bankruptcy court for the Southern District of New York in which Judge Robert D. Drain ruled that the lender, PHH Mortgage, had failed to prove its claim to a delinquent borrower's home and instead wiped out the $461,263 mortgage on the property. Whether this ruling will stand on appeal remains to be seen, but it points to the growing problems with the form that home ownership has assumed in the United States.

Chapter 4: Financialization

1. The limited writings on financialization include Robin Blackburn, "Finance and the Fourth Dimension," *New Left Review*, 39 May/June 2006, 39–70; Gerald A. Epstein, ed., *Financialization and the World Economy* (Northampton, MA: Edward Elgar, 2005); Greta R. Kippner, "The Financialization of the American Economy," *Socio-Economic Review*, Vol. 3, 2005, 173–208; John Bellamy Foster, "The Financialization of Capitalism," *Monthly Review*, Vol. 58, No. 11, April 2007; Thomas I. Palley, "Financialization: What It Is and Why It Matters," The Levy Economics Institute, Working Paper No. 525, December 2007; Randy Martin, *Financialization of Daily Life* (Philadelphia, PA: Temple University Press, 2002).

2. Peter Gowan, "Crisis on Wall Street," *New Left Review* (Jan/Feb 2009): 22.

3. The foremost writers on the cultural aspects of financialization—although they don't use the term—are Frederic Jameson, particularly in *Postmodernism or The Cultural Logic of Late Capitalism* (Durham, North Carolina: Duke University Press, 1991) and the essays in *The Cultural Turn Selected Writings on the Postmodern, 1983–1998* (New York: Verso, 1998), and Mark C. Taylor in

Confidence Games: Money and Markets in a World Without Redemption (Chicago: The University of Chicago Press, 2004).

4. Taylor, *Confidence Games*, 7.

5. Ibid., 7.

6. Kevin Phillips, *Boiling Point Democrats, Republicans, and the Decline of Middle-Class Prosperity* (New York: Random House, 1993), 193–194.

7. Ibid., 194. For Braudel's observation that the growth of finance is a sign of late stage economic power, see Fernand Braudel, *The Perspective of the World* (Los Angeles: University of California Press, 1992), 243.

8. Kevin Phillips, *Arrogant Capital: Washington, Wall Street, and the Frustration of American Politics* (New York: Little, Brown & Company, 1994), 81. See also Gerald A. Epstein and Arjun Jayadev, "The Rise of Rentier Incomes in OECD Countries: Financialization, Central Bank Policy and Labor Solidarity," in Gerald A. Epstein, ed., *Financialization and the World Economy* (Northampton, MA, Edward Elgar Publishing, Inc., 2005), 46–74.

9. Ibid., 82.

10. Robert N. McCauley, Judith S. Ruud, and Frank Iacono, *Dodging Bullets: Changing U.S. Corporate Capital Structures in the 1980s and 1990s* (Boston: MIT Press, 1999), 88.

11. "Banks Try to Stiff-Arm New Rule," *Wall Street Journal*, June 4, 2009, C1.

12. This definition is also adopted by Greta R. Krippner in an important article on financialization. See "The Financialization of the American Economy," *Socio-Economic Review*, Vol. 3, 2005, 173–208. Among Krippner's most important observations is that nonfinancial firms have come to earn an increasing percentage of their profits through finance as opposed to their nonfinance activities. Examples of this include General Electric Company and General Electric Credit Corporation and many other companies that have entered the finance business, from the retailer Target Corp. to the airplane manufacturer Textron, Inc.

13. David Harvey, *The Condition of Postmodernity: An Enquiry into the Origins of Cultural Change* (Cambridge, MA.: Blackwell, 1989), 147.

14. Ibid., 142.

15. Ibid., 147.

16. Ibid., 194.

17. Ibid.

18. Giovanni Arrighi, *The Long Twentieth Century: Money, Power and the Origin of our Times* (New York: Verso, 1994), ix.

19. Arrighi, *Adam Smith in Peking*, p. 161.

20. Ibid., 8.

21. Ibid., 142.

22. Brenner, *The Economics of Global Turbulence*, 307

23. Ibid., 307.

24. Arrighi, *The Long Twentieth Century*, 5.

25. I would like to thank David Gerstenhaber of Argonaut Capital Management for helping me formulate my thoughts about consumption. See Argonaut Capital Management, November 23, 2009, "The U.S. Economy in 2010: Will the Inventory Cycle and a Rebound in the Labor Market Power the Economy Back to Trend Growth?"

26. The end of the gold standard (1973) unfettered the dollar from precious metal backing and laid the seeds for unconstrained credit growth. The economic consequences of the movement off of the gold standard have been incalculable, but the psychic effects have been no less profound. Gold is considered by many to be an anachronistic investment, others (including this author) consider it a psychological one, but nobody should forget that gold is one of the few forms of tangible money extant. Gold is a promise kept. Gold is the antiderivative, the anticredit default swap, the anti-LBO. More important, it is the antidollar, the antifiat currency. And a fiat currency is the ultimate example of a promise, increasingly, a promise that can't be kept. Ironically, gold may be considered old fashioned because it lacks promissory elements. Of course, there are gold futures and gold derivatives, and the very popular SPDR Gold Trust (GLD), but good old-fashioned gold is just a piece of metal that you hold in your hand or store in a vault. It is a tangible thing in a world that increasingly values intangible things. It is grounded in a world where few things are grounded. Most important, it is a physical good that is limited in supply. If the end of the world ever comes, it will be your best friend.

Chapter 5: From Innovators to Undertakers

1. "Get Ready for the Private-Equity Shakeout," The Boston Consulting Group, December 2008, 2.

2. Ludovic Phalippou and Oliver Gottschalg, "The Performance of Private Equity Funds," Working Paper posted August 7, 2005, last revised March 28, 2008. http://ssrn.com/abstract=473221.

3. Source: Estimates by International Financial Services London; Preqin.

4. Michael C. Jensen, "Eclipse of the Public Corporation," *Harvard Business Review*, September-October 1989, 61–73, at 61. While many of Professor Jensen's arguments in support of leveraged buyouts in this article have become outdated by subsequent events during the past 20 years, he was very perceptive in understanding the constructive role these transactions played in the private equity industry's early days. His biggest error was believing that private equity

firms would solve the agency problem rather than simply create new versions of it and in the process badly abuse the trust of their own limited partners.

5. For example, the employment of short-term strategies such as having portfolio companies raise additional debt to pay dividends to their private equity sponsors gave the lie a long time ago to the argument that private equity firms are long-term investors.

6. Hyman P. Minsky, "Schumpeter and Finance," in Salvatore Biasco, Alessandro Roncaglia and Michele Salvati, ed., *Market and Institutions in Market Development: Essays in Honour of Paulo Sylos Labini* (New York: Palgrave, 1990), 112.

7. Jensen, 64.

8. The fact that Chrysler Corp. was not liquidated upon filing for bankruptcy in early 2009 but was instead forced into the hands of the Italian carmaker Fiat S.p.A. was a failure of industrial policy. Post-bankruptcy, the company remained uncompetitive and a candidate for liquidation even after its deal with Fiat. The Chrysler bailout was nothing more than a jobs bill designed to minimize short-term job losses at a time when the U.S economy was experiencing steep increases in unemployment. Policymakers chose an expedient short-term solution (that likely will be unsuccessful) that only exacerbated the long-term problem of excess capacity in automobile manufacturing. As a result, it will take that much longer for the U.S. automobile manufacturing industry to return to profitability.

9. Robert W. Parenteau, "The Late 1990s U.S. Bubble: Financialization in the Extreme," in Gerald A. Epstein, ed., *Financialization and the World Economy* (Northampton, MA.: Edward Elgar Publishing, Inc., 2005), 134.

10. Ibid., 134.

11. By December 2009, these types of financing structures were creeping back into the market, suggesting that a new credit bubble was beginning to build as the Federal Reserve felt it necessary to keep interest rates at an effective zero rate.

12. Ludovic Phalippou and Oliver Gottschalg. Management, "Performance of Private Equity Funds," August 7, 2005, last revised March 28, 2008, Working Paper, University of Amsterdam and HEC Paris.

13. Andrew Metrick and Ayako Yasuda, "The Economics of Private Equity Funds," June 27, 2007, last revised September 9, 2008, Working Paper, University of Pennsylvania, The Wharton School.

14. Robert N. McCauley, Judith S. Ruud, and Frank Iacono, *Dodging Bullets: Changing U.S. Corporate Capital Structure in the 1980s and 1990s* (Cambridge, MA: MIT Press, 1999), 60.

15. For purposes of this discussion, I am leaving aside issues involved in firms engaging in selective disclosure of returns from certain funds and not others,

issues involving valuation of nonpublic securities in these funds, and other complex issues that raise further questions about the validity and reality of their risk-adjusted returns.

16. Steve Kaplan and Antoinette Schoar, "Private Equity Performance: Returns, Persistence and Capital Flows," 2005, Working Paper, University of Chicago and MIT.

17. Phalippou and Gottschalg, "Performance of Private Equity Funds."

18. Alexander P. Groh and Oliver Gottschalg, "The Risk-Adjusted Performance of U.S. Buyouts," 2006, Working Paper, University of Amsterdam and HEC Paris.

19. A fraudulent transfer is a transaction that renders a company insolvent and deprives a creditor of repayment.

20. Among the private equity companies that have recently paid dividends and subsequently defaulted on their debts are Mervyns Department Stores, Simmons Company, Buffets, Inc., Maax Corp., Nellson Nutraceutical Inc. and several companies owned at least in part by the private equity firm Bain Capital—Dade Behring Inc., American Pad & Paper LLC and KB Toys, Inc.

21. "Buyout Firms Profited As Company Debt Soared," *New York Times*, October 5, 2009, A1.

22. In earlier periods, public companies enjoyed a significant advantage in that they could raise debt at significantly lower interest rates than private companies. This advantage disappeared in the early 2000s with the advent of the Sarbanes-Oxley Act of 2002, also known as the Public Company Accounting Reform and Investor Protection Act, which was passed in reaction to a series of accounting scandals at large public corporations such as Enron Corp., WorldCom Inc., Tyco International, Ltd. and Adelphia Communications Corporation. Sarbanes-Oxley significantly increased the cost of being a public company and led many public companies to consider going private to avoid heightened public scrutiny.

23. Gregory Zuckerman, Henny Snyder and Scott Patterson, "Hedge-Fund Crowd Sees More Green as Fortress Hits Jackpot with IPO," *Wall Street Journal*, February 10, 2007, A1.

24. "For the Love of God," *The HCM Market Letter*, June 13, 2007. In his book on the financial crisis, Charles Gasparino writes the following with respect to this topic: "[B]oth Paulson and Bernanke still seemed unconvinced that the credit crisis was anything more than a much-needed correction to teach Wall Street a valuable lesson in risk management. It was their belief that the overall economy, even the banking system (with a few bad apples) was still sound. Private equity firm Blackstone had just become a public company, and other private equity firms were considering the same. It was a

vote of confidence in the markets and the financial system in general." See Charles Gasparino, *The Sellout How Three Decades of Wall Street Greed and Government Mismanagement Destroyed the Global Financial System* (New York: Harper Business, 2009), 281. While Gasparino does not specifically attribute this thinking to either Paulson or Bernanke, he appears to suggest that these were their thoughts. If that was in fact what they were thinking, it is a startling example of just how clueless the men in charge were about what was occurring in the financial system that they were charged with preventing from running off the cliffs.

25. Philip Augur, *Chasing Alpha: How Reckless Growth and Unchecked Ambition Ruined the City's Golden Decade* (London: The Bodley Head, 2009), 110.

26. "Private Equity Suffered its Worst Year on Record in 2008," *Financial Times*, Aug. 1, 2009.

27. See "At Calpers, the Great and Not-So," *Wall Street Journal*, December 9, 2009, C3.

28. "Calpers Has Worst Year, Off 23.4%," *Wall Street Journal*, July 22, 2009, C3.

29. In fairness, many of these investments recaptured most if not all of their losses in 2009. But investments in fixed income are not supposed to experience such dramatic volatility. Volatility generally suggests that the manager has poor risk controls and is otherwise failing to exercise sound investment judgment. Private equity firms should stick to investing in private equity, where they have enough trouble generating decent risk-adjusted returns.

Chapter 6: Welcome to Jurassic Park

1. David Koepp, *Jurassic Park,* a screenplay based on the novel by Michael Crichton and on an adaptation by Michael Chrichton and Malia Scotch Marmo. Final draft December 11, 1992.

2. Gillian Tett tells the story of the creation of credit default swaps in her excellent book *Fool's Gold* (New York: Simon & Schuster, 2009). According to Ms. Tett, the idea for these instruments was developed at a fairly raucous retreat for JP-Morgan's swaps department at the Boca Raton Resort that occurred in June 2004, about a year after the film *Jurassic Park* was released.

3. Edward LiPuma and Benjamin Lee, *Financial Derivatives and the Globalization of Risk* (Durham, North Carolina: Duke University Press, 2004), 133–134.

4. The following is based on the analysis of David Harvey in *The Limits to Capital*, 245–246.

5. "Derivatives Firms Tackle Backlog," *Wall Street Journal*, March 14, 2006, C4.

6. Henry T.C. Hu, "Empty Creditors' and the Crisis," *Wall Street Journal*, April 10, 2009. In September 2009, Professor Hu was named to head the SEC's new Office of Risk Assessment, which will regulate complex financial instruments such as credit default swaps.

7. George Soros, "One Way To Stop Bear Raids," *Wall Street Journal*, March 23, 2009.

8. LiPuma and Lee, 86–87.

9. This is why articles like Matt Taibbi's irreverent story on the stock market bear raids on Bear Stearns miss the point. See Matt Taibbi, "Wall Street's Naked Swindle," *Rolling Stone*, October 14, 2009. It was not the stock market that drove Bear Stearns (and later Lehman Brothers) into distress; it was the credit market, and in particular credit default swaps that were subject to manipulation and in many respects misunderstood and misrepresented by the media.

10. The question of the Federal Reserve's emergency powers is a controversial one. Section 13.3 of the Federal Reserve Act provides as follows: "In unusual and exigent circumstances, the Board of Governors of the Federal Reserve System, by the affirmative vote of not less than five members, may authorize any Federal reserve bank, during such periods as the said board may determine, at rates established in accordance with the provisions of section 14, subdivision (d), of this Act, to discount for any individual, partnership, or corporation, notes, drafts, and bills of exchange when such notes, drafts, and bills of exchange are indorsed or otherwise secured to the satisfaction of the Federal Reserve bank: *Provided*, That before discounting any such note, draft, or bill of exchange for an individual, partnership, or corporation the Federal reserve bank shall obtain evidence that such individual, partnership, or corporation is unable to secure adequate credit accommodations from other banking institutions. All such discounts for individuals, partnerships, or corporations shall be subject to such limitations, restrictions, and regulations as the Board of Governors of the Federal Reserve System may prescribe." There has been a great deal of debate about the actions of the Federal Reserve during the 2008 financial crisis, many of which were considered outside the scope of its traditional powers. Section 13.3 appears to be the primary statutory basis for such actions. Whatever one's view regarding whether the Federal Reserve acted properly, there is little doubt that Congress would have done worse. Accordingly, Congress should never be given power over the actions of the central bank. As argued elsewhere in this book, a non-partisan oversight body would be the most appropriate solution to this issue.

11. Gretchen Morgenson, "First Comes the Swap, Then It's the Knives," *New York Times*, June 1, 2008.

12. The shift of capital away from cash markets was exacerbated by the implementation of the Trade Reporting and Compliance Engine (TRACE) that was

launched in 2002 by the NASD (now FINRA) to require all broker-dealers to report all corporate bond trades to a public trading system within 15 minutes of execution. The transparency that TRACE introduced into the previously opaque corporate bond markets (particularly less-than-investment grade or junk bonds) rendered trading in such bonds far less profitable and drove many small dealers from the markets.

13. Soros, "One Way to Stop Bear Raids," *Wall Street Journal*, March 23, 2009.

Chapter 7: The Road to Hell

1. Harry Markowitz, "Portfolio Selection: Diversification of Investment," *Journal of Finance*, March 1952.

2. Ibid.

3. Bernstein, *Capital Ideas*, 53.

4. Eugene F. Fama, "Random Walks in Stock Market Prices," *Financial Analysts Journal*, September/October 1965, pp. 55–59.

5. This is discussed in Tim Hattan, *The New Fiduciary Standard: The 27 Prudent Investment Practices for Financial Advisers, Trustees, and Plan Sponsors* (Princeton, NJ: Bloomberg Press, 2005), 35–38. Hattan concludes that "financial markets are efficient" and "most investors cannot profit even from inefficient financial markets" (38). This is patent nonsense, and it is frankly shocking that Bloomberg could not find somebody with a remotely twenty-first-century understanding of investing to write its primer on fiduciary duty.

6. At some point, one must wonder how in the world markets are expected to function when they are guided by theories that are based on assumptions that are consistently and completely divorced from reality. It is little wonder that finance is still guided by the false mantras of efficient markets and rational investors when one studies the work of the early pioneers and Nobel laureates whose work has so little to do with the real world.

7. Eugene Fama and Kenneth French, 2004, "The Capital Asset Pricing Model: Theory and Evidence," *Journal of Economic Perspectives*, Vol. 18, No. 3, September 2004, 25,46. Quoted in Peter Bernstein, *Capital Ideas Evolving* (Hoboken, NJ: John Wiley & Sons, 2007), 165–166.

8. Bernstein, *Capital Ideas Evolving*, 173.

Chapter 8: Finance after Armageddon

1. Frederic Jameson, *Postmodernism, or The Cultural Logic of Late Capitalism* (Durham, NC: Duke University Press, 1991), ix.

2. Theodor Adorno, "Education after Auschwitz," 1969.

3. Zygmunt Bauman, *Modernity and the Holocaust* (Ithaca, NY: Cornell University Press, 2000).

4. Jeff Madrick, "They Didn't Regulate Enough and Still Don't," *The New York Review of Books*, November 5, 2009, 54.

5. Andrew Ross Sorkin, "Obama Faces a Tough Crowd Bringing a Bitter Pill to Wall Street," *New York Times*, September 16, 2009, C1.

6. For example, economist Robert Shiller has performed extensive research demonstrating that the prices of different types of financial assets can diverge from underlying economic value for extended periods of time. See Robert Shiller, *Irrational Exuberance* (Princeton: Princeton University Press, 2000), chapter 9. While Professor Shiller focused his argument on stock prices in the 2000 edition of this book, he updated his argument for the second edition (published in 2005) to include real estate prices. This research led to the development of The S&P/Case-Shiller Home Price Indices, which have become the most widely respected source of data on housing prices in the United States.

7. "A Regulator of Banks Gives Them a Scolding," *New York Times*, September 24, 2009, A1.

8. The December 2009 proposal by the Chancellor of the Exchequer Alistair Darling to impose a 50 percent tax to be paid by banks on banker's bonuses (in addition to the taxes paid by the bankers themselves) is a step too far, however. Such a tax return the United Kingdom to the days of confiscatory tax rates and will ultimately discourage free enterprise. There are better ways to tax speculative and socially unproductive activities, such as the Tax on Speculation proposed later in this chapter.

9. On January 14, 2010, President Obama introduced a proposal to tax banks for the bailout. The proposal would levy a tax on the nondepository assets of banks with more than $50 billion of such assets. The purpose of this tax would be to recover the cost of the bailout for the American taxpayers. This proposal is inadequate from several standpoints. By only taxing the banks, it ignores the complicity of many other speculators who benefitted from the reckless financial practices that led to the financial crisis, such as hedge funds and other investors who continue to speculate in naked credit default swaps and other dangerous financial instruments. It is widely known by knowledgeable market professionals that the vast majority of trading in such instruments is done for the purpose of speculation, not for the purpose of hedging underlying positions. Accordingly, this proposal gives a free pass to much of the speculative activity that comprises the most profoundly flawed practices in the system. The Tax on Speculation is more precisely aimed at unproductive activities which, if permitted to fester, will continue to push the U.S. economy down the road to ruin. The tax also lets the banks off easy. The $120 billion price tag over 10 years is a drop in the bucket compared to the trillions of dollars of damage that their reckless practices imposed on the American economy. Recapturing just the cost of the TARP does not go far enough to compensate society for

the damage that modern financial practices have imposed. This tax does not go nearly far enough in imposing a financial responsibility on these public utilities.

10. For example, Federal Reserve Governor Edward M. Gramlich publicly urged an investigation into abusive mortgage practices in the early 2000s but was derailed by Alan Greenspan despite the fact that the Federal Reserve clearly had the authority to conduct such an inquiry. See Edmund L. Andrews, "Fed Shrugged as Subprime Crisis Spread," *New York Times*, December 18, 2007.

11. Source: Federal Reserve.

12. "U.S. Clears 66 Executives for at Least $1 Million in Total Pay," *Bloomberg News*, October 23, 2009.

13. "Plan Aims to Curb Dangerous Risks," *Wall Street Journal*, A4, October 23, 2009.

14. Lucian A. Bebchuk, Alma Cohen, and Holger Spamann, "The Wages of Failure: Executive Compensation at Bear Stearns and Lehman 2000–2008," Working Draft, November 22, 2009.

15. Matthew Benjamin and Christine Harper, "Volcker Urges Dividing Investment, Commercial Banks," Bloomberg.com, March 6, 2009.

16. Compare William R. White, who argues that, "major structural shifts within the financial sector have encouraged procyclicality: securitization, globalization, and consolidation." "Should Monetary Policy Be 'Lean or Clean'?" Federal Reserve Bank of Dallas, Globalization and Monetary Policy Institute, Working Paper No. 34, August 2009, 17. Unlike White, I do not expect securitization to return to prominence for an extended period of time. However, the digitalization of finance the ability to deconstruct financial instruments into 1s and 0s—that is the underlying technology of securitization remains a dominant force that contributes to procyclicality by blurring the differences between debt and equity and between traditional asset classes. The conflation of different asset classes tends to make different types of securities—for example, stocks and bonds—correlate to a far greater extent than investors expect. This results in the failure of diversified portfolios to protect investors from drops in one asset class, such as equities, because other parts of their portfolios such as bonds join in the decline.

17. See, for example, William R. White, "Should Monetary Policy Be 'Lean or Clean'?" Federal Reserve Bank of Dallas, Globalization and Monetary Policy Institute, Working Paper No. 34, August 2009.

18. As an aside, leverage does nothing other than increase the profitability of an already profitable investment. It does not turn a bad investment into a good investment, or render a good investment a better investment. Leverage simply magnifies the nonleveraged return on an investment. In general, a

useful investment philosophy is that an investment that is unattractive without leverage will also be unattractive with leverage. Certain investment strategies, such as credit arbitrage, create relationships between debt instruments that yield very small returns that are then leveraged up enormously (10 or 15 times) to produce decent returns. These strategies have generally ended in tears when financial crises have struck and wiped out years of returns in the blink of an eye (such as Long Term Capital Management).

19. One way to understand this is to think about two different rates of interest—the market rate and the natural rate. The market rate is just what it sounds like—the interest rates that are set in the market. The natural rate would be considered to be the prospective growth rate of the economy. Some economists believe that the market rate fell below the natural rate as long ago as 1997 and that the gap between the two continued to increase right through the financial crisis of 2008. See William R. White, "Should Monetary Policy Be 'Lean or Clean'?" Federal Reserve Bank of Dallas, Globalization and Monetary Policy Institute, Working Paper No. 34, August 2009; D.M. Knight, "General Manager's Speech," on the occasion of the BIS Annual General Meeting, 30 June 2008, Basel, Switzerland.

20. Richard Russell, *Dow Theory Letters*, March 22, 2000, 3.

21. Source: Credit Suisse, *2009 Leveraged Finance Outlook and 2008 Annual Review*, January 20, 2009, 33.

22. Michael E. Lewitt, "New Math or New Economy? Some Ruminations on the 1999 Stock Market Bubble," *Trusts & Estates*, February 2001.

23. White, 19.

24. Roger W. Garrison, *Time and Money: The Macroeconomics of Capital Structure* (New York: Routledge, 2001), 120.

25. Whether this obfuscation was deliberate or not remains a complex question and lies at the heart of whether what occurred at Enron Corp. was truly criminal in terms of the laws that govern corporate disclosure. Malcolm Gladwell makes the very interesting argument that Enron in fact disclosed significant amounts of information about its off-balance-sheet entities in its public filings with the SEC. The problem, Gladwell argues, is that these entities were so complex in nature that the disclosure was basically difficult if not impossible for the average investor or regulator to understand. Accordingly, he poses the possibility that it was inappropriate to claim that Enron's executives violated laws regarding corporate disclosure because they did, in fact, disclose this information; the problem was that nobody understood it! See Malcolm Gladwell, "Open Secrets Enron, Intelligence, and the Perils of Too Much Information," in Malcolm Gladwell, *What the Dog Saw* (New York: Little, Brown and Company, 2009), 149–176. This article first appeared in *The New Yorker* on January 8, 2007. There were other problems with the

Enron prosecutions, including the legal issue of whether the crime of "theft of services" was properly applied in the case (a question that will come before the United States Supreme Court in the 2009–2010 term in regard to the conviction of former Enron executive Jeffrey Skilling). Gladwell's argument raises serious and troubling questions about the nature of corporate disclosure as corporations engage in increasingly complex transactions.

26. Peter Wilmott, "Hurrying Into the Next Panic?" *New York Times*, July 29, 2009.

Conclusion: "This Is Later"

1. Cormac McCarthy, *The Road* (New York: Alfred A. Knopf, 2006), 24.

2. "At World's End, Honing a Father-Son Dynamic," *Rolling Stone*, May 27, 2008.

3. McCarthy, *The Road,* 46.

4. Walter Benjamin, "Theses on the Philosophy of History," in Hannah Arendt, ed., *Illuminations* (New York: Shocken Books, 1968), 255.

BIBLIOGRAPHY AND OTHER SOURCES

Acharya, Viral V., and Matthew Richardson, ed. *Restoring Financial Stability*. Hoboken, NJ: John Wiley & Sons, 2009.

Adorno, Theodor. "Education After Auschwitz," 1969.

Anders, George. *Merchants of Debt: KKR and the Mortgaging of America*. New York: Basic Books, 1992.

Anderson, Perry. *The Origins of Postmodernity*. New York: Verso, 1998.

Arrighi, Giovanni. *The Long Twentieth Century: Money, Power and the Origin of our Times*. New York: Verso, 1994.

Arrighi, Giovanni. *Adam Smith in Peking: Lineages of the Twenty-First Century*. New York: Verso, 2007.

Augur, Philip. *Chasing Alpha: How Reckless Growth and Unchecked Ambition Ruined the City's Golden Decade*. London: The Bodley Head, 2009.

Baran, Paul A. and Paul M. Sweezy. *Monopoly Capital: An Essay on the American Economic and Social Order*. New York, Monthly Review Press, 1967.

Bartlett, Sarah. *The Money Machine: How KKR Manufactured Power & Profits*. New York: Time Warner Books, 1991.

Barbera, Robert J. *The Cost of Capitalism: Understanding Market Mayhem and Stabilizing Our Economic Future*. New York: McGraw-Hill, 2009.

Bauman, Zygmunt. *Modernity and the Holocaust*. Ithaca, NY: Cornell University Press, 2000.

Benjamin, Walter. *Illuminations*. New York: Harcourt Brace & World, Inc., 1968.

Berle, Adolph A., and Means, Gardiner C. *The Modern Corporation and Private Property*. New Brunswick, NJ: Transaction Publishers, 2007.

Bernanke, Ben S. *Essays on the Great Depression*. Princeton, NJ: Princeton University Press, 2000.

Bernstein, Peter. *Capital Ideas: The Improbable Origins of Modern Wall Street*. New York: The Free Press, 1992.

Bernstein, Peter. *Against the Gods: The Remarkable Story of Risk*. New York: John Wiley & Sons, 1996.

Bernstein, Peter. *Capital Ideas Evolving*. Hoboken, NJ: John Wiley & Sons, Inc., 2007.

Biasco, Salvatore, Roncaglia, Alessandro, and Salvati, Michele ed. *Market and Institutions in Market Development Essays in Honour of Paulo Sylos Labini*. New York: Palgrave, 1990.

Blackburn, Robin. "The Subprime Crisis." *New Left Review* 50 (Mar/Apr 2008).

Blackburn, Robin. "Finance and the Fourth Dimension." *New Left Review* 39 (May/June 2006).

Braudel, Fernand. *Civilization and Capitalism, 15th–18th Century, Volume I, The Structures of Everyday Life*. New York, Harper & Row, 1981.

Braudel, Fernand. *Civilization and Capitalism, 15th–18th Century, Volume II, The Wheels of Commerce*. New York: Harper & Row, 1982.

Braudel, Fernand. *Civilization and Capitalism, 15th–18th Century, Volume III, The Perspective of the World*. New York, Harper & Row, 1984.

Brenner, Robert. *The Boom and the Bubble: The US in the World Economy*. New York: Verso, 2002.

Brenner, Robert. *The Economics of Global Turbulence*. New York: Verso, 2006.

Cassidy, John. *How Markets Fail*. New York. Farrar, Straus and Giroux. 2009.

Cendrowski, Harry; Martin, James P.; Petro, Louis W.; and Wadecki, Adam A. *Private Equity: History, Governance, and Operations*. Hoboken, NJ: John Wiley & Sons, 2008.

Chancellor, Edward. *Devil Take the Hindmost: A History of Financial Speculation*. New York: Farrar, Straus, Giroux, 1999.

Cheffins, Brian, "The Eclipse of Private Equity," Working Paper No. 339, Centre for Business Research, University of Cambridge, March 2007.

Cooper, George. *The Origin of Financial Crises: Central Banks, Credit Bubbles and the Efficient Market Fallacy*. New York: Random House, 2008.

Coxe, Donald. *The New Reality of Wall Street*. New York: McGraw-Hill, 2003.

Duncan, Richard. *The Dollar Crisis: Causes Consequences Cures*. Singapore: John Wiley & Sons (Asia) Pte Ltd, 2003.

Epstein, Gerald A. ed. *Financialization and the World Economy*. Northampton, MA: Edward Elgar, 2005.

Faber, David. *And Then the Roof Caved In: How Wall Street's Greed and Stupidity Brought Capitalism to its Knees*. Hoboken, NJ: John Wiley & Sons, 2009.

Faber, Marc. *Tomorrow's Gold: Asia's Age of Discovery*. New York: CLSA Books, 2002.

Fama, Eugene, and French, Kenneth. "The Capital Asset Pricing Model: Theory and Evidence," *Journal of Economic Perspectives* 18(3) (September 2004): 25–46.

Fama, Eugene F. "The Behavior of Stock Prices." *Journal of Business* 37(1) (January): 34–150.

Fama, Eugene F. "Random Walks in Stock Prices." *Financial Analysts Journal* (September-October): 55–59.

Foster, John Bellamy "The Financialization of Capitalism." *Monthly Review* 58(11) (April 2007).

Ferguson, Niall. *The War of the World: History's Age of Hatred*. London: Allen Lane, 2006.

Fleckenstein, William A., and Sheehan, Frederick. *Greenspan's Bubbles: The Age of Ignorance at the Federal Reserve*. New York: McGraw-Hill, 2008.

Fox, Justin. *The Myth of the Rational Market: A History of Risk, Reward, and Delusion on Wall Street*. New York: HarperCollins, 2009.

Fraser-Sampson, Guy. *Private Equity as an Asset Class*. Hoboken, NJ: John Wiley & Sons, 2007.

Gasparino, Charles. *Blood on the Street: The Sensational Inside Story of How Wall Street Analysts Duped a Generation of Investors*. New York: Free Press, 2005.

Gasparino, Charles. *The Sellout: How Three Decades of Wall Street Greed and Government Mismanagement Destroyed the Global Financial System*. New York: Harper-Business, 2009.

Garrison, Roger W. *Time and Money: The Macroeconomics of Capital Structure*. New York: Routledge, 2001.

Gladwell, Malcolm. *What the Dog Saw*. New York: Little, Brown and Company, 2009.

Goodman, Laurie S.; Li, Shuman; Lucas, Douglas J.; Zimmerman, Thomas A.; and Fabozzi, Frank J. *Subprime Mortgage Credit Derivatives*. Hoboken, NJ: John Wiley & Sons, 2008.

Gowan, Peter. "Crisis on Wall Street." *New Left Review* (Jan/Feb 2009).

Grant, James. *Money of the Mind: Borrowing and Lending in America from the Civil War to Michael Milken*. New York: Farrar Straus Giroux, 1992.

Grant, James. *The Trouble With Prosperity: The Loss of Fear, the Rise of Speculation & the Risk to American Savings*. New York: Random House, 1996.

Groh, Alexander P., and Gottschlag, Oliver. "The Risk-Adjusted Performance of US Buyouts." Working Paper, Montpelier Business School, HEC School of Management, Paris, 2006.

Hartcher, Peter. *Bubble Man: Alan Greenspan and the Missing 7 Trillion Dollars*. New York: W.W. Norton & Company, 2006.

Harvey, David. *The Limits to Capital*. New York: Verso, 1999.

Harvey, David. *The Condition of Postmodernity*. Cambridge, Mass: Blackwell Publishers Inc., 1990.

Hattan, Tim. *The New Fiduciary Standard: The 27 Prudent Investment Practices for Financial Advisers, Trustees, and Plan Sponsors*. Princeton, NJ: Bloomberg Press, 2005.

Hedges, Chris. *Empire of Illusion: The End of Literacy and the Triumph of Spectacle*. New York: Nation Books, Inc., 2009.

Hitchins, Christopher. "He's Back: The Current Financial Crisis and the Enduring Relevance of Marx." *The Atlantic* (April 2009): 88–95.

International Monetary Fund, "The State of Public Finances: Outlook and Medium-Term Policies After the 2008 Crisis" (March 6, 2009), www.imf.org/external/np/pp/eng/2009/030609.pdf.

Jameson, Frederic. *Postmodernism or, The Cultural Logic of Late Capitalism*. Durham, NC: Duke University Press, 1991.

Jameson, Frederic. *The Cultural Turn: Selected Writings on the Postmodern, 1983–1998*. New York: Verso, 1998.

Janis, Irving L. *Groupthink*. Boston: Houghton Mifflin Company, 1982.

Jensen, Michael C. "Eclipse of the Public Corporation." Harvard Business Review (September–October 1989).

Kaplan, Steve, and Schoar, Antoinette. "Private Equity Performance: Returns, Persistence and Capital Flows." Working Paper, University of Chicago and MIT (2005).

Kaufman, Henry. *On Money and Markets*. New York: McGraw-Hill, 2000.

Kaufman, Henry. *The Road to Financial Reformation: Warnings, Consequences, Reforms*. Hoboken, NJ: John Wiley & Sons, 2009.

Kauffman, Stuart. *At Home In The Universe: The Search for the Laws of Self-Organization and Complexity*. New York: Oxford University Press, 1995.

Keynes, John Maynard. *The General Theory of Employment, Interest and Money*. New York: Harcourt Brace & Company, 1964.

Kindleberger, Charles P., and Laffargue, Jean-Pierre ed., *Financial Crises: Theory, History & Policy*. New York: Cambridge University Press, 1982.

Kindleberger, Charles. *Manias, Panics and Crashes: A History of Financial Crises* Revised Edition. New York: Basic Books, 1989.

Kippner, Greta R. "The Financialization of the American Economy." *Socio-Economic Review* (2005).

Koepp, David. *Jurassic Park, a screenplay*, based on the novel by Michael Crichton and on an adaptation by Michael Crichton and Malia Scotch Marmo. Final Draft December 11, 1992.

Kolakowski, Leszek. *Main Currents of Marxism*. New York: W.W. Norton & Company, Ltd., 2008.

Koshman, Josh. *The Buyout of America: How Private Equity Will Cause the Next Great Credit Crisis*. New York. Penguin Group. 2009.

Le Bon, Gustave. *The Crowd: A Study of the Popular Mind*. Marietta, GA: Cherokee Publishing Company, 1984.

LiPuma, Edward, and Lee, Benjamin. *Financial Derivatives and the Globalization of Risk*. Durham, NC: Duke University Press, 2004.

Littell, Jonathan. *The Kindly Ones*. New York: HarperCollins, 2009.

Lowenstein, Roger. *When Genius Failed: The Rise and Fall of Long-Term Capital Management*. New York: Random House, 2000.

Mandel, Ernest. *Late Capitalism*. New York: Verso, 1978.

Markowitz, Harry. "Portfolio Selection." *The Journal of Finance* 7(1) (March 1952): 77–91.

Markowitz, Harry. "Market Efficiency: A Theoretical Distinction and So What?" *Financial Analysts Journal* (2005): 17–30.

Martin, Randy. *Financialization of Daily Life*. Philadelphia: Temple University Press, 2002.

Marx, Karl. *The Eighteenth Brumaire of Louis Napoleon*. New York: International Publishers, 1972.

Marx, Karl. *Capital*, Volume I. New York: International Publishers, 1967.

Marx, Karl. *Capital*, Volume II. New York: Penguin Group, 1991.

Marx, Karl. *Capital*, Volume III. New York: Penguin Group, 1991.

Marx, Karl. *Grundrisse*. New York: Penguin Group, 1973.

McCarthy, Cormac. *The Road*. New York: Alfred A. Knopf, 2006.

McCauley, Robert N., Ruud, Judith S., and Iacono, Frank. *Dodging Bullets: Changing U.S. Corporate Capital Structures in the 1980s and 1990s*. Boston: MIT Press, 1999.

Metrick, Andrew, and Yasuda, Ayako. "The Economics of Private Equity Funds." (June 27, 2007. Last revised September 9, 2008. Working Paper, University of Pennsylvania, The Wharton School).

Minsky, Hyman. *John Maynard Keynes*. New York: Columbia University Press, 1975.

Minsky, Hyman P. *Stabilizing an Unstable Economy*. New Haven: Yale University Press, 1986.

Mitchell, Lawrence E. *The Speculation Economy: How Finance Triumphed Over Industry*. San Francisco: Berrett-Koehler Publishers, Inc., 2007.

Morris, Charles. *The Trillion Dollar Meltdown: Easy Money, High Rollers, and the Great Credit Crash*. New York: Public Affairs, 2008.

Muolo, Matthew, and Padilla, Mathew. *Chain of Blame: How Wall Street Caused the Mortgage Crisis*. Hoboken, NJ: John Wiley & Sons, 2008.

Napier, Russell. *Anatomy of the Bear*. New York: CLSA Books, 2005.

Nielsen, Kasper Meisner, "The Return to Pension Funds' Private Equity Investments: New Evidence on the Private Equity Premium Puzzle," Job Market Paper, 2006, Copenhagen Business School.

Nesvetaiova, Anastasia. *Fragile Finance: Debt, Speculation and Crisis in the Age of Global Credit*. New York: Palgrave Macmillon, 2007.

Otteson, James. *Adam Smith's Marketplace of Life*. New York: Cambridge University Press, 2002.

Palley, Thomas I. "Financialization: What It Is and Why It Matters." The Levy Economics Institute of Bard College, Working Paper No. 525, December 2007.

Panitch, Leo. "Thoroughly Modern Marx." *Foreign Policy* (May/June 2009).

Phalippou, Ludovic, and Oliver Gottschlag, "Performance of Private Equity Funds." (August 7, 2005. Last Revised March 28, 2008), Working Paper, University of Amsterdam and HEC School of Management, Paris.

Phillips, Kevin. *Arrogant Capital: Washington, Wall Street, and the Frustration of American Politics*. New York: Little, Brown & Company, 1994.

Phillips, Kevin. *Boiling Point: Democrats, Republicans, and the Decline of Middle-Class Prosperity*. New York: Random House, 1993.

Polyani, Karl. *The Great Transformation: The Political and Economic Origins of Our Times*. Boston: Beacon Press, 1944.

Posner, Richard A. *A Failure of Capitalism: The Crisis of '08 and the Descent Into Depression*. Cambridge, MA: Harvard University Press, 2009.

Rasmussen, Dennis C. *The Problems and Promise of Commercial Society: Adam Smith's Response to Rousseau*. University Park, PA: The Pennsylvania State University Press, 2008.

Ritholtz, Barry. *Bailout Nation: How Greed and Easy Money Corrupted Wall Street and Shook the World Economy*. Hoboken, NJ: John Wiley & Sons, 2009.

Ross, Ian Simpson. *The Life of Adam Smith*. New York: Oxford University Press, 1995.

Sharpe, William F. "Capital Asset Prices: A Theory of Market Equilibrium Under Conditions of Risk." *The Journal of Finance* XIX(3) (September 1964): 425–442.

Shiller, Robert J. *The Subprime Solution: How Today's Financial Crisis Happened, and What to Do about It*. Princeton, NJ: Princeton University Press, 2008.

Sheehan, Frederick. *Panderer to Power: The Untold Story of How Alan Greenspan Enriched Wall Street and Left a Legacy of Recession*. New York: McGraw-Hill, 2009.

Shiller, Robert. *Irrational Exuberance*. Princeton: Princeton University Press, 2000.

Simmel, George. *The Philosophy of Money*. New York: Routledge, 1978.

Smith, Adam. *The Theory of Moral Sentiments*. New York: Barnes & Noble Publishing Company, 2004.

Smith, Adam. *The Wealth of Nations*. New York: Random House, Inc., 2000.

Sorkin, Andrew Ross. *Too Big to Fail*. New York: Viking. 2009.

Soros, George. *The New Paradigm for Financial Markets: The Credit Crisis of 2008 and What It Means*. New York: Public Affairs, 2008.

Soros, George. *The Crisis of Global Capitalism: Open Society Endangered*. New York: Public Affairs, 1998.

Soros, George. *The Alchemy of Finance: Reading the Mind of the Market*. New York: Simon & Schuster, 1987.

Taleb, Nassim Nicholas. *Fooled by Randomness: The Hidden Role of Chance in Life and Markets*. New York: Random House, 2004.

Taleb, Nassim Nicholas. *The Black Swan: The Impact of the Highly Improbable*. New York: Random House, 2007.

Taylor, Mark C. *Confidence Games: Money and Markets in a World Without Redemption*. Chicago: University of Chicago Press, 2004.

Tett, Gillian. *Fool's Gold*. New York: Simon & Schuster, 2009.

Thompson, E.P. *The Making of the English Working Class*. New York: Random House, 1963.

Thompson, E.P. *The Poverty of Theory & Other Essays*. New York: Monthly Review Press, 1978.

Warburton, Peter. *Debt & Delusion: Central Bank Follies That Threaten Economic Disaster.* London: Allen Lane, 1999.

Wessel, David. *In Fed We Trust: Ben Bernanke's War on the Great Panic.* New York: Crown Business, 2009.

Wheen, Francis. *Marx's Das Kapital: A Biography.* New York: Grove Press, 2006.

Wheen, Francis. *Karl Marx.* New York: W.W. Norton & Company, 1999.

White, Eugene N. ed. *Crashes and Panics: The Lessons From History.* New York: New York University Press, 1990.

White, William R. " Should Monetary Policy Be 'Lean or Clean'?" Federal Reserve Bank of Dallas, Globalization and Monetary Policy Institute. Working Paper No. 34 (August 2009), p. 17.

Wolf, Martin. *Fixing Global Finance.* Baltimore: The Johns Hopkins University Press, 2008.

Wood, Christopher. *Boom & Bust: The Rise and Fall of the World's Financial Markets.* New York: Atheneum, 1989.

Zizek, Slavoj. *First as Tragedy, Then as Farce.* New York: Verso, 2009.

ABOUT THE AUTHOR

M ichael E. Lewitt is the president of Harch Capital Management, LLC, a money management firm headquartered in Boca Raton, Florida. Since 1990, he has been the author and editor of *The HCM Market Letter*, a monthly analysis of financial markets that is read worldwide. His work has appeared in the *New York Times*, *The New Republic*, and the Spanish newspaper *El Mundo*, where he writes a bimonthly column on economics and finance. Mr. Lewitt studied at Brown University, Yale University, and the New York University School of Law. He lives in South Florida. A complete collection of his writings on markets and finance can be found at www.hcmmarketletter.com.

INDEX